Telling Stories to Change the World

Telling Stories to Change the World is a powerful collection of essays about community-based and interest-based projects where storytelling is used as a strategy for speaking out for justice. Contributors from locations across the globe—including Uganda, Darfur, China, Afghanistan, South Africa, New Orleans, and Chicago—describe grassroots projects in which communities use narrative as a way of exploring what a more just society might look like and what civic engagement means. These compelling accounts of resistance, hope and vision showcase the power of the storytelling form to generate critique and collective action. Collectively, these projects demonstrate the contemporary power of stories to stimulate engagement, active citizenship, the pride of identity, and the humility of human connectedness.

Rickie Solinger is a historian and curator, and author of books including *Pregnancy and Power: A Short History of Reproductive Politics in America* (NYU Press, 2007) and *Wake Up Little Susie: Single Pregnancy and Race before Roe v. Wade* (Routledge, 1992, 2000).

Madeline Fox is an educator and researcher enrolled in the Ph.D. in Social Personality Psychology at the Graduate Center of the City University of New York.

Kayhan Irani is a community arts practitioner who in 2007 was awarded a certificate of recognition by New York City mayor Michael Bloomberg for her arts work in immigrant communities.

D0223559

The Teaching/Learning Social Justice Series
Edited by Lee Anne Bell
Barnard College, Columbia University

Telling Stories to Change the World

Global Voices on the Power of Narrative to Build Community and Make Social Justice Claims

**Edited by
Rickie Solinger, Madeline Fox,
and Kayhan Irani**

Routledge
Taylor & Francis Group

NEW YORK AND LONDON

First published 2008
by Routledge
270 Madison Ave, New York, NY 10016

Simultaneously published in the UK
by Routledge
2 Park Square, Milton Park, Abingdon, Oxon OX14 4RN

Routledge is an imprint of the Taylor & Francis Group, an informa business

© 2008 Taylor & Francis

Typeset in Minion by RefineCatch Limited, Bungay, Suffolk
Printed and bound in the United States of America in acid-free paper by
Edwards Brothers, Inc.

Library of Congress Cataloging-in-Publication Data
Telling stories to change the world : global voices on the power of narrative
to build community and make social justice claims / edited by Rickie
Solinger, Madeline Fox and Kayhan Irani.—1st ed.
    p. cm—(The teaching/learning social justice series)
    Includes bibliographical references.
    ISBN 978–0–415–96079–3 (hb : alk. paper)—ISBN 978–0–415–96080–9
(pb : alk. paper)—ISBN 978–0–92806–6 (ebook)   1. Community life.
2. Storytelling.   3. Social change.   I. Solinger, Rickie, 1947–   II. Fox,
Madeline.   III. Irani, Kayhan.
    HM761.T45 2008
    307.1′4—dc22

                                                                2007047265

ISBN 10: 0–415–96079–7 (hbk)
ISBN 10: 0–415–96080–0 (pbk)
ISBN 10: 0–203–92806–7 (ebk)

ISBN 13: 978–0–415–96079–3 (hbk)
ISBN 13: 978–0–415–96080–9 (pbk)
ISBN 13: 978–0–203–92806–6 (ebk)

Mien Homeland

The sun alights in the west and the west burns.
In parched California, we dig to China, total pop.: one.
The chap who dwells there hoists us up and burps us.
We chant his praises; proffer our princess,
the oath of succession, on the morrow, the throne.
Pissed, our crown prince insists on his birthright.
Orange tree for the son on his left palm,
one for the son-in-law on his right, the king decrees:
Whose fruits first is sovereign.

Up with the sun, the local one espies a mandarin
globe in the clutches of the prince's branches.
Spinning like earth swifter than perception, or slower,
he plucks the sucker and pastes it to his.
Now king, first thing, he holds court and posthaste
banishes our clan to the hinterlands of Laos.
Tigers, centipedes, jungle elephants: we survive millennia
in mountaintop mist till the Americans fly over
the Plain of Jars, carpet bomb and bring us home.

I tell our story to make sense to my family
of a world on fire, the road ahead.

                                        David Hellman

Note: 30,000 Mien refugees resettled in the United States after the American war in Indochina. Versions of this story were told by Mien elders in refugee camps in Thailand prior to resettlement.

Acknowledgments

The editors thank Zachary Fabri, Heather Jarrow, Catherine Bernard, Jennifer Heath, and Lee Bell for their enthusiastic assistance of various kinds. The editors also wish to express their respect and appreciation for project participants and observers all over the world who made time to let readers of this book know about their work.

Contents

Part IV
The Power and the Limits of Stories

Series Editor's Introduction

The Teaching/Learning Social Justice Series explores the many ways people engage diversity, democracy, and social justice in classrooms and communities. "Social justice" is the umbrella for texts that address broad concerns of democracy, equality, diversity, and justice. "Teaching/learning" emphasizes the essential connections between theory and practice. The series invites attention to both popular education as well as education in formal institutions. Central are the stories and lived experiences of people who strive to critically analyze and challenge oppressive relationships and institutions, and to imagine and create more just and inclusive alternatives. My hope is that the series will balance critical analysis with images of hope and possibility in ways that are accessible and inspiring to a broad audience of educators and activists who believe in the potential for social change through education and who seek stories and examples of practice, as well as honest discussion of the obstacles to dismantling oppressive ideas and institutions.

Telling Stories to Change the World realizes this goal through assembling a broad and engrossing array of narratives by people from diverse communities around the world who appropriate storytelling as a means to assert their knowledge, experience, and claims on justice. As someone who has been interested in the storytelling method to engage young people and their teachers in exposing and confronting racism in curriculum and school practices, the promise in this form to generate critique and collective action is near and dear to my heart. In my work, I use story types as a critical lens to examine historical and contemporary patterns that sustain and subvert racism in this society. Through examining stock and concealed stories, reclaiming and generating resistance stories and contributing new counter-stories, the youth I work with assert their right to shape schools and communities to meet their needs.

The editors of *Telling Stories to Change the World* offer vivid and compelling accounts of resistance, critique, hope, and vision from communities whose stories are often invisible, concealed, trivialized, or erased by the dominant society to show us the myriad ways in which people have reclaimed and reshaped a traditional art form in the service of their ideas and demands for justice. Appropriately, the editors critique our cultural fascination with individual, solipsistic stories as they consider why this tool seems so appropriate to so many at this time in global history. Through historicizing and problematizing storytelling they reflect on the complications of using stories to interrupt rather than reinscribe what they call the Oprahatic fascinations of the current milieu. In so doing, they articulate the limitations as well as conditions under which storytelling can organize challenges to entrenched power and images of alternative possibility.

I appreciate the editors' insistence that we always situate ourselves in the stories we tell, especially important when we retell the stories of others. How do we honor the historical, national, political, cultural, social, and personal context in which stories are generated and the particularities of location they intend to address? We in the U.S. are no strangers to the misinterpretation and often cooptation of the stories of others for our own gain—this has been an ongoing struggle of those involved in participatory action research in and with marginalized students, schools, and communities. *Telling Stories to Change the World* complicates and clarifies the responsible retelling of stories and respect for the purposes of those who generate them.

I hope that this work inspires conversation, self-reflection, a decentered notion of our roles and capacities as educators, researchers, civic actors, and activists grounded in the local yet implicated in global struggles for equality. I hope it inspires others to action—using storytelling for their own collective purposes or for generating new ways of expressing and enacting claims to recognition, rights, and justice.

Lee Anne Bell
Barnard College, Columbia University
October 2007

Introduction

Telling Stories to Change the World collects twenty-three essays about the ways that social justice activists, artists, and project leaders all over the world—in a village in northern Afghanistan; in a smaller village in Germany; in Philadelphia, Mississippi; in Chicago and Kampala and New Orleans and elsewhere—are insisting on the power that stories have to generate hope and engagement, personal dignity and active citizenship, the pride of identity, and the humility of human connectedness. The storytelling projects in this volume—and the dozens of other projects we learned about in the process of collecting—illustrate that the beginning of the twenty-first century is a historical moment in which narrative is more broadly recognized than ever as a significant, simple, crucial vehicle for reawakening, disseminating, and sustaining social justice impulses.

Telling Stories to Change the World is a collection of essays about community-based and interest-based projects in which groups of people are using stories as a grassroots tactic for making social justice claims. HIV-positive mothers in Kampala, Uganda; teachers and students in the Lower Ninth Ward of New Orleans; "disabled" performers in San Francisco; Maya youth in Guatemala are claiming public voice and public space to make community-based, collective claims for their value and their rights as persons and for the forms of social justice they require to fully realize that value.

The essays in *Telling Stories* describe projects in which storytellers—using dance, exhibition, archives, ancient scrolls, community meetings and community theater, newspapers, the internet, children's drawings, and other formats—create narratives that draw on personal history and also resonate beyond singular lives, invoking history, in order to claim immigrant rights or the value of community or everybody's right to physical safety and education. These projects honor the past and imagine the future. They explore meanings of civic engagement and generate creative visions of justice. Often, the participants in "Telling Stories" projects are using narrative as a way to transform identity from *victim* to *agent* to *public critic*, a person with full legal status in the public square.

Nineteen of the essays in *Telling Stories* are project based and the other four—focusing on the commodification of trauma stories in South Africa; the use of autobiography as a stimulus for organizing in the American South and Guatemala; the stories of Cuban exiles; and stories in law—are more speculative, considering the power and also the limits of storytelling for social justice and other clarifying purposes.

This introduction continues with short statements from each of the three editors, Rickie Solinger, Madeline Fox, and Kayhan Irani, describing what each of us was looking for, as we began searching around the world for people who could write about the grassroots projects they were developing. Each member of our editorial trio came to *Telling Stories* with a distinct orientation, a situation which conditioned the corners each of us looked in, and for what.

Following these individual statements, we will comment on what we learned generally about why people are telling stories for social justice around the world and also comment on how people are identifying, marshalling, and deploying various kinds of resources to make community-based projects. We conclude the introduction with an observation about the authorship of the essays in *Telling Stories* and a note about how we found the projects and the way the essays are organized into sections.

Rickie Solinger:

My ideas about rights and citizenship and the public square were born at the edges of the civil rights and anti-war movements in the 1960s. So were my ideas about what makes a convincing story about the needs and rights and capacities of ordinary people. The stories I found believable then—and still do—suggest, among other things, that fairness matters a lot and that racism and sexism and poverty have been far more powerful causes of "social problems" in the United States than the bad behavior of individuals. The stories that I carried out of the sixties also suggested that groups of ordinary people can frame powerful, convincing narratives that explain and can sometimes help achieve their goals for a fairer and more just community.

For the past generation, our contemporary, Oprahatic culture has overshadowed these sixties-style stories about social justice and activism. Now the stories in the U.S. public square (think "memoir" and "reality TV", for example) are mostly about individuals making their own singular lives. We tune in and hear confessions of individual pain or individual glory.

Not surprisingly, these Stories of Self resonate with—and reinforce—the narratives that our national leaders tell these days about the point of being an American: Here, everyone can achieve the American Dream, a status that promises each of us our own personal *success story*. Recent political campaign rhetoric (the Republican variety most insistently) says that anyone who doesn't own one of these stories is a victim only of her own bad choices. Within this highly political frame, we are asked to believe that the most important purpose of public policy is to protect the public purse (and private taxpayers) from the depredations of bad choicemakers; or put another way, to protect the private property of the winners, men and women who fulfill their civic duty simply by being winners.

I don't believe that the only stories Americans like to encounter in the public square are stories about individual pain or glory or stories that cast the highest form of freedom as the freedom to be personally wealthy, or famous.

I came to the *Telling Stories* book project interested in finding powerful examples of community-based groups figuring out how to use stories and public storytelling not to isolate and valorize individualism but as a way to frame and broadcast social justice claims, and as a way to define a set of tactics for achieving a more just community.

Looking for examples, the editorial trio found out that, yes, groups around the world are using all kinds of narrative forms for envisioning and articulating such goals as revitalizing the environment, reclaiming history, encouraging civic engagement, and, most generally, for creating opportunities to build coalitions and take concerted action.

For me the *Telling Stories* volume is not an attempt to revive the romance of the 1960s civil rights movement, a golden moment when people in community felt "empowered," partly because they were able to generate a coherent and convincing narrative about freedom. Rather, this volume is a record—and a set of inspirational examples—of how people all over the world today are honoring and adapting and extending many community-based narrative traditions for the purpose of claiming public space, building audience and activist communities devoted to the common good.

Madeline Fox:

For years, I have worked as an organizer, in the U.S. labor movement and in Ireland. I brought my perspectives as an organizer with me as I launched the search for storytelling projects. From this standpoint, I looked for work that is accessible, practical, rooted in doing and creating consequences.

But before I was an organizer, I was raised on the storytelling stages of community theater where being in the audience and hearing stories is as moving and powerful as jumping up on stage and telling stories. One person's ordinary story, expressed through art, can resonate across boundaries. In the work of assembling this book, I sought out projects that exist in the confluences of story, art, and organizing.

From where I stood as an organizer, I thought about justice as a point out in front—a vision of the future. Because the project participants we encountered insisted that using storytelling to accomplish tomorrow's justice was not enough, I came to think about "justice" as a here-and-now goal, as well. For one thing, project ethics seemed to insist on supporting those who become vulnerable in the midst of the organizing process. The voter-rights project, for example, took care to honor each participant's process as director of her own script even while remaining focused on the goal of increasing civic participation among the voting-eligible population generally. Again and again, across cultures, mediums, and ages, these projects show us that participants' individual experiences of justice and dignity must not be compromised for the greater goal of group justice. These projects make the case that both are possible and necessary.

As projects appeared on my computer screen, I looked for, and found, new relationships between story, art, and organizing. I read about people working together toward justice, building relationships strong enough to incite the kinds of risk-taking that's required to build movements. In the organizing I know, relationship-building is often approached one on one in living rooms and other familiar spaces. Around the world, though, the ancient intimacy of storytelling is being harnessed simply and effectively to build authentic relationships in courtrooms, on stages, and through books and electronic media. This recognition—that storytelling can be key to organizing—felt obvious and, at the same time, it was a revelation. I could think of many ways the labor movement uses workers' stories to organize—and has for decades. (We made grand efforts to include a union essay in this volume, without success.)

The editorial team is made up of a historian, an artist, and an organizer (the butcher, the baker, the candlestick maker). But, these borders are lightly drawn. The historian is also an artist and an educator. The artist is also an organizer and a writer. The organizer is also a researcher . . . and a student. Because of my backgrounds, I understand my true orientation to this project is as a learner. Defining my criteria, searching for projects, talking with project participants, I determined, first, to listen well, then to take action. And, that is what a room full of *Telling Stories to Change the World* projects requires: humility and an orientation towards listening and learning. Whatever our backgrounds and from whatever angles we approach this work, we ask that you listen deeply, carefully, and with complicated ears to the stories these projects tell.

Kayhan Irani:

As an *artivist* my life is dedicated to presenting the arts as a channel—for artist or audience—to engage with social justice issues. But I find that a good deal of my time is spent trying to convince people of the value, validity, and practicality of using the arts to do social justice work. So when I became an editor of the *Telling Stories* volume, I was struck with a missionary zeal: this book was, finally, the opportunity to bring truth to non-believers. I would find projects created with such clarity of mission and implemented with such strategic precision that the reader would be immediately transformed. My single-minded passion to find proof that art *works* was set into motion. With these blinders on, I ventured forth.

I can see now that I was lucky not to have spoiled my adventure by sticking with such demanding, yet vague, prescriptions. My initial mistake of looking at the end product to provide truth—instead of looking at the beginning of the process for the truth of the situation—was remedied when I began to read the amazing submissions. Out of the multiple contexts (a prison, a daycare center, a refugee camp) and multiple goals (to learn skills, to secure resources for children, to understand local history) emerged a set of modern myth-making endeavors with common elements: each project is deeply meaningful, instructive, and inspirational to the communities which created it. Each community engaged in "myth-making" by deploying stories that reflect the community's needs and values, project their hopes and dreams, and offer supremely practical guidance.

Let me talk about the Zuni language and culture project since this is the project I was most resistant to—and most demonstrates my transformation. Upon first reading it in my prescriptive, missionary mode of thought, I dismissed this work as a language project that was nice but not a clarion call. Where was the quantifiable change? Who were the victors? Most of the community has lived in a time of water scarcity, pollution, with a slowly disappearing river. How could they, then, see this river as a meaningful part of their lives, as a robbed treasure?

But then I saw that the Zuni language makes the invisible visible. The painful depletion of the river, and of the people's lack of access to it, becomes apparent through the Zuni stories. These stories reawaken the relationship between the people and the physical features of the land, and a new comprehension emerges—from the old. Important names are spoken once again. Important places become sacred again, and the pain of alienation is overcome by the passion for honor and connection. Coming back to the mother tongue, literally speaking the same language, revitalizes claims for ownership and stewardship and creates something out of nothing.

All the projects illustrate how change comes not from outside qualifiers and quantifiers, measures that social scientists recognize, but rather from the creation of a collective will. The community identifies the problem and makes it matter, reordering and restructuring key concepts, old stories, relationships. Engaging with these projects in Lahore, New Orleans, New Mexico, Guatemala, and elsewhere is a way of understanding how groups are bringing out, bringing up, and bringing back values of justice and fairness into their communities.

The *Telling Stories* project has connected me with a tiny sample of what is growing in this field of civic and political participation. I hope you can see into the work, as I have begun to do, and bring out possibilities. *Telling Stories* has changed my perception of my own work, and perhaps, in the end, it was I who was saved!

*   *   *

In the essays here, groups of people create narratives that identify obstacles to freedom, to health, to safety, to dignity. In response to the obstacles, these groups develop "stories," vehicles for voices and visions that implicitly or explicitly claim a better world. We present reports here from groups figuring out ways to build audience, figuring out how to offer up their stories in settings that will make a difference. Must the essays' authors or the volume's editors grapple with the relationship between "telling stories" and "truth-telling"? Are the authors, the editors, and the participants responsible for assessing the impacts of this kind of storytelling? For the purposes of the *Telling Stories* volume, do we need to know if the individual life, the community, the world has been changed—and if so, how much—because the stories have been told?

Our answers spring from the spirit of the projects themselves. Teenagers in New Orleans, warehoused in a financially and educationally bankrupt high school, and a couple of their teachers, dream up a pre-Katrina project—documenting the stories, street by street, of the Lower Ninth Ward. Today the set of books that the Neighborhood Story Project produced tell about the lives of people who lived there before the storm. The books have become precious remains. A practical solution to a dire indignity, with unexpected results.

An archive at Smith College about important, activist women in the United States holds almost no papers of women of color activists. Loretta Ross and others go to work, in the most practical way, raising money, getting permissions, collecting papers. Now the concept of *archive* (whose remains are worthy?) and the stories that some historians of women can draw on to define the past have changed forever. In Darfur, a killing field bereft of world media, and an Australian pediatrician determined to "get the story out." The pediatrician realizes that the story-pictures that children make of the killing fields can carry the atrocities into worldwide consciousness.

These essays are largely about how groups of people around the world are selecting storytelling, broadly defined, as a vehicle for launching practical solutions. We are focused, like the practitioners, on the impulse to reach for narrative, less on questions of truth or standpoint or even results.

Embedded in the selection of storytelling-as-vehicle are several layers of optimism. First, participants share the stance that telling stories requires voice and requires listeners. Imagining and then realizing both voice and audience are profoundly political acts that trump coercive silencing and break into enforced isolations. Second, telling stories of indignity, tragedy, hope involves the teller in acts of transformation: experience and identity become mutable. The story can have a different ending from the one we already know. You can "hear" the story differently from me. We can compare. We can rewrite/re-enact/redraw and retell it again. The story becomes a way of remaking the world; being a storyteller in these contexts means being an activist.

Claiming storytelling as an expression of optimism is first cousin to claiming storytelling as ennoblement. In the world before now, when physicians in Atlanta coerced young women of color to ingest fertility-limiting agents, often in harmful forms, and when gay youth in Chicago could not make their claims for human dignity in private family settings or in public venues, and when disabled artists had no hope of performing lives, then Authority was all in the hands of physicians and parents and teachers and "normal-bodied" artists. The authors of the essays in *Telling Stories* are nearly all making the case for storytelling as a vehicle for claiming Authority and for situating the teller as Expert. The immigrant storytellers in the Hudson Valley, the youthful resisters against the wages of genocide in Guatemala, the Muslim women as historians are using stories—relying on new and old narratives—to justify claiming the right to speak with dignity and knowledge and consequence in public. Storytellers here are taking the right, too, to contradict the physicians and anti-immigrant politicians, the old authorities who always held all the power. The storytellers are speaking differently about the polity and about the ingredients of public health. They are including human rights perspectives and positioning themselves as experts in these matters.

When the storytellers boldly use the first person, they are sometimes claiming expertise and sometimes also claiming space for intimacy, even or especially in public. When an incarcerated woman begins a story with "I," she is, for one thing, explicitly inviting the listener/reader to "know" her, to imagine her humanity. When she says "I" and the next incarcerated storyteller starts her story with "I," too, and then the next, we begin to imagine a community of incarcerated women, speaking to us and also to each other (even across the dehumanized spaces of isolated "I"s), building community in the midst and against the insanity of imprisonment.

Getting familiar with projects around the world, we have come to see that when the project developer or the community group settles on storytelling as part of the process of redress and revival, the crime (or the violation) must be *speakable*. In recent times, in the United States, most people have come to accept that rape can occur within marriage, for example. Now when a husband rapes his wife, the wife—who is no longer simply "a wife," and is now also a "rape victim"—has the possibility of speaking to authorities, speaking out in various venues about this sexual crime that her husband committed against her, and the community will be more likely to understand what she is talking about, and probably more sympathetic, than it would have been in the past. Also, being a "rape victim" gives the storyteller a new, legitimate legal status and a platform from which to claim rights and redress.

Thus, in Kampala, Uganda, previously shamed and silenced HIV-positive mothers work together, in public, to prepare "memory books" for their children today, so that even as orphans in the near future, these children will know the stories of their families. Today in Kampala, HIV status is more public tragedy than private shame, so stories are possible. The women who direct the Memory Book Project are respected and can take public space to do their work. Families, too, make space, knowing that HIV-positive mothers want to define what constitutes a "resource" to bequeath, to whom.

Zuni Indians in Arizona are passionately focused on saving their language and revitalizing the Zuni River, both entities currently near death. Imagining the viability of linguistic identity and the viability of the environment as organically linked emblems of demographic endurance is a project that speaks volumes about twenty-first-century concepts of community health.

We have puzzled over "why now?" Why has narrative become so useful a tactic for making social justice claims? This question engages issues about the ubiquity of interest in "self" and "identity" in growing numbers of cultures. It surely raises issues about the globalization of solipsistic cultural forms via the movies and the web, the seductiveness of the memoiristic impulse, the lure of confessional "reality" entertainment and infotainment. Using stories to make certain claims simply and obviously draws on some of the most favored forms of popular culture. But the power of narrative in the service of social justice also fits in with the "good" flipside of twenty-first-century solipsism: when you're claiming rights in this right-claiming era, it's always best to start with your personal story, because who can argue with that? Your own story is ultimately inviolate. It is your truth. From Phoenix, AZ to Springfield, MA to Lahore, the storytelling circle is something old made new again.

Finally, wherever we've looked, the storytellers are expressing an additional strain of optimism: that ordinary people are artists when they want to be, especially when they *need* to be; that shaping and making stories is art; and that the art of storytelling can work. The optimistic strain affirms that storytelling can change the world. Reclaiming history, cleaning up the river waters, making girls into teachers, fighting against racism and xenophobia—these projects are too important to leave to the droning politicians and their cronies. Ordinary people all over the world turn to artful storytelling, to make their most indelible mark on the cause.

*   *   *

At one point, as we perused essays from around the world, the editorial trio called the outcome they imagined, the anthology, "a handbook." But handbooks promise nuts-and-bolts, replicable tactics, recipes, scenarios, special props. As we became familiar with our subjects, we saw that this heavily resourced concept "handbook" couldn't capture the ways that many groups are essentially making something out of "nothing." In this section of the introduction, we will try to convey some of the ways that project participants are identifying, marshalling, and deploying various kinds of "resources"—often immaterial—to make community-based projects.

Most fundamentally, many of the essayists and participants identify tradition and group-knowledge as the most powerful resources they own. Putting these resources into words and actions, as stories, and making art out of them, is the most direct and effective way, many of the essayists write, to make the claim.

In Mississippi and in Roth, Germany and elsewhere participants are clear that another fundamental resource is the willingness and ability to speak across barriers. Sometimes this involves unearthing and airing toxic histories. Sometimes it means communicating honestly with longtime enemies. In all of these cases, it seems to mean giving birth to a new language that can tell a new story in the interests of community and justice, a story that couldn't be told before the barriers were breached.

Here the personal story has nothing to do with solipsism. It gets spoken as an instrument of survival and not only an instrument of personal survival but as a way of making community survival more likely. Here the "resource" is a fluid orientation between private and public; there is no separate category of "privacy," because the personal decisions that people make and can make are always shaped by the framework of official policies and laws and other forms of constraint. Laying bare the connection between the personal and the public is a crucial strategy for making sense of the world and telling stories about it. Silence, the anti-resource, is the cost of believing that these worlds can be separated.

When communities make narrative the vehicle for calling attention to urgent matters, they deploy a special set of resources, some more material than others. In the face of total eclipse, sometimes, or even in the shadow of obliteration, storytellers shape and fill narrative with elements of documentation: ancient objects, diaries, drawings, photographs, costumes, testimonies of many kinds. Even under the most dire threats, communities can deploy resources that facilitate inserting their voices/images into the media. The greatest resource in these cases is the ally—the ally from an unmarked community—who knows how to work the media. The greatest resource is the ally who is not only unmarked and knowledgable, but the one who comes with credentials so credible and interesting—such as the Australian pediatrician in Darfur—that worldwide media is engaged. Sometimes the issue is so pressing that even the media doesn't require a heavily credentialed outsider. But this is rare.

Where it's possible, communities sometimes decide to make a direct claim on the polity, suddenly identifying themselves as owners of a resource that was there all the time, but which never before seemed theirs for the taking. For example, in Tucson, Arizona, a group of traditional non-voters became voters and practitioners of civic education through storytelling that focused on the impact of government policies on the lives of individuals.

Historically, subordinated people have told subversive stories on their oppressors. Sometimes the stories have been so subversive that whole new thought-systems and language-systems have had to be made up to express them. They've also required space. Essayists write about commanding public spaces in which traditionally sequestered or shunned populations can tell subversive stories. Others describe using traditional gatherings for subversive purposes. Inside these venues, "dependent" people sometimes assume positions of authority and enact their power, rehearsing, perhaps. In

Guatemala and Lahore and Afghanistan and from prisons, storytellers are using subversive varieties of "ancient arts" in the service of public health.

* * *

Some romance dictates that all the authors of the essays shall be "authentic voices." The authors shall be the claim-makers, the community-based activists, themselves. In the romance, these writers, in rural China and India, in the Lower Ninth Ward, in Cell Block 54, the young girl-teachers in the mountains of northern Afghanistan, the new immigrants in the Hudson Valley, and the homeless teenagers in Chicago are all familiar with The Routledge Essay-Form: four thousand word-limit, no problem. But in book-making reality, the editorial trio recruits the Afghan man who sets up the teacher-making project; the Justice Now employee who recruits incarcerated women to make the CD and works with incarcerated poets and singers and storytellers from beginning to end, assembling talent and resources. We find the university-based expert in racial reconciliation who sits with the folks in Philadelphia, Mississippi, as they break their forty-year silence and tell stories to each other about the murders of Cheney, Schwerner, and Goodman.

Sometimes, the authors are more strictly "of" the community. A man we know delivered a tape recorder to the HIV-positive women of the Memory Book Project in Kampala. The women spoke, roundtable-fashion, into the recorder for a good, long stretch about their work, so we were able to shape an "essay" out of their real voices. A woman who is herself the daughter of a Holocaust survivor from Roth, Germany assembled an essay from the writings of five people, including her survivor-father and two women in Germany, all of whom contributed to making an exhibition-story about the eradication of Jews from that small town. Again, in New Orleans, we found pastiche: the teachers and one of the students at the heart of the Neighborhood Story Project concocted a multivocal essay. The Zuni writers are as close to their material as one can be. So are the members of Sins Invalid; the initiators of the Depo Diaries Project; and Ms. Loretta Ross, who models, generates, inspires, and honors storytelling to change the world in places that will endure.

Where there is apparent distance—the writer is a visitor, an outside expert, a student of the terrain—we asked for transparency. The writer had to locate herself. And we suggested she incorporate participant-voices lavishly. Distant or close, the chapter authors all share our interest in examining the impulse to tell stories in community, with purpose.

Two questions arise. First, how did we locate projects in northern Afghanistan and New Orleans, Kampala and Chicago, and the Chinese countryside? And then, if storytelling is occurring all over the world, why these projects and not others?

After the fact, it is magic. We brought a gigantic map of the world into our workroom and stuck pins in all the places where friends and co-workers and activist-buddies told us about projects. Soon the essays materialized, in hand from Guatemala and Lahore and Darfur, from behind prison walls. In the actual process, though, the three editors occupy overlapping but quite distinct spheres. And each of us individually occupies many overlapping spheres, working in various ways on social justice issues of many kinds and knowing others here and abroad who do the same. This made for a fruitful team. One of us is especially well endowed with friends and contacts around the world. One of us is a researcher, drunk on electronic access to everything, and interested in many domains. One of us, especially, knows folks devoted to community-based activism and devoted to storytelling. Finding the essays was about making those in our complex networks aware that we wanted to find out about storytelling projects—and then sitting back with delight when the projects kept showing up.

Earlier we noted that we located a great many more projects than we included in this volume. We read about and admired storytelling for social justice in Montreal, in Toronto, in the Caribbean, in the Pioneer Valley of Massachusetts, and within the structure of a labor union in Texas. We found storytelling projects in Cairo and Sydney, Palestine and Belgium and Des Moines and Denver, and deep in the jungles of the Philippines. Sometimes finding a person to shepherd the essay onto paper was impossible. Sometimes there was another issue, sometimes there was no space. In the end, finding projects was not difficult; they are everywhere. Even finding the very apt projects that we chose for the book was not difficult. You just have to look. People are telling stories everywhere to change the world.

* * *

Finally, a note about the organization of *Telling Stories to Change the World*. The book is divided into four parts. The first part, "The Language of the People Was Born," collects projects that focus on preservation—of language and environment, of history, memory, community, health, personal, and group resources. These projects are about keeping what matters alive. The second part, "This Needs Urgent Attention," gathers the projects that formed under specific and immediate threat: community disintegration, crisis suicide, various assaults on human rights. These projects are built for protecting and defending the targets of assault and shoring up the community. They also aim to alert the world. Each of the projects in the third part, "Weaving Freedom into New Tongues," springs from a revolutionary idea: a world without prisons, for example; the intrinsic dignity and civic power of Muslim women, historically; the beauty and artistic capacity of "disabled" performers. The fourth division, "The Power and the Limits of Stories," is set apart, with its own brief introduction, as this part considers the problems and possibilities of storytelling, complicating, we hope, whatever conclusions the reader may have come to already.

I

"The Language of the People Was Born"

Stories in the Service of Healing, Tradition, Cultural Vitality, History

1

Zuni River—*Shiwinan K'yawinanne*
Cultural Confluence

EDWARD WEMYTEWA AND TIA OROS PETERS

Edward Wemytewa; courtesy of A:shiwi A:wan Museum and Heritage Center

E:lah:kwa ho'n a:wan a:łashshina:we, dem don lił dek'ohan'an a:dey'ona. Ho'n a:wan don bena: ihdohk'yana:we. Hon yam anikwa:w akkya, dem le:w a:na' hon yam Shiw'an bena:w dap haydoshna:w akkya, hon oneyał k'okshi'kona' i:yona: ya:k'yana:we. Ishałde'ma Shiw'an bena:w dap haydoshna:w ya:nish a:deya'dun'ona.

This began to be made in a long ago time, when the ancient A:shiwi ancestors emerged from a damp underworld womb within Mother Earth and entered this world. The Ancestors traveled great distances of space and consciousness, and their relationships with the water, land, and collective spirit, evolved with them as they journeyed across the body of Mother Earth. Expressing primal responses in rhythm with the land and waters, *Shiwi'ma bena:we*, the language of the people, was born. During that era the ancient ones were guided through the land and instructed by *K'yan Asdebi*, the Water Strider, to live in the Middle Place, *Idiwana*, near *A:shiwi K'yawinanne*, the Zuni River. From this confluence of culture and story, land and shimmering water, the A:shiwi, the Zuni, were nurtured and today remain bonded to this place, knowing ourselves as the *Dowa Shiwan an chawe*, the Children of the Corn Priest.

A:shiwi ulohnan dewuso'ya a:deyaye. For a thousand centuries the Zuni River and the landscape sustained the A:shiwi. Life blossomed. Animals, plants and the people flourished along a rich riparian region. The health of the Earth was reflected in the vibrancy of the many Zuni villages that dotted the river-banks and high mesa areas. Relationships were defined and strengthened through a multitude of clanships like eagle and macaw, tobacco and turkey, sun and corn. Sometimes these long ago days were also very difficult. But mostly, these are remembered as harmonious and dynamic times for the A:shiwi who articulated a unique identity and worldview through complex rituals and spiritual engagement that resonated with the seasons of sun, wind, and rain. A:shiwi existence unfolded with great beauty, as vivid and promising as a butterfly freshly emerged from a chrysalis.

Cornmeal was offered in the glow of early morning light and sweet water percolated to the surface from deep underground springs, providing spiritual and physical sustenance. *Ko'n yado: ho'n a:wan Yadokkya Datchu dewankwin yela:nakwayle:'a.* An intricate webbed path of dreams and songs, storytelling and ceremonies laced together the spiritual and mundane worlds as grandfathers and grandmothers taught the younger generations about the confluence of life with the River. Women and children carried water in painted clay pots from the Zuni River, tending waffle gardens that grew cilantro, chili, onions, beans, and melons sustaining the people in the arid high desert. The people traded turquoise, salt, and stories with neighboring communities and far away tribes. Men hunted in the wooded mountains for elk and deer. They planted corn and squash, praying for the blessings of peace and rain. Offerings were given to the ancient ones, which the Zuni River conveyed as it flowed to

Kołuwala:wa, the final, everlasting place downriver. Nurtured by the Zuni River—*Shiwinan K'yawinanne*, the world was in balance.

The A:shiwi roamed and occupied 15.2 million acres from the wooded mountain range in the east, now known as the Zuni Mountains, to the flatland areas in the west, now known as the state of Arizona. All of this is what we still know and recognize as our aboriginal homeland. And it was a beautiful place rich with thriving gardens and fields, not just what some anthropologists would claim were little patches of onions or cilantro in dusty backyards where the people could barely scrape a meager living. At one time, when the Spanish conquistadors first eyed the wealth of A:shiwi lands, the Zuni watershed was intact and the River flowed freely through our territories. It fed streams and springs that nurtured more than 12,000 acres of agricultural land rich with corn, wheat, and alfalfa fields, that were cultivated and sustained the people. Not to mention that the River supported an abundance of wildlife which nourished Zuni cultural sustenance and a rich ceremonial life.

Peace was severed when the conquistadors Coronado and Oñate invaded Pueblo territories, cutting into our homelands, and dismembering the Ancestors with swords, greed, and God. Taking slaves, burning crops, all in search of gold when the real wealth was in corn, the power of the River, and in harmony found with the Natural World. Christian missionaries and settlers closely followed the invaders, ravenous for Native spirits and desperate to seize non-existent Zuni gold. Upon seeing the thousands of well-irrigated, thriving acres with the complex system of canals and ditches, their hunger for gold turned to a thirst for the most precious commodity in a desert ecosystem, water. Harsh change came to the land and to the A:shiwi as the people saw the first glint of steel blades in the hot sun and heard the anguished sound of children crying.

Incursions into vulnerable tribal homelands continued. The Zuni River was dammed and diverted by the Ramah Cattle Company empowering Mormon missionary settlements upriver in the late 1890s, impounding thousands of acres of water and altering the natural life and flow of the watershed. Meanwhile, other Anglo settlers and ranchers began clearcutting the forests, causing a dramatic increase in the amount of runoff in the drainage of the Zuni watershed, resulting in topsoil erosion and near total decimation of the ecosystem. The sun no longer shimmered on the Zuni River.

The Zuni River is a sacred waterway. It is an umbilical cord for Zuni people, a nurturing conduit linking the A:shiwi with a spiritual destiny, carrying prayers and offerings to *Kołuwala:wa*, our final, everlasting home. Only certain Zuni tribal leaders visit this special place during the summer solstice as part of the homecoming dance, a ceremony involving the Rain Dancers and their escorts from the village. The people await their return and anticipate hearing vivid descriptions of the blessed pilgrimage. As they return, the pilgrims share stories of what they saw and experienced during the journey to Zuni Heaven.

It is these stories that echo in the dreams and memories of the people, linking together past and present, a mirror for the future.

With the ebb and flow of the pilgrimages, the image of the numinous Zuni Heaven landscape is renewed within us. We decipher meaning from words and word patterns to redefine and create "the place." It is a necessary cultural process in building collective vision and tribal cohesion because the particular sacred landscape we talk about is off limits and not to be visited by just anyone in the village. In actuality, the majority of Zuni people will never see the treasured *Kołuwala:wa* in their lifetime with their own eyes, because of the associated religious taboos. Most Zunis will only know of this special place through the reflections of the spiritual leaders who are entrusted to be the link between worlds.

From such stories we know the landscape as a wetlands having two distinct mountains, a valley and a lake—a place serene and distant, as distant as a time when the *Kokko* (Kachinas) roamed the land, a time that could be equated to the world of dinosaurs. Zuni people recount dreams of this particular land-scape, with such familiarity and respect that reinforce tribal identity with something intimately connecting and awesome. For the A:shiwi, it is not necessary to see *Kołuwala:wa* but rather to trust the words shared by the leaders who see and walk gently upon the land, the land where we had lived in ancient time, where we witnessed a daunting event. The waterway was men-acingly alive at one time, a place where lives of children were lost to the River, and so marks a special resting place. Perhaps that is why the A:shiwi cry with mixed emotions of joy and sorrow when we see someone return from a four-day foot pilgrimage, someone who had actually walked upon the very sand and river rock of *Kołuwala:wa*.

There is a piece of an early Zuni story, of a brave little boy and his loving grandmother who lived in an ancient village *Kyadi:kya*, near the Zuni River and were transformed into swans by a white bear, a spirit visiting Zuni from the Place of Forever Snow. The bear-spirit told them, "*During the summer, you will go north, to my land—the Place of Forever Snow. We will be all there together. When winter comes, you will return back here to Kyadi:kya. There is a river below your house, and there in the water, you two will land . . . Your feathers will be so white like snow, and when the villagers are drawn in by your beauty, they will come to see their own feelings . . . You will make the people understand . . . This is how you will protect your Mother, by traveling from place to place.*"

As the story goes, the two beautiful white swans traveled from place to place, watching over the land. In the summertime they traveled north to the Place of Forever Snow, and in the winter they flew to Zuni lands and warmer weather, bringing other birds and their incredible beauty so the land wouldn't be lonely. Occupying the world that links the Earth and sky, birds are an indicator species, telling us what our lives have become and sometimes, of our destiny. We know them as our relatives through clanships of eagle and turkey, crow and macaw, and through traditional stories like this one, that link the A:shiwi with collective memories and a history of place, being, and purpose. But today, there is only a dry riverbed after decades of impact from the Ramah Dam and other incursions by non-indigenous settlers and ranches. Swans no longer travel from the Place of Forever Snow, to grace the lake near the Zuni village of Blackrock, or to dip their bills for food in the Zuni River.

In the early 1900s, the seeps and springs around *Koluwala:wa*, the convergence of the Zuni River and Little Colorado River, were drying up, and Zuni leaders raised serious concerns. The sacred place of dream and memory that was once lush with thick grass and flowers, that provided for the gathering of birds, wetland and fur-bearing animals and fish, and formed a foundation of Zuni spiritual life, began to die. Signs of this tragedy could be seen everywhere by experienced and knowing eyes. In subsequent religious pilgrimages, the leaders talked about the lake (*Hadink'yaya*) being void of turtles. Fewer animals and migratory birds came to nourish themselves there anymore.

The dam was expanded and fortified. It took decades to drain what was once a vibrant, moving waterway that sustained thousands of people and animals, to emptiness. 1982 was the last time the Zuni River flowed freely and flooded the village since the Ramah Dam was built. The precious waterway on which the community has relied for centuries died in its sleep as some vulnerable children do, a Sudden Infant Death. Only an empty riverbed remains where the river once flowed. Now our land is always thirsty. What was once a rich landscape awake with gardens, wheat and cornfields, animals and birds, is a parched land that only tears can soften today. *K'yawe denkya. Hish kwa' k'oksh'amme.*

Sadness lays hard on the land. Commodification and diversion of a most sacrosanct element, Water, the Zuni River, is not only an assault on the ecosystem and the people, but on the ability of our distinct culture to continue to grow and flourish, and of the Earth to regenerate and sustain us. Our lands are being plundered and our resources exploited for profit, with impunity. Precious watersheds that give birth to our lakes, springs, and streams and enable life in our communities are under attack. Polluted by toxins, dammed and diverted, the vital waters that nurture us and have assured our survival since ancient time are being killed by unquenchable greed, forcing us into poverty and pushing us further to the edge of existence. *Ma'che'k'wat dem k'yawina'kyadap, k'yawe yalolo'ankya, yadokkya k'yawina'kowa yadopba.*

To survive on our lands, the tribe wants wet water and not just water on paper. Reduction in development upstream will provide potential for instream flows through the Zuni reservation and on to *Koluwala:wa*, and bring ecological balance. Water is necessary to reinvigorate farming where it will be economically viable for the farmers and families relying on livestock.

The Zuni Tribe is using much of its resources to re-establish the wetlands, reaffirming the fact that springs are held in the greatest reverence for their life-giving properties and that many of the most important plants and animals in Zuni culture are wetland obligated species. Through asserting Federal rights and pursuing land claims settlements as well as through tribal memory and stories, the A:shiwi are fighting for our land, water, and cultural rights. Yet a frontiersman hostility meets Zuni community members who attempt to advance aboriginal water rights, hearing threats from those who siphon from the watershed like, "someone's going to get killed around here." Without place, the very structure of the people will erode away, and without the people's collective memory, the place will erode away unnoticed.

In earlier days, storytelling by elders was as common as the flowing Zuni River. *Halona*, close to the River, was the gathering place for Zuni elders who exchanged stories of daily accounts, historical events, or fables, just created. Like the River, this too has stopped. Only every once in a while do stories still trickle through the Zuni village.

It is unfortunate that what was enjoyed by so many in childhood, the shimmering flow of the River, the vitality of gardens and countless cornfields, and the cherished sight and sound of the storytellers, is no longer as available to Zuni children. This is where the Idiwanan An Chawe Theater Project comes in, to demonstrate the use of the *shiwi'ma bena:we*, the Zuni language. Fortified with the songs, stories, and place names, recalling ancestors who walked along the River, planted corn in the flood plains, and molded adobe bricks along the eastern shores of the Zuni River, the project works at the grassroots level to bring Zuni language acquisition skills and fluency to its community of 10,000 citizens.

Through this project, the entire community can still hear Zuni stories in the Zuni language, reinforcing the context of traditional culture and collective memory. Contemporary theater and artistic expression merge with traditional Zuni stories and knowledge, forming a unique language and cultural revitalization tool, aimed at social justice for Zuni people, history, and homelands. It is in this way that the people can still experience the tradition of storytelling and remember the flow of the River. These two precious resources, critical to A:shiwi existence, can be salvaged. It is not too late.

The Zuni are among many hundreds of other tribal communities on the frontlines of this struggle to recover the richness of land, community, and culture. Today, sacred areas of prayer, healing, burial, and history that resonate with the memories and consciousness of our peoples, places marked by the ancestors, are threatened with imminent destruction. Native homelands, waterways, and prayer sites are under assault. What was once a rich, diverse landscape is being stripped of its life-giving purpose, made barren, and struggling to survive. At this very moment, Indigenous peoples across the Americas are engaged in a mismatched battle for environmental justice and cultural recovery. The intimate connection and respect for such places has been challenged with brute force throughout Native America.

Seventh Generation Fund (SGF) is an Indigenous peoples' non-profit organization that has been involved in sacred sites protection and cultural revitalization for nearly thirty years. Emerging out of the political power and social justice movements of the 1960s and 1970s, the SGF has worked side by side with grassroots Indigenous communities in supporting community-based initiatives to design and implement culturally relevant strategies for cultural renewal and environmental justice. Through the SGF Affiliate Program, emerging grassroots community projects such as the Idiwanan An Chawe Theater Project receive integrated program and technical assistance, and financial support to grow and develop innovative Indigenous projects that directly serve community needs and express traditional Native vision and values.

We share this essay with you during an urgent time. Thousands of Indigenous languages of the world are quickly slipping into oblivion, and with that loss comes the death of distinct cultural knowledge and tribal worldviews, as well as possible claims to secure ancient places and waterways defined in the language and described in story. Tribes and community-based Indigenous organizations working to protect sacred places, retain aboriginal water rights, and sustain sovereignty are not only found in treaties and agency documents, but such knowledge survives in the memories, oral traditions, songs, and place names that live in the tribal languages. The Zuni language is under threat of extinction, just like the Zuni River, in the next generation, even though it is in far better shape than many Native languages in North America that are seeing a sunset of conversational fluency and adaptive capacity at the community level during this generation. The increasing loss of traditional, esoteric understanding and the rich concepts of Indigenous ecological knowledge not only impacts Native people but also indicates the potential devastation for all societies of life.

This chapter has been collaboratively created by two writers who are linked to a high desert ecosystem and the cool midnight sky where countless generations of our grandfathers and grandmothers have dreamed and danced, prayed and fasted, and farmed and hunted in the vast lands we know as *Idiwana*, the Middle Place. One author is a fluent, Native speaker and writer of Zuni whose first words were in his tribal language, *shiwi'ma bena:we*. Not only engaged on the frontlines to renew and sustain the beauty and efficacy of the Zuni language for future generations through his founding of the Idiwanan An Chawe Theater Project, he is also in the struggle to recover the Zuni River at the local, state, and federal agency levels. The other writer, Executive Director of the Seventh Generation Fund, is also a Zuni. Learning the language of her people as part of the language renaissance that is sweeping Native America, she also knows and recognizes that language acquisition is essential to understanding the nuances and depth of her tribal identity, and is, itself, an essential expression of sovereignty.

You may find that this chapter did not always lead you in a straight line journey of words and thoughts going from point 1 to point 2 to point 3. You may even find repetition or rhythm. This was as intentional as it is natural. Laguna Pueblo author Leslie Marmon Silko illuminates on this in saying, "*Pueblo expression resembles something like a spider's web—with many little threads radiating from the center, crisscrossing one another. As with the web, the structure emerges as it is made, and you must simply listen and trust, as the Pueblo people do, that meaning will be made.*" We hope that this essay helps immerse the reader in a structure that follows patterns of the oral tradition, as much as it takes aim at Western linear thinking and challenges the impacts of globalization, subverting them on behalf of tribal peoples and sacred places everywhere, through a unique and transformative Native narrative. And, we ask that you trust this essay to lead you on a pathway of compassionate understanding, and that it encourages you to take action for social, environmental, and cultural justice for the A:shiwi, for all Indigenous peoples, and for the Earth herself. *Hon yam Awidelin Tsitda handakłishna:wa.*

Edward Wemytewa is a former Zuni Tribal Councilman, and his connection to his Zuni cultural heritage is through art and language. He is a founding director of Idiwanan An Chawe, a storytelling theater. A playwright, performer, and visual artist, Edward's prize-winning paintings and sculptures have been exhibited in museums in Arizona and New Mexico.

Tia Oros Peters serves as Executive Director of the Seventh Generation Fund for Indian Development, an Indigenous peoples' organization working for social, cultural, and environmental justice for Native nations. She earned a B.A. in Law & Society from UC Santa Barbara, and an M.F.A. in Creative Writing from Antioch University.

Further Reading

Founded in 1977, Seventh Generation Fund for Indian Development is the oldest continually operating, identity-based fund dedicated to Native grassroots empowerment, community action, leadership development, cultural revitalization, and tribal sovereignty in the United States.

Seventh Generation Fund: www.7genfund.org

2

The Memory Book Project in Kampala, Uganda

"We're Not Going to Die Today or Tomorrow"

MARGARET SSWEANKAMBO, NAOME KUTEESA, NABUMA MARGARET, AND KASUJJA JOYCE; EDITED BY MADELINE FOX

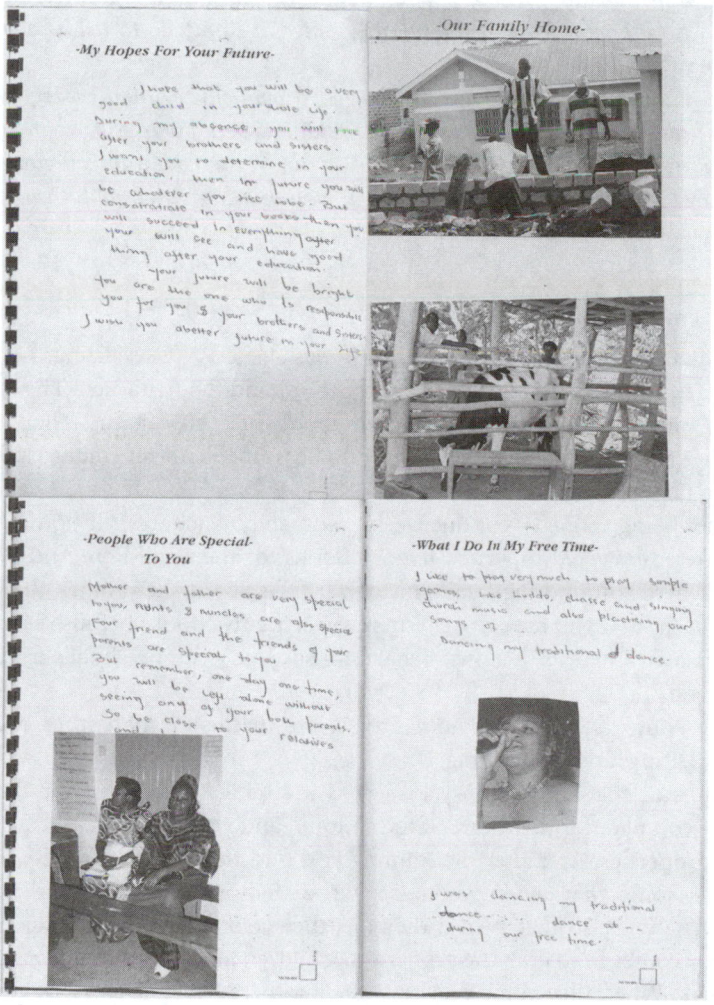

Pages from a Memory Book, lent by Stephen Shames

Editor's Note

In August 2005, we received a large envelope in the mail from Kampala, Uganda. The envelope contained two audio tapes and a spiral-bound book with a photocopied cover titled, "Memory Book."

Inside the "Memory Book" were pages telling the story of a child's life, written by her mother. Each page had a title: "The Story of Your Family," "Your Birth," "My Favorite Memories of You." And more pages providing important information for the child like: "My Education," "My Working Life," "My Health," "Information about Your Father," "Important Friends," "Our Family Home." Each page had been carefully completed with hand-written entries, photos, and newspaper clippings.

The shells of the audio tapes were broken and yet when we put them in the tape player we heard the voices of four Ugandan women, all HIV positive, gathered around a tape recorder in a community center in Kampala to tell us about the Memory Book Project.

On a continent fighting against the AIDS epidemic without nearly enough global support, in a country struggling to retain its own progressive approaches to combating AIDS, from the small offices of an innovative community organization, Margaret Ssweankambo, Naome Kuteesa, Nabuma Margaret, and Kasujja Joyce share with us their story.

The Memory Book Project

The Memory Project is a project which was started after realizing that there was a gap between [mothers living with AIDS] and their children. They had to find a way of talking to their children about their HIV status. They started together and got ideas that they needed to be trained and get empowered to be able to talk to their children.

After being trained—for one week—women go back to their homes where they are empowered to write Memory Books for their children. And this is a book where you find the family history. It talks about the mother, the father, and the child. If you have five children you write five books because each child has his own interests, his own behavior—so, you write five books for all the children.

The contents of the Memory Project are disclosure, parenting, Memory Book writing, and will writing.

You find that the Memory Project is a coping mechanism for the children—you plan for the future of the children and you also look at security for their properties. And after the training you find that by the time the women go back home, they are empowered to write Memory Books for their children, and write wills, so that even if they die, their properties are well shared and nobody comes in to grab the properties. Children also get a training after their mothers. When they come they say their mothers have talked to us and now we understand what is happening in our family. "We know how to care for our sick mothers or sick fathers and we can now be able to support our parents with the income-generating activities so that even if they pass away, there is no gap." And they remain in one home, so anybody who wants to support them, supports them from that one home. The children are no longer being shared by the relatives. Because you would find that if one child goes to a good family, she lives there a happy life. And the other one goes to a poor family, she would never go to school. So these children would never know each other.

So, one goal of the Memory Project is to keep the families united. And another is to share with the children the fact that the mom is HIV positive. And the third is to tell their family history.

If you die with a young baby, when you have a written a Memory Book for this child, when she grows, she reads this Memory Book and she can understand where she originates from. But, if you don't leave any writing, nobody will talk about that and they will never talk about any good thing the mother did. So, you talk about education if at all you went to school, the working-time, and if you have photographs you put [them in] so at least children as they read the Memory Book, at least they find that though my mother died HIV positive at least she had gone to school—she was a nurse! But, when we used to die, people would just say, "Oh. She has died of AIDS." And that is the end of the story. So, children just come away with a miserable mind. But if you have written something—"I have been a teacher," "I went to such and such a school," then you put in your photographs while you are still young and the photos as you grow up and then photos by the time you will die.

And then it comes to the father. In most cases you find that the in-laws don't want to give you the history about the spouses. Because, by the time the man dies, they blame us for killing the man, of having brought the disease in the home. They don't believe that maybe it's the man who brought the disease in the home. Most cases they blame the women. It's the women who have killed their brethren. So, they never like to give the information about the father. It's good to write the Memory Book before both of you die. And the father gives you the right information. If the father was a teacher or a farmer, they put that thing there. At least the child can know that, my father had a farm although the cows are no longer there now.

The good thing about the Memory Project is that when you are making the Memory Book you can include advice for your children—either boys or girls. You just write a word of advice so when the child comes to the adult stage, he can read that advice. For example, you can write that, "Please, do not have sex before marriage. Control yourself. AIDS is a bad disease. I have suffered so much, it is painful, I don't want you to experience what I have experienced. So, please behave and be on guard."

The Memory Book has also helped us to teach our children how to look after us when we are bedridden. Our children now know how to look after us when we are sick and where we get medication. When I fall sick, my child can get my book and take it to where I get medication.

On Stigma and AIDS in Uganda

A long time ago we used to not tell our children. The children used to hear it from the neighbors and then they would just come running. They said, "This one has said, Mom, you have HIV/AIDS." So, they used to take it as an abuse. But, when you tell them yourselves, then you sit, you get an entry point, you start to talk, you tell them—"I'm HIV positive, but I'm not dying today or tomorrow." So that they can have hope that you are not dying today or tomorrow. "And, if I'm sick you can take me to health care, and if I'm very sick, you go and get the nurses and they will come and treat me from home." So, they know where you get your drugs from. When you write a will, you don't show it to them, you give it to your lawyer, or you take it to where you get your drugs from. So that as soon as you die, those people can come in to support these children. By the time you die, you die a peaceful death.

But, if you keep quiet, and you take your drugs from the toilet, then even if you get sick your children will not support you. And when they see you eating an egg, then they say, "Mommy's very greedy. She eats the egg alone!" But, now they say, "Leave her egg. We need her life so that she can be able to support us." And that's why I even have a little money to live all these thirteen years.

The Memory Project reduces stigma at our neighbors' homes, in our communities . . . Because after disclosing my status to you, even if you come laughing at me that I am HIV positive—I don't care.

I tell them [about my status] so that I can save some other people's lives. Because if you disclose your status to other people, you can save two or three people. They come [and say], "Oh, I'm going to be very careful. How did you get the virus?" And then you start telling them the whole story. So, Memory Project also reduces stigma.

Making the Memory Book

When you have big children, you call the child whom you are writing the book for, you sit together with the child if the child is big. But with the small ones, you just write it because they don't understand what it is. And, if you tell a small child I am HIV positive, he will go and say, "You see, Mommy has said this," and then it will affect you so much. But with the big children, they will understand what it is. As you write the Memory Book, the child will say, "Ah, Mommy, this photo is not good. You put a nice photo. I know you are living with HIV, but please, put a nice photo where you are dressed up well." And sometimes the children, when you are adding information about the children, they will say, "I'd like you to put this photo of me." And, then when it comes to Hopes, writing what hopes you have for that child. [For example,] Cozulo was telling us that before his father died, he told him that he would be a very good doctor and now you see he is working very hard because his father said he'd be a good doctor.

The most challenge which we have seen in this Memory Project [is] where you find the mothers who are HIV positive and some children who are HIV positive and disclosing your status to the child is difficult. Telling the child that, "My daughter, you are HIV positive." The child has very many questions, "Mommy, I've never had sex. How does it come that I am HIV positive?" That is a very sensitive question, and it may take you twenty days before you are able to answer that child. So the mothers who have children living with HIV/AIDS really find it very hard. But, with the training in the Memory Project they got empowered and they were able to talk to their child. It took them a long time, but they were able to tell their children. After telling them that you are HIV positive but you are not dying today or tomorrow. AIDS is manageable and you can be able to live for quite a long time, provided you follow the rules and the advices given to you by the counselor and the doctor. And now, as we speak, the drugs are available and we have hope of living long and our children are happy that they see us looking nice. What they ask is, "Long time ago, people with HIV/AIDS used to be very thin, but I see you growing fat. What's happening?" I say only that I have been living Positively, and the Memory Project training empowered me so much to be able to talk to my children. And my children have supported me so much.

On How the Memory Project has Impacted Lives

Before I [talked about] my HIV status with my children, it was really difficult for the children. And, after disclosing I say, "My dear, the rice and food I bring, I'm getting this from Nsambya Home Care Clinic. Nsambya Home Care Clinic is supporting us with food aid, so that we can be able to survive." And, children will ask you whenever you become sick and see you with the medicine in your bag, "What's this drugs for?" I could not tell them because I didn't want them to know that I am HIV positive. But, after disclosing I say now, "These drugs, I get them from Nsambya Home Care Clinic, and if I'm sick you can go there and tell the counselors to come and take me to the hospital." And, that's why I've been able to live for ten years with HIV.

Our children are our treatment supporters. They help us with treatment. When you are taking the drug, the pill may be at night. When it comes to night, the children remind us "Mommy, it's time for drugs, it's coming to eight at night." They bring water and then they bring the pill. So, our children are helping us because of the Memory [Project] training, after the disclosure.

Margaret Ssweankambo (MS) interviews Nabuma Margaret (NM)

MS: My dear, beautiful, lady. Before you were trained in the Memory Project, how were you finding this situation in your home between you and the children?

NM: The situation was very bad because my children didn't know my status and I was planning how I was going to tell my children because my children were very young then, and I couldn't break that sad news to them. But, after getting the Memory Project training, I was empowered and I gained strength to break the news to my children and that helped me very much.

MS: After the breaking the ice to your children, how did you feel?

NM: [laughter] I felt so much relieved. All my heart was washed, and I was OK and fine.

MS: Did you have any funny questions from the children?

NM: Yes. My last born, who is called Hilda, asking me, "Mommy, but Uncle told me that my father died of TB and now you are telling me that you are HIV positive. Does it mean our dad also died of AIDS?" I said "Yes" to that girl. And that's when they came to know that their father also died of AIDS and I started explaining each and everything.

MS: Did you have any blame for your husband before getting the training in the Memory Project? Blaming him that it was him who brought the disease?

NM: Yes, of course [laughter]. I got that blame because I was very very very faithful to my husband. I was [laughter] blaming him that maybe he was the one who might have brought the virus. But, after the Memory Project training, I couldn't blame him anymore.

MS: So far how many books have you written for your children?

NM: Two, and remaining four, because I have six children—four biological children and two adopted children. But, I wish, let me pray to God, I wish to write the other four more books.

MS: Have you been able to write a will?

NM: No. In the Memory Project I have failed to do that. Maybe it is because I don't have anything. I have not been able to make a will.

MS: Have you been able to select a foster parent for your children to take care of your children after you have passed away?

NM: I have failed to do that. But, I feel good because my first born is nineteen years now. Now I think my first born can look after [the other children].

MS: Has she got a job?

NM: Ah, no.

MS: Then, how is she going to be able to look after the young siblings?

NM: I pray to God to bring another person who is like Uncle Steve [Shames] to help that first born to go to the University.

MS: Have you ever tried to talk to some of your relatives, like a sister or aunties, to find out whether they will be able to take care of your children if, at all, you are no longer alive?

NM: I have tried. But, everyone is telling me that, "You see, we are in a single or double rented room. I can't add any child to my family. So, maybe you can take those children to their father's family deep in the village in Masaka?" I can't do that, because if I had done that, my children wouldn't have gone to school.

MS: So, now, when do you think you will be able to write the will, because it is really important for you to write a will? Although you say you have nothing, even if it is a photo, or your own clothes and you haven't told the children where you want to be buried. Children should know! Because, your brother might come and say, "We are taking our sister." Then, the in-laws will say, "We are taking the dead body of our wife." And then the children will be confused. But, when you write a will for them, then the one with the will will say, "This lady say she be buried at the place of her husband." And, people will obey the will.

The Memory Project has helped so much because the fear we had reduced. As soon as the husband dies, oh you think even the next day you are going. But, now, we know we no longer die, we can stay for quite a long time and now when we talk to your children and your children support you. And as your children support you, you also talk to your relatives so they can support you—those who can. And this really made us to live! If you tell them, when you see me like this—I need milk. Then your brother will understand that you really need it. But, if they don't know that you are HIV positive, they will not understand that you need the milk. And, when they hear that you are sick, at least those who are supportive, they come very fast to support the family and the children no longer stay very miserable with no food, no water, the mother is sick and the children are very worried. They [the children] used to end up going to the streets. Now, they have hope that at least our mother will live, the brother is helping, and the Nsambya Home Care Clinic is coming in with the medicine—so, for them life goes on.

Reaching Out in the Community

Now, me, I work as a volunteer for Nsambya Home Care Clinic. I go around from the client to take to them medicine. And, I look after them when they are very sick. I can go to get the doctor. And, others, they come and ask you, "What are you using?" They come for advice. So, I advise them—"You go and get tested for HIV." After that they go and they attend the clinics.

The Memory Book Project helps me to go out to look for others [who are HIV positive] because I don't fear. I go there straight and I advise them to go to the hospital.

You'll find that the people in the community now admire us who have attended the Memory Book Project and they wish they could have a training also so that they are able to leave a will for their children, although they are not HIV positive. So you find it has made a very great impact in the community.

We have become trainers; although we are HIV positive, we are trainers. We train those who are not HIV positive.

Margaret Ssweankambo, Naome Kuteesa, Nabuma Margaret, and **Kasujja Joyce** are all taking antiretroviral drugs and living healthy, vibrant lives in Kampala. They are volunteers with the Stephen Shames Foundation (see below). The Memory Book Project was started by the National Association of Women Living with HIV and AIDS (NACWOLA) in 1997.

Margaret Ssweankambo is a nurse, HIV/AIDS counselor, and community activist. She teaches sewing to teenagers, looks after a score of non-related orphans, and is Benon's aunt.

Naome Kuteesa is the mother of four children including Moses and Afuwat, who are students in Concern for the Future.

Nabuma Margaret is a volunteer at TASO, The AIDS Support Organisation. She is an activist, HIV/AIDS counselor, and mother of Hilda and Derrick.

Kasujja Joyce is a Peer Counselor in HIV/AIDS and she volunteers at Nsambya Home Care. She is the mother of Paddy, Michael, Wasswa, Moreen, Brian, and Freddy, and she looks after Jackson.

Further Reading

The Stephen Shames Foundation raises funds for and partners with Concern for the Future, a successful Ugandan-run educational program, which in a few years has transformed the lives of seventy-five very smart, motivated AIDS orphans, child soldiers, working children, and young people in refugee camps.

Concern for the Future: www.concern4future.org
Stephen Shames Foundation: www.stephenshames.org

3
Telling the Truth
How Breaking Silence Brought Redemption to One Mississippi Town

SUSAN M. GLISSON

Philadelphia, Mississippi; Kate Medley

On June 21, 1964, Father's Day that year, three young men, one black and two white, drove into Neshoba County, Mississippi, to investigate a church burning. They were the first of a wave of young people who would make up the staff of the Mississippi Summer Project, more well known as Freedom Summer. A campaign coordinated by four major civil rights organizations, the project aimed to register masses of black voters in the notoriously "closed society," and to test the nation's commitment to political inclusion and real democracy.

The state's power structure and many of its white citizens did not welcome these "invaders," as they came to see the freedom workers, and a newly reorganized Ku Klux Klan worked in concert with the white supremacist and state-funded Sovereignty Commission to monitor, intimidate, and eliminate the perceived threat. The three young men, intent only on supporting a local black community as it overcame fear and harassment, walked into this whirlwind and reaped the deadly consequences.

After investigating the church ruins and attempting to visit parishioners who had suffered beatings before flames consumed the church, the three civil rights workers—James Chaney, Andrew Goodman, and Michael Schwerner—drove back toward Meridian to the Congress of Racial Equality (CORE) office that Michael and his wife Rita Schwerner coordinated. As they drove, Philadelphia policemen stopped them, ostensibly for speeding. Held in jail long enough for Lauderdale and Neshoba Klansmen to gather an assassination team, the three young men were released around ten o'clock that evening and never seen alive again.

As the nation was gripped by the 44-day search for the bodies—and as white Mississippi officials declared the disappearance a hoax—the town of Philadelphia experienced a different kind of "invasion," this time an influx of FBI agents and military personnel and journalists. Hundreds of newspaper articles and magazines dissected and criticized the town's race relations and community mores for a national audience. Only a few local whites spoke out publicly against the murders, even though many knew the names of Klan members and participants in the murders. One native son reflecting years later on the climate at the time has said, "Growing up in Philadelphia, Mississippi helps me understand Nazi Germany." He described a tremendous penchant in those days to conform to authority. He reported hearing as an adolescent, " 'Those kids shouldn't have been murdered but they also shouldn't have been here.' "

After the bodies had been found buried in an earthen dam, and after outsiders had left the community—some to pursue cases against the murderers—knowledge of the case dissolved into a public secret. Everyone knew about the event but no one talked about it. Children who grew up in Philadelphia heard whispers of murder, when adults gathered to talk about old times and thought the kids were out playing. But as surely as winter slips into spring, the murders became a season out of time and mind. The silence infused the town and guilt hovered like clouds. Many children, some who understood that an evil had occurred there, left home. But many used the silence to initiate changes. Some adults and children facilitated a quiet and relatively smooth process of public school integration in Philadelphia. And black and white children began to grow up together. Public facilities became open to all, and in time, local blacks campaigned for and won public office.

Still the secret of murder dogged the way local people and outsiders thought of Philadelphia, Mississippi. Presidential candidate Ronald Reagan used the reputation of Neshoba as a place committed to white supremacy to cement his "Southern strategy" in 1980, for example. On August 3 of that year, Reagan delivered an early campaign speech at the Neshoba County Fair, at a campground less than five miles from the earthen dam where the three young men had been buried by Klansmen. Among many exhortations to the crowd, Reagan declared, "I believe in states' rights," echoing the white supremacist mantra of the 1950s and 1960s. Many observers across the nation interpreted Reagan's visit and his declaration in that haunted place as a barely coded message in support of white supremacy and racial discrimination. Just over fifteen years after the murders, the image of the president at Neshoba communicated a conflicting and troubling message to the nation.

The clouds slowly began to lift twenty-five years after the crime. A group of local leaders, many of whom had been teenagers when the murders occurred, held an interracial memorial ceremony. Then-Secretary of State and native son Dick Molpus apologized to the families of the victims, who had been invited to town for the occasion. For many, this public apology, the first by any Mississippi public official, felt like someone had opened the window of a house that had been closed up for way too long. Following closely on the heels of the ceremony, the local newspaper editor, Stanley Dearman, flew to New York and interviewed Carolyn Goodman, the mother of one of the slain civil rights workers, Andy. In a lengthy article, Dearman shared Goodman's remembrances of her son. To many in the community, Andy became more than a faceless victim for the first time. He became a son and a brother and a friend, a person with hopes and dreams and courage. A person who did not deserve to die. Rays of sunshine began to shine down on Neshoba, highlighting glimpses of truth and redemption.

But still, the town's reputation as a bastion of racism lingered. After all, Philadelphia was still a place that allowed murderers to walk freely among the people. In truth, another fifteen years passed by before real change would come.

In the fall of 2003, two old friends ran into each other on the courthouse steps. One was black, one white. These men had gone to school together, worked together at the newspaper as interns to Mr. Dearman. Both had grown up in the shadow of the murders. Leroy Clemons had just been elected to chair the county National Association for the Advancement of Colored People (NAACP). He campaigned on a platform of addressing the murders. Jim Prince had just returned home to run the newspaper. The two men quickly determined to pressure local leaders to acknowledge the upcoming fortieth anniversary of the murders in some appropriate way.

Early in 2004, Clemons and Prince formed a task force with the full support of the city, county, and tribal officials. They invited a university-based non-profit institute that specializes in racial reconciliation to help facilitate the task force's work, which they initially identified as commemorating the fortieth anniversary. (I am the director of this non-profit center.) But both men hoped for more. They wanted to issue a call for justice. But they weren't sure the larger community would approve of that goal. And so, at the first meeting in April of the new task force, blacks and whites sat around a table and began to talk about the public secret.

For the African Americans in the room, this new discussion had been long overdue. Each year Mt. Zion United Methodist Church, which had on that fateful day in 1964 been burned in order to lure the civil rights workers to town, held a memorial service for the victims and demanded an accounting for the murders. Few local whites attended these services.

At the first task force meeting, local blacks were eager for action, for a public demand for accountability. They suggested a march through town. The whites in the room shrank visibly in their seats. For them, marches meant direct protest and rioting. They countered with a proposal for a community resolution. Now it was the black participants' turn to resist. Resolutions were just words on a page. They wanted action. It was clear that while both groups agreed to sit at the same table, unanimity about next steps would be difficult to achieve.

The group decided to open the meetings to the public. Jim Prince initiated a series of editorials and articles about the upcoming anniversary as one way to raise awareness in the town and to clear the clouds. We moved from the local chamber of commerce boardroom to the fellowship hall of the First United Methodist Church and in one session asked the attendees to say why they were there. The stories that tumbled out were powerful and moving. The variety of voices spoke to the different sectors of the community and laid the ground for breaking the old silence.

Jewel Rush McDonald is the daughter of Georgia Rush and sister to John Thomas Rush, members of Mt. Zion beaten by Klansmen the night of the church burning in 1964. She wept as she spoke of her family's fear that summer, that Klansmen would return to "finish the job," to keep them from identifying their assailants. She told of hiding clothes in the chicken coop in case the house was burned and they needed to make a quick escape. And she spoke of leaving Mississippi and its racism behind, only to return decades later when her mother fell ill. She was determined now to make Philadelphia her home but wanted justice, not just for "those three boys," but for her mother and brother, too.

Nettie Cox Moore, an African American woman from Philadelphia, joined at the urging of Leroy, despite her deep distrust of whites. Nettie had been a school teacher in the local system and had begun teaching civil rights history in the 1960s and wearing dashikis to class. Rumors that she was a militant precipitated her firing, so Nettie was not inclined to believe that any whites shared her beliefs. She was quiet in the early meetings but soon learned that the whites in the group were as outraged about the murders as she. When the time came that she told Leroy she might, in fact, like some white folks, she helped transform a fragile peace into an enduring civic bridge.

After reading about what we were now calling the Philadelphia Coalition in the newspaper, Deborah Posey decided to see "if it was for real." Posey is a white, rural, working-class woman who married into the family of one of the murderers. She initially believed what her husband's family—and her culture—claimed: that the three workers were "Communist infiltrators," "dirty," and not worth grieving over. But one day, she saw a picture of the three men. They looked clean and decent and, somehow, she began to question everything she'd ever believed in. Weekly prayers at a stone memorial she built by hand at the murder site just off Highway 19 cemented her determination to do something. She hoped that faith would help cleanse her community.

Fent DeWeese had been one of the few whites who regularly attended the Mt. Zion memorial service. He spoke about how Dick Molpus's apology in 1989 had begun to relieve the guilt of the whites of his generation. And he consistently pushed the group to be aggressive in pursuing a trial.

James Young was one of the first black children to integrate Philadelphia Elementary, just two years after the '64 murders. Being in this cohort was a difficult experience that could have caused Young to hate whites forever. Yet he does not, and he rose to hold the chairmanship of the Neshoba County Board of Supervisors, the first African American to do so. His membership in the Coalition underscored the new political clout that black Mississippians held. It also reflected Young's belief that the relationships built between Coalition members are its most important accomplishments because these relationships express the healing power of the Coalition's work.

Guy Nowell is a white banker, quiet and reserved. He spoke of embarrassment as he shared why he became a member of the Coalition. He has endured shame all these years because whites hadn't stood up against the Klan and had allowed murderers to go free. In June 2004, at the Coalition's public appeal for justice, Nowell attempted to apologize to David Goodman, Andy's brother, for the murder. Goodman, in his gentle way, assured Nowell that no such apology was necessary. It was, as Nowell recounted the next day, the first time he hadn't felt ashamed to be from Neshoba County.

Each member had a powerful story. We spent a majority of the early Coalition meetings listening to the words members said publicly for the first time, watching as relationships formed and deepened across racial lines. These stories made the path to unity apparent. The group determined to issue a call for justice to the state of Mississippi and pressure local officials to join them. The call for justice led to unanimous endorsements from the Chamber of Commerce, the City Council, and the County Board of Supervisors.

After this, the group members developed ever-stronger connections to each other, even while the group as a whole continued to bear the suspicion of some civil rights veterans and family members of victims who did not trust this new push for atonement from the long-silent community. During one contentious meeting, some of these veterans challenged the motives of the group. Members literally sat with their arms around each other as they responded to the charges in unity.

Armed with clear community support for a trial, the Coalition met with the local district attorney. And in September, 2004, it invited Carolyn Goodman and her son David to join in a meeting with the state attorney to push for a trial. In that meeting, the community again shared its stories, trying to get the attorney general to understand the cost of the murders, the shame—and fear for the town's moral well-being. And Carolyn Goodman shared her story, of the ultimate sacrifice of a mother to a cause she raised her son to support. According to the attorney general, this meeting cemented his commitment to bring the case to trial.

On January 6, 2005, the Day of Epiphany in the Christian calendar, the state of Mississippi brought the first murder charges in the 1964 murders. On January 7th, I sat in the Neshoba County Courthouse between Leroy Clemons and Jewel Rush McDonald, as district attorney Mark Duncan accused reputed Klansman Edgar Ray Killen of taking the lives of three human beings. Jewel and I held hands and wept, mostly for joy at some measure of justice finally coming. We also wept in sadness as we remembered her mother and brother, both now deceased, who'd been beaten by Killen's Klan brethren forty years before at Mt. Zion Church. Leroy was stoic throughout the arraignment; later he would tell reporters he'd been certain that the indictment was coming: "Neshoba County has been ready to remove the stigma that haunts it."

And this is what we learned, that underneath the silence of decades about the murders, there were citizens who were waiting for someone—for a group of community members—to speak up, to tell the story of the civil rights workers' lives and to condemn their deaths. As we gathered together on the evening after the public call for justice in 2004, the members of the Coalition related their new-born feelings of relief and pride in their community. The white mayor shared an encounter with a black attendee at the previous day's service. When she saw his name tag and confirmed that he was the mayor, she said she had one question. "All these years," she said, "I've heard of the clouds over Neshoba County." She went on to ask, "Where are they? Today, all I can see is sunshine."

The coalition made a commitment early on that their work wasn't just in the interest of justice in *this* case. It was about making Neshoba better for everyone. In the battle to build a stronger, healthier community, the Philadelphia Coalition has undertaken an educational reform project to teach local children about civil rights history. The group does not want to teach the traditional "savior narrative" that most students learn. This civil rights curriculum aims to offer Philadelphia children a sense of their own empowerment. It wants to define "civic engagement" in the tradition of local black activists throughout the state's history. It wants to make visible the heroes that Hollywood doesn't make movies about. These definitions of "community interest" have carried the group forward.

From the inception of the Philadelphia Coalition, its work has been marked both by hopefulness and by controversy. While its members struggled to build trust among each other across years of silence and suspicion, others attacked the Coalition, some even accusing its participants of being Klansmen. In the end, the attacks from outside the community forged a bond of determination that allowed this band of thirty to move their community from public silence to public condemnation of the murders in less than three months.

The story of Neshoba County is an American one. It has the heroes and villains that have marked this nation's conflicted journey through racial terrain since its founding. But mostly, this story is about complicated human beings, none of whom are perfect but all of whom are trying hard to discern a path to a better community for all. After the vicious murders enacted by a cabal of local law enforcement, state officials, and a racist vigilante group, after forty years of largely public silence on the indignity of the crime, few expected a new day in Neshoba County or a model coming out of Neshoba that can be useful across the country. The fact is, because some in the group came together to denounce these crimes and to commit to a healing process, the group has modeled a challenge for the whole country: to acknowledge its hypocritical appeal to the principles of democracy and freedom while continuing an oppressive legacy of slavery.

On June 26, 2005, a New York *Newsday* column declared that "Mississippi is America now." The backhanded compliment was meant to bestow upon Mississippians the dubious honor of having achieved legitimate membership in the Land of the Free. But Mississippi has always been America, with its racial violence and insincere pledges to a gospel of freedom. That this state now shows us all a way out of the racial morass may be surprising. But really, this development is appropriate. Indeed, it was the young activists of the Student Nonviolent Coordinating Committee (SNCC) and CORE like Michael Schwerner and James Chaney who believed that Mississippi would be the proving ground for America's stated commitment to democracy.

Racism is not just in the past. One need only witness the consequences of poverty and race laid bare in the aftermath of Hurricane Katrina to see that racism lives and breathes in the heart of America. But so too does oppression's greatest enemy—the ability of an organized, empowered, and enlightened citizenry to topple discrimination and to build a beloved community.

Too often Americans look for white male heroes. Too often the media create them. In the rush to anoint a new "hero" responsible for the latest developments in Neshoba County, the work of the Philadelphia Coalition has often been slighted. And so the complicated story of real growth in Mississippi, one of "the last bastions" of racism, has been completely ignored.

Our story, then, is an American one, of individuals overcoming great obstacles to make their lives and communities better. Because this story is set in Mississippi, the elements of hope and redemption are especially profound and moving. The Philadelphia Coalition is far from having achieved what the group thinks of as ultimate victory—an integrated, egalitarian community. Indeed, momentum is complicated as the group tries to define other common agendas. But we have made significant and historic progress, guided by faith that the real democracy we envision represents the culmination, finally, of the American Dream.

Susan M. Glisson is the executive director of the William Winter Institute for Racial Reconciliation at the University of Mississippi. She co-authored (with Sam Chaltain and Charles Haynes) *First Freedoms: A Documentary History of the First Amendment Rights in America* (Oxford University Press, 2006) and edited *The Human Tradition in the Civil Rights Movement* (Rowman & Littlefield, 2006).

Further Reading

William Winter Institute for Racial Reconciliation: www.olemiss.edu/winterinstitute

4

"Our Ancestors Danced Like This"

Maya Youth Respond to Genocide through the Ancestral Arts

CZARINA AGGABAO THELEN

The musicians of Sotz'il dressed as the divine energies of the four directions, including Ixmukane (leftmost) and Yaxb'alam E (middle); Victorino Tejaxún

Sacred fire of the Serpent's dance:

We invoke the circle
To receive the power of the four cardinal points
and to bring Heaven to Earth.

Our steps are an offering.
Our art is the walk of our lives.

Here we collect the textures of our days:
Feathers, stones, weavings, tecomate, petate,
Corn, clay, branches, leather, fire.

We sound the music that invigorates our being:
Birdsong, the cascade of water,
The breeze whispering through dry leaves,
The indomitable blaze of the drum,
The peal of turtle shells,
The melody of steps in the cornfields.

We name the names of the sacred energies.

Fusing form with fertility, we Create.

By what miracle do we kindle
What creates life and beauty from Nothing?

Nothing more than the heat of our heart
Stirs our dance.

If only we could always live with such purity of intention!
—the piercing wail of the conch shell—

Ours is the elemental task:

To dig up what has been buried under a half thousand years of
Indignities, atrocities, massacres, and colonizations of our being . . .

Therefore:

We give breath to the half-forgotten melodies
That escape from the lips of our elders.

We construct instruments that only exist
Frozen in murals and museums.

Under our steps, our Mother Earth reminds us
That our ancestors danced like this.

Perhaps it is as Confucius said:
"I merely transmit, I do not create;
I love and revere the Ancients."

By giving form to our dreams,
We break out of what limits us.

Raising our songs to the sun,
We give light to that which, for centuries,
Has been waiting to be born.

Story contributes to social justice struggles by affirming the value of oppressed peoples' cultures and re-igniting their embattled will to survive and defend their land and way of life against the destructive forces of oppression, racism, degradation, and genocide. Where once the Maya peoples in Guatemala had to struggle for social justice solely through physical defense and political action, the next generation is now incorporating the power of story. The Maya youth theater group Sotz'il resurrects an ancestral story that has been forced into near oblivion by Guatemalan colonial powers because of its empowering Maya cultural symbolism and theme: the cycle of a people's resistance, survival, regeneration, and ultimate liberation. This essay explores why Sotz'il's theatrical presentation of the ancestral story of Kaji' Imox has such deep resonance with the contemporary Maya movement for social justice in the wake of the recent genocide. Their story is a testament to the fundamental role of a culture's creative forces in renewing the life of a people even as horrifying waves of greed and empire threatened to extinguish it.

Surviving Two Waves of Genocide

Nearly 500 years ago, the Spanish began their invasion of the Mesoamerican Mayas' lands. As they moved south from the Aztecan stronghold of Tenochtitlán, they were preceded by European diseases that messengers and regional traders unsuspectingly carried. Smallpox and other epidemics laid waste to many Maya communities before the Spanish even set foot on the land of the Maya Kaqchikeles, one of over two dozen Maya nations that survived the colonization. Under the subsequent Spanish domination, the Kaqchikel people and all Maya peoples across Mesoamerica were cruelly persecuted.

Their ceremonial and governance centers were ransacked and their villages were destroyed. Forced into slavery, the Mayas had to haul on their shoulders the materials for the construction of the new Spanish empire, from the Atlantic ports to the Pacific coast. The wave of death resulting from this inhumane treatment threatened to extinguish the Maya population.

On top of the physical torment, the Spanish tried to break the spirits of the surviving Mayas to gain their complete submission to the colonization process—including the new empire's labor needs, its aspirations of religious conversion, and its Machiavellian objective of killing once and for all the Mayas' resistance and struggle for their land. The Maya culture, and their spirituality in particular, were targeted. A drastic set of laws was imposed that forced them to practice Catholicism and prohibited many potent expressions of Maya culture. Bishop Diego de Landa ordered the destruction of all Maya books in a fanatic campaign to wipe out Maya spirituality. In the most infamous incident in 1562, he burned 5,000 Maya sacred objects and statues and over 2,500 codices (hieroglyphic texts) that contained thousands of years of history, scientific data, and cultural legacy. Landa himself recounted, "We burned them all, which they [the Maya] regretted to an amazing degree, and which caused them much affliction."

Ever since the Spanish invasion, the Mayas have continued to suffer the brunt of the Guatemalan government's policies of exclusion and exploitation, and they have increasingly been forced to cede their land to wealthy Ladino ("non-Maya", according to Guatemalan definitions) landowners. In the late 1970s, about halfway through Guatemala's 36-year internal armed conflict, the left-wing revolutionary movement's push for a more equal land and power distribution in Guatemala began to resonate with many Mayas. Yet almost immediately after significant numbers of Mayas began to join the revolutionary movement, the government began campaigns that razed entire Maya communities, disregarding their status as civilians. The military sought to wipe out the "seeds of resistance," and Maya *culture* was deemed to be that. Thus Maya spiritual leaders were targeted, and the practice of Maya spirituality was forced underground. Maya men who wore their traditional clothing were considered suspect. Asserting one's identity as Maya was considered a sign of insurrection to the government's death squads.

As a result, in the early 1980s, the Maya peoples suffered a second wave of genocide and unspeakable atrocities. Over 400 Maya villages were burned to the ground by the Guatemalan government's forces, and their inhabitants were raped and butchered. In many cases, all the villagers would be forced into the village church, and then the soldiers would burn the church to the ground, oblivious to the people's screams of agony. *Under such overwhelming oppression and genocidal forces, with their land-based subsistence culture at stake, how do a people survive?* . . . because such circumstances make an easy slide into despair and self-destruction.

In response, some Maya community leaders attest that the unabiding practice of their culture was at the heart of maintaining their ancestors' will to survive during the Spanish colonization.

In the current post-war era, the youth group Sotz'il adds another dimension to the cycle of resistance and survival by creating the first play in a Maya language since the colonization. By reclaiming a potent ancestral story about their cultural legacy, they inspire their community to transform the current oppressive system into one that does not mutilate their Maya values and culture, but rather celebrates it. After so many waves of destruction and death, Sotz'il's experience illuminates the miracle of fertility and regeneration—to transcend physical limitations, continue the ancestral line, and inspire new births and creations, in art and elsewhere—touching us with the brilliance of life itself.

Generations of Resistance—"We Must Find Another Path!"

The experience of the parents and grandparents of the youth who founded Sotz'il epitomizes the national experience of repression, resistance, and transformation into a more just society of their collective making. The grandfather of one clan sought to improve his community's well-being through development projects. Through community committees that wrote proposals and solicited funds from international donor agencies, he was the leading force behind bringing potable water to Sotz'il's rural community. In turn, at the age of ten his son Anastasio was recruited to be secretary to help the elders of the committee with their written transactions. Years later, after starting his own family and studying at night from middle school through college, don Anastasio eventually became a teacher and a leader in the bilingual education movement that seeks to make Maya languages and cultures a cornerstone of education in their communities. Now don Anastasio is the father of some of the founders of Sotz'il, and these values have been passed down to his children.

However, his experience of "The Violence"—as the height of the repression in the early 1980s is colloquially referred to—was equally influential.

Simply for being a community leader, he was persecuted. "The military went around monitoring who were the leaders of local groups," says don Anastasio, who at that time was a captain of the local soccer team and president of the local development committee that over the years organized to obtain a community auditorium, a child sponsorship program, and electric light for the community. "I remember that I had some diplomas, the ones that they give you as recognition at an activity. I had to bury them so that the military wouldn't identify me as a member of a committee."

Still, he ended up in the hands of the military on an easy afternoon while playing soccer. His name and photo were on a list the military maintained of those leaders they wished to "disappear"—that is, clandestinely assassinate. He escaped that day, but he immediately went into hiding. The next day, his house was surrounded by military soldiers. They pursued don Anastasio for six months. By then, his third child had been born, so he made daring visits to his young family under the cover of night:

> My family suffered. They had a lot of shocks of fright because of the persecution. During my nighttime visits, my neighbors would warn me, "Get out of the house! The army is coming! They are going from house to house to register people!" And we would flee with our children.
>
> We would hide in some small pine grove, sometimes in the midst of our cornfields, sometimes farther away. We brought with us a large sheet of plastic, or something to cover us. We stayed out there for a long time, until dawn started to break at four or five in the morning. Only then did we return to the house.

This persecution indelibly marked don Anastasio's wife and children, as well as his work. For several years, his organizing became political, as the physical defense of the community became an increasingly pressing need. Eventually, this community defense project converted into a movement to gain local power in the mayorship and town council. "This was a time of so much unity. Thus, the Civic Committee was born. We wanted to *do* something. We couldn't keep going along with a system of political parties that takes advantage of the vote of the people, and in the end doesn't do anything. As a result, we succeeded in electing the first indigenous Mayor of Sololá in ninety-five years. And we kicked out the military base and installed a university on that land."

However, as the years wore on, the rural Maya communities suffered from the painful divisions sown by the war and repression. Consequently, don Anastasio's vision of how social change is achieved, and how he participates in that process, has evolved:

> I have come to think that I have my responsibility with my family. Above all, if we don't educate our youth, it is a shame. We *must* fight what is not correct—the social injustices. But we also must find a way —to not continue sacrificing lives. I tell the youth now, "We must appreciate life."
>
> Recently, they killed a man here. When the community met, I told everyone, "Look, let's do something. I believe there's another way! No more violence, no more orphans, no more widows. It doesn't suit the community!"
>
> As a teacher, I've realized that if things stay as they are [that is, dictated by violence and force], it becomes a psychological problem. I've had this experience with schoolchildren. It's difficult to see. So that's

why I told the community, "No more violence! If we continue like this, what will our children inherit? We don't believe that being violent offers us anything. No—we must find another path."

Another Kind of Inheritance: Don Anastasio's Political Resistance Becomes Sotz'il's Art

In addition to these early childhood experiences with their father, don Anastasio's children had their own experiences of discrimination and oppression within Guatemalan society that moved them to create Sotz'il with other youth of their community. In the case of Lisandro, the coordinator of Sotz'il:

> [The dominant urban culture] was another system, another way of life. Some friends and I began to dance according to the trends that we saw in the media. At that time, it was techno, rap, and hip-hop. So we began to dance in the clubs. More than anything, it was a show. But there came a time when I asked myself, "What am I doing? Nothing! Sure, the youth like this, but—I'm from a rural area." And to jump into city life—I could do it, but it wasn't my world. Even more, the people there were very discriminatory. They didn't like to see someone from the mountains coming here to dance in front of them. So, I went back home.

At the same time, Lisandro also felt the brunt of discrimination in other settings. First, he and ten of his classmates were kicked out of a politically progressive, Catholic boarding school for questioning the religion and its impact on Maya culture. Yet, these schools are among the few high school options for poor Maya youth. Lisandro reflects, "This experience marked me. It proved to me that this system is not made for us [Mayas]."

Also at this time, he saw a Ladino-produced ballet about Tecún Umán, the legend of a Maya K'iche' warrior who was defeated at the time of the colonization and who the Guatemalan establishment proclaims to be the national hero. "We were always told, in school and in Guatemalan society, about Tecún Umán. The Folkloric Ballet came to do a show about him near our community. I didn't like the way in which they represented indigenous people in their dances. They portrayed Tecún Umán as a timid indigenous person, an indigenous person who makes you laugh."

Yet, the impact of oppression and the crush of stunted opportunities had devastating consequences on Lisandro. He catapulted into depression and alcoholism at the young age of eighteen.

"The days didn't matter to me, nothing mattered," he recalls.

Then, tragedy struck. Lisandro's younger brother died while working at a construction site in the nearby tourist mecca of Panajachel. He was only seventeen years old, and was already a very gifted artist. His brother's unfulfilled potential forced Lisandro to re-evaluate his own life.

He was aided by a propitious encounter with *The Annals of the Kaqchikeles*—a colonial-era text about the last governors of the Kaqchikel nation. This epic story of the grandeur of pre-Hispanic Kaqchikel civilization is exactly the opposite of the demeaning representations of Mayas that are promoted in Guatemalan national life. Reading *The Annals of the Kaqchikeles* inspired Lisandro to create a theater group that strengthens cultural identity by presenting dignified stories of their ancestors and recuperating "the true spirit and musical aesthetic of the Maya Kaqchikel world."

The Miracle of Creation: "Directly from Our Context"

Bursting with youthful energy, a handful of mostly high school students officially founded Sotz'il in August 2002. But it soon became apparent that the challenges had just begun: They had no money. They felt discouraged at having no Western musical training. Furthermore, how would they represent the Maya? The only widespread representations of the Maya are degrading or portray a "lost" culture that is disconnected from its present-day descendants. Disheartened, everyone gave up.

Sotz'il could have had a very short history. But Lisandro describes a timely moment of insight:

> Later, we realized that to want to do something doesn't mean that we have to follow what's on the TV or radio. Rather, we can begin from our OWN context! So we thought, "OK, what do we have here? What about marimba, and the old melodies?"

While searching for traditional outfits that the group could wear for their music and dance performances, they met a respected community elder and described their project to him. He was willing to lend them some of the traditional outfits because he believed in the group's vision. He presented only one request, which the group took to heart: "Don't portray the degrading stereotypes of our culture," he said. "Portray its dignity. Portray the ancestral line." Inspired by the elder's endorsement, the group set about changing the expectations of what Maya art is, and of what they, as youth in an adult-dominated world, could do about it.

The group started with a phase of investigation. The practice of the ancient Maya arts had largely been wiped out by the fanatic Spanish campaigns, so Sotz'il had no living predecessors who could teach them the tonalities, footwork, rhythms, and aesthetic of ancient Maya music and dance. To resurface these practices, they had to resort to learning about them through the only surviving documentation: the remaining four Maya codices and the archeological record. So Sotz'il plowed through all the books they could access. A well-known mural at the archeological site of Bonampak in Mexico was especially inspirational to them. It portrays a dancer facing a line of six musicians, all bearing pre-Hispanic instruments that no longer exist. The group decided to replicate the dancer's outfit and the instruments based on their depiction in the mural. (In fact, during their performance, the group enters the stage in the same order as the musicians on the Bonampak mural.)

The group then began to flesh out some of the remaining ancient melodies that have survived the centuries of oppression and genocide. They researched the oral histories of their communities and consulted with elders who played the *marimba*, wood flutes, *tun*, drum, and other traditional instruments whose playing technique is only passed down along family lines. Yet, they taught Sotz'il, even though "we don't even have a musician in our family lines!" as Lisandro notes.

The lack of funding did not deter Sotz'il. They simply turned to the materials of their land, and they themselves constructed the instruments they saw depicted in the ancient murals. They trained themselves in dance by replicating postures they found in the four codices and the movements they saw in the natural world around them. They also did their own "costume design" based on the outfits they saw depicted in the archeological records. Some of it required weaving in odd shapes—unlike the rectangular weavings that are produced on the traditional backstrap loom. Unfazed, the group members enlisted one of their mothers to experiment with weaving these pieces. She in turn manifested her creative talents by producing complicated weavings in triangular shapes and the gap-toothed form of castle turrets.

In this way, the group engaged in an act of creation that is reminiscent of the miracle of life itself: birthing beauty out of "no-thing"—the concept of zero which the Mayas themselves formulated.

And having thrown themselves wholeheartedly down this road, Nature responded as though affirming their choice of direction. Things fell into place. The same mother went to ask the community elder don Francisco to teach Sotz'il members how to play the traditional *marimba*. He wasn't home when she visited. Years ago, he had retired from playing when his Evangelical pastor suggested that this music was "of the devil" and had caused the cancer in his thigh. He had even sold his antique *marimba de tecomate*.

Yet, a week later, don Francisco appeared at Sotz'il's house. He offered to teach them how to play the *marimba*. "He was one of our great teachers who motivated us to continue," reflects Lisandro.

Then, Victor Barillas, a theater director from the capital whose vision complemented that of Sotz'il, volunteered to work with them.

"All of our environment, including the community itself, made us change so that we could form the theater group," says Lisandro. "The youth could have had all the enthusiasm in the world, but if the society itself, our context, had not told us, 'DO IT!' we would not have succeeded."

Sotz'il also decided to present their emerging play in Kaqchikel. "Using

Spanish might have facilitated the experience of many audience members. But if we did that, our play would not be Maya."

"Here I Will Tell the First Stories"

Three years after Sotz'il's founding—after crafting their instruments, training themselves to play them, gathering melodies, developing dances, and pairing with Victor Barillas for theater direction—it was time to finally engage the powerful and transcendent story of *The Annals of the Kaqchikeles* and, in particular, that of the great Kaqchikel leader Kaji' Imox. Lisandro reflects,

> The community organizing that the previous generation did was like the "first front," because they were under severe, constant repression. The only way to confront that was to organize, to join together. That is, if you have five families by your side, it's immediately noticeable if someone disappears, and why—[also] who did it.
>
> This "front"—these organizations—opened many spaces, and the new generations are occupying them. Now we *can* project a vision of the future.
>
> At first, our youth group faced a lot of frustration. We would make music—but *for what?* There came a moment when I felt it was necessary to be able to say to the state and to municipal and national authorities, "This is bad!" But I thought I couldn't.
>
> Then we realized that one of the functions of art is to declare our vision and protest. "Protesting" through art is different. It's visual, and aural. It's much more complete. In art, you can't walk around with a combat-hardened face, saying, "I am strong! We must do this!" No. One must have even deeper feelings about the injustice to protest through art.

Sotz'il decided that they first needed to reclaim the stories about the great Maya leaders who have been kept out of the Guatemalan schoolbooks and "official" state history. Lisandro comments:

> We sought to counter the way in which we as indigenous people are represented in Guatemalan society. It's ridiculous . . . That's why people think that we're backward! . . . It makes me think that the character of Tecún Umán was created simply to call us stupid, ridiculous, idiots, clowns, like we don't know anything.
>
> Yet it's totally the opposite. We have our own stories. We have a history that we've been prohibited from seeing and hearing.

In reaching back to investigate and tell these stories, Sotz'il has uncovered a narrative in *Kaji' Imox* that is intriguingly resonant with recent Guatemalan history. Sotz'il's play presents the dilemma: *How will Kaji' Imox guide the Maya people from near-extinction and ensure the perseverance of the great Maya culture?*

The story of Kaji' Imox is not merely of historical interest. The genocide and forced assimilation of the past thirty years eerily parallel the attempted breaking of Maya resistance nearly 500 years ago. The multicultural audiences who watch Sotz'il's play are also implicitly invested in this story: as Mayas, Ladinos, or members of the international community that work in Guatemala, each audience member's socioeconomic position in Guatemala today is a direct result of the actions taking place in the story, and, ultimately, of Kaji' Imox's decision about the direction of Maya peoples' resistance. Yet, Kaji' Imox's story and its implications have largely been repressed by many Guatemalans—because colonial Spanish rulers forced the Mayas to "forget," or at least to abandon their public re-enactments of the story. By resurrecting this story in public life, Sotz'il articulates yet another response to the recent genocide and the continuing attempts to invalidate and erase Maya culture through oppression and coerced assimilation.

Thus, before delving into the narrative of this great Kaqchikel leader, Sotz'il places the story into its cultural context, since that is exactly what the Spanish colonizers and Guatemala's contemporary rulers have tried to suppress. They dedicate the first quarter of their play to portraying the creation of the Kaqchikel nation in order to ground *Kaji' Imox* in the profound roots and symbols of Maya culture, thereby affirming Maya culture and identity.

"The start of the play addresses the questions, 'How does life begin? What existed before movement?' *Nothing.* We begin with silence—the dimension of zero—that is both the beginning and the end," comments Lisandro.

The bat—the *nawal* (spirit guide) of the Maya Kaqchikel people—emerges from one of the four corners with a bowl of fire—the symbol of life and wisdom. He arches his body and arms over the fire, silently and slowly transforming his shape through a series of postures as he moves to the center of the stage, bringing the fire to the center of a circle formed by four dancers seated at each of the cardinal points. That circle embodies the communal, holistic Kaqchikel way of life that is brought into being when the hearth-fire arrives at its center.

"Then, sound begins—through breath, and air, and the four sounds of the conch shells from the four corners of the earth. This paves the way for movement: Like a flower, the circle opens up," notes Lisandro.

By building their play around the sacred fire and the *nawales*, Sotz'il makes a powerful and controversial statement of Maya identity. Since the Spanish invasion, Christian churches in Guatemala have demonized (or appropriated) references to fire and the *nawales* since they connect Mayas to their ancestral non-Christian spirituality. Yet *Kaji' Imox* places fire and the *nawales* in their proper context as a source of life, energy, inspiration, and harmonious co-existence with nature, fellow humans, and the Creator. Moreover, at every presentation a Maya priest tends to the fire to keep it from extinguishing during the play. For Sotz'il, the sacred fire is not merely symbolic—it is essential to the dancers' energy.

The play also includes a re-enactment of the Maya ballgame, a sacred ritual that was sport, art, and science. "The ballgame is like life to us. But when the Spanish enter the scene, the rules of the ballgame change, just like the rules of the game of life changed with the Spanish invasion," says Lisandro.

Also in the first act, the importance of telling the story of Kaqchikel history is reinforced as a musician sings the opening lines of *The Annals of the Kaqchikeles*: "Here I will tell you the first stories of our grandfathers, when there was nothing in the forests, in the valleys. There were only birds, rabbits, animals . . ."

Another musician narrates the birth of the Kaqchikel nation and their ancient travels that bring them to their homeland. In a country marked with a severely skewed land distribution since the Spanish invasion—which is the root cause of both the Maya's present poverty and the excruciating struggles for a more just system—this scene affirms the Maya Kaqchikeles' historic right to their lands.

Cutting the Noose

The play then portrays Kaji' Imox's abrupt rise to power when the elder Kaqchikel governors are killed by diseases brought by the Spanish before they

Even though Kaji' Imox (right) had turned himself in to the Spanish colonizers to stop the terrorization of the Maya Kaqchikel people, he refused to bow down to the colonizers' domination and way of life; Ulises Rodríguez

even set foot on Kaqchikel soil. Immediately Kaji' Imox is thrown into the greatest challenge that the Kaqchikel nation had ever faced—the Spanish invasion, which brought "an ambition that had never existed here before," according to Lisandro. Yet Kaji' Imox acts as an astute strategist. He doesn't just attack, says Lisandro:

> The Spanish had already defeated the Aztecs, the Pipiles, the peoples of the South Coast, and even the neighboring K'iches. It would be silly to confront them again using the same strategy! So, instead, he receives the Spanish *before* they arrive at Iximche'—not because he is naively friendly, but in order to better analyze the strengths and functioning of his opponent: What does he eat? What are his capabilities? How does he think, how does he analyze, how does he act?

Then, based on this information, Kaji' Imox directs the Kaqchikel people to flee from their capital city and begin their decade-long armed struggle from the mountains, where the Spaniards' key advantage—their horses—can't function. "This is a powerful act of resistance," says Lisandro. "Fighting from the mountains requires many things: feeding soldiers; making tools and weapons . . . They suffered hunger and thirst. *That's* where the resistance of our people truly began—not with the thirty-six years of civil war, as the URNG [the leftist guerrilla organization] declares!" A beautifully choreographed scene portrays the Kaqchikel warriors gracefully climbing trees as lookouts. Their formidable resistance from the mountains is evoked by their hiding among six-foot tree branches dressed with beads, shells, and feathers whose rattling unnerves and intimidates the Spanish opponents. Yaxb'alam E, the divine energy of war, watches this and encourages Kaji' Imox to keep up his successful campaign from the mountains.

After a decade of struggle, because Kaji' Imox's military resistance still appears infallible, the Spanish invaders led by Pedro de Alvarado decide to take revenge on the Maya civilian communities who till their fields in the plains. "That's when Pedro de Alvarado begins to harass the surrounding communities in order to force Kaji' Imox to surrender. He begins to torture, enslave, and massacre the villagers," says Lisandro.

News reaches Kaji' Imox of the Spanish's campaign of terror against the Kaqchikel villages. He is confronted with a wrenching choice: to continue his successful military resistance from his stronghold in the mountains, so that he can repel the Spanish invasion and safeguard Maya Kaqchikel lands; or to surrender himself, in order to alleviate the cruel reprisals that the Spanish are inflicting against his people. How will he decide?

According to the Maya worldview, there are some decisions that we as human beings cannot make alone. We must consult the ancestors and divine energies that mediate our existence in order to see the long-term consequences of our actions. And in this case, Kaji' Imox's one decision will affect the survival of an entire civilization.

So, Kaji Imox consults the divinities of the four cardinal points: Should he turn himself in to the Spanish? What will become of his military resistance movement if he does? What will become of his people if he doesn't?

The divinities weigh the options. Yaxb'alam E, the great warrior energy, continues to urge Kaji' Imox to be strategic and fight from the mountains.

The great grandmother Ixmukane chimes in. She accuses Yaxb'alam E of having abandoned the villagers with his military strategy. Another energy jumps in and recommends surrender. The fourth vociferously disagrees. Their voices rise in chorus and they begin to talk over each other. How will they decide?

Finally, they all point to Yaxb'alam E. Yaxb'alam E doesn't want to make this decision. He is a warrior and a warrior doesn't surrender easily. But, this is a joint decision—representing the Maya value of community decision-making and democracy. So Yaxb'alam E advises Kaji' Imox to turn himself in, so that his people won't continue to suffer.

This verdict ensures certain torture and execution for Kaji' Imox, but he courageously agrees to follow the wisdom and foresight of the divine energies and his ancestors. He surrenders himself to the Spanish.

Even as prisoner, though, Kaji' Imox can't abandon his culture. He and the other captured Maya leaders continue to pray according to Maya custom, and they put a Christian statue above their altar so that their true spiritual practices will go undetected by the Spanish, cloaked in the veneer of Catholicism. However, when fellow leader Beleje' K'at is executed for defending the ancient Maya texts, this compromised way of life becomes too much to bear for Kaji' Imox. He throws the Christian statue to the ground, throwing off his acceptance of Spanish domination over the Maya way of life.

Kaji' Imox is promptly condemned to execution—in secret, because his captors realize that to do so in public would simply fan the flames of rebellion. In the final scene, two Spaniards lead Kaji' Imox onto an empty stage to be hung. Minutes after the deed is done, though, the play alludes to Kaji Imox's unique form of resistance as his character reaches up, breaks the noose from his neck, and tosses it away. With serene integrity, Kaji' Imox walks off-stage, where once again he dons the headdress of the Jaguar *nawal* and, with a melodic whistle, calls to all the other *nawales* to do a final, joyous dance as the audience applauds and the play concludes.

A New Cycle

The question remains: How did Kaji' Imox's surrender help his people? Did the Spanish persecute the Mayas less after Kaji' Imox turned himself in? Lisandro comments,

The Mayas continued to suffer. What was possibly alleviated was the degree of persecution. But the tribute continued, as well as the slavery. If we look at it this way, Kaji' Imox's surrender could appear to have been in vain. But also, we have to keep in mind that at that time, the Mayas were in the process of being exterminated . . . The epidemics weakened all the Maya nations. So did the wars, and the slavery. On top of that, the frustration, desperation, and repression diminished the population. And if Kaji' Imox hadn't turned himself in? Perhaps we wouldn't be here today talking about it! [*Laughs ironically.*]

In our culture, to die is to be born again. It's to pass into another dimension. By turning himself in, Kaji' Imox showed that he had completed another cycle. His death meant that he entered into yet another cycle of life. That's what the cutting of the noose symbolizes. *The resistance of the Maya peoples emerges again.*

The last chapters of Kaji' Imox's life run remarkably parallel to the past thirty years of Maya peoples' history in Guatemala. For example, the Spanish reprisal against Maya villages for Kaji' Imox's resistance, "simply for being Maya," appears similar to the Guatemalan army's tactic in the early 1980s of taking reprisal against civilian Maya villages in its "scorched-earth" campaign. Also, in an act that recalls Kaji' Imox's resistance from the mountains, some survivors of the 1980s massacres chose to resist the genocidal strategy of the army by forming communities in the jungle and the mountains called the Communities of the Population in Resistance (CPRs). They remained non-combatants, but they refused to leave their land. Land is the basis of Maya culture, and the CPRs proclaimed, "Our culture is our resistance."[1] So they lived in hiding and were constantly on the run from the army's pursuit. Ironically, the CPRs lived this incredibly difficult way for over a decade, mirroring Kaji' Imox's ten years of resistance from the mountains.

Another compelling parallel is that the evolution of don Anastasio's ideas of social change mirrors Kaji' Imox's transformation. Furthermore, many of Sotz'il's youth members have also become progressive educators who are struggling within the school system for their vision of Maya education—that is, pedagogy based on their community's language and values. Their production of art with Sotz'il is an extension of their daytime work in the classroom. They make the connection that the arts are fundamental to a truly community-based education, because students in marginalized communities must value their culture if they are to take their lessons to heart. The group demonstrates that the arts help create that value, and that the act of creation strengthens their community. Moreover, Sotz'il's play is a much-needed antidote to the absence of Maya stories, culture, and values on TV and the radio and the bombardment of advertising spurred by materialist trends in Western culture. By representing Maya stories in a public forum, Sotz'il shows Maya youth that they have a valuable alternative to assimilation into the competitive system promoted by commercial media, and that it *is* possible to present their own expressions, voices, way of life, and values to fulfill themselves and their communities.

Sotz'il members are models of this. They pursue their artwork within their rural community even though it is difficult to find paid jobs there. They participate in the duties of community life, farm their ancestral land, and maintain their families and households. Their art is the walk of their lives, not a pretense. Perhaps this is the embodiment of the kind of resistance that Kaji' Imox's story symbolizes: Celestino, who plays the title role, comments, "Kaji' Imox decides to give up the resistance of war, and take on another kind of resistance. He turns himself in, and thus lives under captivity until the Spanish execute him—but the Maya people survive, practicing our culture without assimilation. And we have survived in the 500 years since."

In this way, Kaji' Imox's selfless integrity and ultimate surrender to defending his people and culture throughout ever-more-daunting obstacles—and his resulting regeneration—is a powerful symbol for the youth of today's Maya movement, just as much as during the colonial era when stories and re-enactments of Kaji' Imox's story were banned by the Spanish rulers. Telling this ancestral story in a public forum is a forceful declaration of the Mayas' existence as a people with their own culture, ways, and history. This is exactly what genocidal forces seek to deny and repress—because they cannot extinguish nor completely suppress a people if they are loudly proclaiming their right to exist and practicing their power of regeneration. Lisandro concludes, "Because Kaji' Imox did this, the Maya have never accepted a new way of life."

Czarina Aggabao Thelen is a Pinay dancer and community organizer. She has lived in Guatemala as a human rights observer and Fulbright scholar. She writes about indigenous peoples' cultural activism and organizing for ancestral land recovery. She previously was a Senior Organizer with Mothers On the Move in the South Bronx, NY.

Note

1   Please see photographer Jonathan Moller's powerful book *Our Culture Is Our Resistance: Repression, Refuge, and Healing in Guatemala* (New York: powerHouse Books, 2004).

Further Reading

"Sotz'il: Maya Kaqchikel Music and Dance"
E-mail (Spanish): gruposotzil@yahoo.com
E-mail (English): Contact the author at czarina@alumni.brown.edu

5
An Unlikely Alliance
Germans and Jews Collaborate to Teach
the Lessons of the Holocaust

DEBORAH ROTH-HOWE, HERBERT L. ROTH,
GABRIELLE SCHMITT, ANNEGRET WENZ-HAUBFLEISH,
AND RABBI ROBERT STERNBERG

Introduction
By Deborah Roth-Howe

As the daughter of Holocaust refugees, I inherited a painful and burdensome legacy from my parents. The memories of those years of anguish under the Nazi regime, however, are not mine. I was born well after the war ended, in "the land of the free and the home of the brave." Yet, as I grew to adulthood and gave birth to my own children, my parents' experiences in Nazi Germany took a more central role in my journey to understand who I am as a parent, as a Jew, and as a citizen of the world. My parents' memories had a big impact on me. And my understanding of their memories has an impact on the next generation. And so it goes.

In this chapter, five individuals reflect upon their reasons for working together to create a permanent exhibition, "*A Reason to Remember:* Roth, Germany 1933–1942," on display at the Hatikvah Holocaust Education Center in Springfield, MA. Each of these individuals contributed to the creation of the exhibit, which tells the story of the five Jewish families who lived in the small, rural village of Roth, Germany prior to Hitler's rise to power. In great detail, the exhibit shows how Nazi rule systematically destroyed the lives of these German-Jewish families.

The chapter begins with my own voice, as the daughter of Holocaust refugees, trying to find a way to put the terrible pain and suffering of these innocent families to constructive purpose. Next are the recollections of Herbert L. Roth, my father, sharing his experience of being made "other" as a Jewish boy and teenager in Nazi Germany. Following are narratives from two German women, Gabrielle Schmitt and Annegret Wenz-Haubfleish, both residents of Roth, who worked long hours over many years to remember and honor the Jewish families who fled or were deported from their village. And, finally, Rabbi Robert Sternberg, Director of the Hatikvah Holocaust Education Center, discusses why teaching the lessons of the Holocaust is not merely a lesson in history, but given the prejudice and racism that continue to pervade our world, a vital lesson in survival.

Deborah Roth-Howe:

I am the daughter of Holocaust refugees. Though that fact was not uppermost in my mind as I wove my way through childhood and adolescence, it became a more prominent piece of my identity as I attained adulthood and became a parent myself. What legacies was I consciously and unconsciously passing on to my children? How could I help them understand what happened to their grandparents and relatives in Nazi Germany, but not instil in them fear or distrust of the current generation of Germans?

These questions prompted me to attend a panel discussion at my synagogue that included children of Holocaust survivors sitting next to and speaking with children of Nazis. I could not begin to understand how these individuals could sit side by side under one roof. Yet there they were. Together, and in solidarity, they spoke about the guilt, rage, fear, and grief they inherited from their parents' participation—as victims and as perpetrators—in the Holocaust. A Jewish presenter, whose mother was a concentration camp survivor, put her arm around the daughter of a notorious Nazi as this woman described her father's crimes against humanity.

It was a transformative moment for me. It stimulated me to look at the prejudice I carried against Germans and Germany—a prejudice I "inherited" from my parents, both of whom were born in Germany, fled the Holocaust, and had relatives and friends murdered in concentration camps. It prompted me to become active in work that, for the first time, pushed me to move past the conscious and unconscious fear and anger I carried within me.

Over the next five years, I became very involved in German-Jewish dialogue. That work brought me to Berlin, and subsequently into German and American classrooms, talking with students about the meanings of the Holocaust. Eventually, it brought me to my father's place of birth near Frankfurt, Germany. The tiny, rural village of Roth had a population of 500 residents in the 1930s. That included thirty-one Jews, comprising five families.

Jews had lived in this village for more than 250 years. The small Jewish community was well integrated into the life of the village: the Jewish children attended the two-room schoolhouse with the other village children; Jews earned their livelihood working with their non-Jewish neighbors. Prior to Hitler's rise to power, the thirty-one Jews in Roth were able to "live Jewishly"—eat Kosher food, attend synagogue, follow Jewish law and ritual, and so forth—while simultaneously engaging in the daily life of their fellow German citizens.

That harmony, however, was destroyed in a meticulous, carefully designed, state-sanctioned, step-by-step process that led to the deportation and deaths of fifteen members of Roth's Jewish community. The others were fortunate enough to escape and flee to other countries.

No Jews have lived in Roth since 1942, when the last deportation brought those still alive to ghettos and concentration camps where they were murdered. No evidence of the 250-year history of Jewish life in that particular village was apparent after 1942, except for the dilapidated and empty synagogue.

The synagogue in Roth still exists because a farmer who lived next door to this Jewish House of Worship begged the Nazis not to burn it down on Kristallnacht, November 10, 1938, when Nazis burned thousands of synagogues throughout Germany and Austria. He feared that the flames would damage his property. The Nazis agreed and returned with hatchets but could not cut through the support beams. Throughout and after the war the building stood, serving as a warehouse for grain and falling into a state of serious disrepair.

As one of very few synagogues left standing after Kristallnacht, the synagogue was designated a historic building in 1987, and soon thereafter plans were underway for its renovation. No Jews have resided in Roth since their final deportation in 1942, but the synagogue was restored as an education center and memorial to the Jewish families who either fled or lost their lives under Nazi rule. Renovations were completed in 1998. The village invited my father and the few other Jewish survivors from Roth to return for a special commemoration ceremony. I attended the ceremony with my father and mother, and we were far more moved than we had expected to be. Speakers honestly addressed the town's shameful history. In conjunction with the opening of the newly renovated synagogue, a teacher from a local high school had put together a display, documenting the fate of four of the eleven Jewish children who had fled or been killed by the Nazis.

Though I could not read the German text, the display's photos alone told a powerful story of individuals whose lives were destroyed, slowly and painfully, throughout the course of the Nazi regime. I wondered: if this display and its accompanying documents were to be translated into English, could it be a powerful educational tool for American students? Would they be able to identify with a child who had a family, lived in a particular house, played soccer, acted in a local theater group? Would such an exhibit allow the current generation of middle and high school students in America to understand the human devastation of the Holocaust? And if so, could we create an exhibit that would draw parallels between what happened to Jews in Europe under Nazi rule and what is happening to other groups in targeted areas of the world today?

I brought the idea to Rabbi Sternberg, Director of the Hatikvah Holocaust Education Center in Springfield, MA. He thought the idea was a good one. He strongly believed that the stories of the Jews of Roth matter.

- They matter because the Jews of Roth, like all victims of war and genocide, deserve to be remembered as individuals with whole lives—not only as victims.

- They matter because those families who were murdered in their entirety have no descendants. Nevertheless, they must be remembered and their humanity returned to them. With no descendants to do that work, we must find ways to prevent their "disappearance" from our collective memory.
- They matter because Roth, Germany had an authentic Jewish community. The community itself deserves remembrance and its place in history.
- Finally, the stories of the Jews of Roth matter because they represent a microcosm of what occurred to millions of Jews and other victims of Nazi atrocities.

Rabbi Sternberg and I believed that understanding the history of the Holocaust and how it unfolded would make it possible for people to understand how passivity and self-preservation allowed a previously civilized and cultured nation to transform itself into one of murderous intent. We became determined to expand upon the display in Roth and create an exhibit that clarified the vital difference between responding to injustice as an activist and remaining a bystander. We were committed to creating an exhibit that helped visitors make the link between discrimination against Jews under the Nazi regime and discrimination against "others" in the United States and throughout the world today. We wanted people to grasp what British philosopher Edmund Burke meant when he said, "All that is necessary for evil to triumph is for good people to do nothing."

The exhibit "*A Reason to Remember: Roth, Germany 1933–1942*" is now celebrating its third anniversary. Approximately 10,000 visitors have viewed it over the course of the first three years. Visitors' responses have been comforting and inspiring, including comments such as: "*. . . The main theme* [of the exhibit] *expresses the undying strength, hope, and determination we humans can have*" and "*. . . I feel it is imperative and even necessary to know and understand the history of all people so that I may be able to recognize patterns that may repeat over time.*"

These responses confirm my belief that exhibits like this one *can* touch people deeply and raise their consciousness about the injustices that surround us. The exhibit underscores and illustrates the truth that we must be aware of the plight of others, we must protest loudly when *anyone's* civil rights are abridged, and we must grasp the fact that our individual well-being is directly linked to the well-being of everyone across the globe.

Herbert L. Roth:

The seeds of the exhibit "*A Reason to Remember*" date back to 1996, when a group of residents in and near the small village of Roth in Hessen (Germany), my birthplace, formed an organization (Arbeitskreis Landsynagoge Roth) dedicated to the restoration of the former synagogue as a cultural center in memory of the former Jewish residents of the village. The group was successful, and in March of 1998 the restored synagogue was formally opened. In cooperation with the local high school, the activists in Roth created a display recording the lives of four of the five Jewish families, including my own. The display included a great number of documents from the Nazi period, edicts and decrees crafted to transform *and eventually destroy* every aspect of our lives.

The display impressed me greatly. It graphically displayed the Nazi-driven process of isolating the Jews before they were deported. For example, included was a newspaper article from 1935 falsely branding my father—a man who was well liked and well respected—a parasite and exploiter. After this article was published, in the context of ubiquitous Nazi propaganda in the press and on the radio, my father's business rapidly declined, and soon he could no longer support his family.

The display portrays a world that inexorably turned against us. Most villagers, *our friends and neighbors for decades*, no longer greeted us or the other Jewish residents of the village. When my grandmother died in 1937, no Christian neighbor attended the funeral. The local cabinetmaker refused to build a coffin for her. This was in sharp contrast to what happened when my mother died in 1934, and most of the village came to mourn with us.

During this period from 1935 through 1937, when I was 12–14 years old, my peers said I could no longer play on the school soccer team. I was devastated. In school, we had one teacher who spoke briefly about the Jews every single day. He always said something really bad, for example that Jews were thieves and committed racial defilement. I didn't know what he meant. After his short speech, he would always say "Present company excepted." "Present company" was me, so no one could forget that a Jew was in the room. By 1937, I and the other Jewish children in the village were not permitted to attend the village school. My normal life had ended.

The Jews of Roth were law-abiding citizens who had lived harmoniously with their Christian neighbors for 250 years. Never during that time had any Jew been indicted for violating the law. Nevertheless, we were driven out of our homeland or deported to be murdered. How was this possible in a Western country which produced many of the greatest thinkers of the last century? The reasons are many. For me, the most important were *Silence* and *Indifference*. The German people living during the Nazi period, with a few notable exceptions, failed to honor their Christian teaching, and thereby made possible this unprecedented historic catastrophe, the Holocaust. By their silence and indifference, the German people blessed the extermination of European Jewry.

For me, personally, the restoration of the synagogue and the creation of the exhibit "*A Reason to Remember*" fulfilled my wish that those who perished from my village should not be forgotten. Over time, however, my interest has evolved into the conviction that the only meaningful and lasting contribution we who survived can make is to teach the lessons learned from the Holocaust to future generations Let us teach our children **never to remain silent or indifferent when hate and discrimination are taught, justified, or sponsored by any organization, and especially by their government**.

Gabrielle Schmitt, Art Teacher, Gymnasium Niederwalgern, and current Chairperson of the Arbeitskreis Landsynagoge Roth:

When I moved to Niederwalgern, a village next to Roth, in 1984 to become a high school teacher, I had no idea what was awaiting me. Soon I found the book *Die mit Tränen säen, Seeing through Tears*, by Peter O. Chotjewitz, published in 1980, describing the life of Jews in a small German village.[1] I was deeply moved by this story about the Jewish way of life in the German countryside. I had never heard of it before. How was it possible that nobody at church or in school had ever talked about it . . . not even my parents?

My interest was aroused. I began to look for traces of these people where I lived and worked. I remember clearly when I stepped into the synagogue in Roth for the first time. Beneath all the dust, the last bits of grain, and the cobwebs, I could see the building in its original beauty. The inscriptions were faint, and the sky painted on the ceiling of the synagogue was peeling, but nevertheless I was deeply touched. I asked myself, "Who were the people who belonged to this synagogue? What was their life like? Where are they? Are there survivors?" It was then that I began my research.

In 1996, I and others studying the history of the Jews of Roth founded the Arbeitskreis Landsynagoge Roth. We decided to restore the synagogue, despite some resistance in the village. The local district, which had bought the building, funded the extensive renovations. We asked ourselves, "How can we fill this place with life?"

We wanted the synagogue to be a place of remembrance, of learning, and of cultural events. I deepened my knowledge about the former Jews of Roth and explored their families' fates. In 1996 I met Herbert and Elsa Roth. Many meetings were to follow that one. Each of these meetings, some including their children and grandchildren, has enriched my life enormously.

When the synagogue was reopened in March of 1998, my students read aloud the names of the Jewish villagers who had been deported and murdered. They placed candles around the ceramic Star of David, which I had created and in which I had etched the names of each individual from Roth and the neighboring villages who were murdered by the Nazis. This Star of David, which permanently resides in the synagogue, connects the Jews of Roth forever with this holy place.

The synagogue has once again become an active place: exhibitions, concerts, readings, and a writing workshop bring people there to meet, to learn, and to commemorate the past. The guided tours offer visitors a window into our difficult past. And, importantly, the high school in Niederwalgern makes it a priority that students visit the synagogue and learn about the village's former Jewish community and its demise.

A new dimension of my own personal work is becoming clear to me. Those who suffered from and lived through the Holocaust have reached the last phase of their lives. I have taken on the responsibility of telling their story to the younger generation, in Germany, to make sure that they will not be forgotten.

Annegret Wenz-Haubfleish, Archivist and Co-Founder of the Arbeitskreis Landsynagoge Roth:

I was born in Roth in 1960, fifteen years after the end of World War II. I first learned about Jews in Sunday School from the stories of the Old Testament. At school and in the 1970s, as a university student, I learned about the Third Reich and the Holocaust. However, teachers and professors taught this on a very general level and did not encourage us to study local, regional, or oral histories. The book entitled *Dig Where You Stand*, written by Swedish author Sven Lindquist, stimulated many groups to explore their local history, often with special focus on the Holocaust.[2] Also at this time, a famous film called *The Holocaust* on German TV had a great impact on many Germans, including myself. I was already in my twenties when I became interested in finding out what had happened in my own village. I met others working in archives, conducting interviews, and attempting to get addresses of local survivors of the Holocaust.

Unexpectedly, in 1987, our local pastor gave me a manuscript written by Herbert L. Roth on the history of the Jews of Roth and asked me to translate it from English into German. At the same time, the idea emerged from our working group that the local government should buy the synagogue from the farmer who owned it in order to restore and preserve it as a memorial for those who perished in concentration camps. Although people in the village still called it "the Jews' temple," at that time they were far from thinking of preserving this structure as a memorial. We worked hard to find politicians who shared our goal and who would provide the necessary funding. The restoration began in 1993. It would take five years of work before the renovations were complete.

Personally, I was motivated to preserve this piece of rural Jewish culture in Germany in order to create a place of remembrance and of mourning; and to recreate a place of learning. I wanted to honor the eleven Jews from Roth who managed to emigrate to South Africa, the United States, and England and the fifteen people who perished in concentration camps. Hitler's goal had been to destroy every trace of Judaism in Europe. I wanted to do my part to prevent Hitler, so many years after the end of World War II, from reaching his goal.

I was also determined to draw attention to the ways that the synagogue makes tangible the violence from which the Jews suffered. Visitors to the synagogue see the damage that was inflicted upon the building during the time of National Socialism in Germany and they begin to ask questions. And thus the synagogue has really become a place for learning, and, hopefully, a place for helping prevent a totalitarian regime like Hitler's from ever rising to power again in Germany.

As one part of the commemoration ceremonies, one of the high school teachers created a well-researched display, illustrating the fates of four of the Jewish children who had lived in the village. For the survivors—and for all of us—the display represented the first time that their lives and the lives of their relatives were officially and publicly remembered in the village. Their persecution and suffering were depicted on large panels, and the silence regarding their fate was broken. One could see that Roth was not a village of innocents. Hitler's regime functioned everywhere, regardless of how small and unimportant the place. It functioned in Roth much the way it functioned throughout Nazi Germany.

Today, citizens of Roth understand that those murdered or exiled were not abstract individuals, but former neighbors. Visitors learn what it means for an individual to lose his or her democratic and human rights. Nowadays, this is a crucial issue in Germany. Social problems are increasing. We have high unemployment rates; our educational system is not as good as it used to be; poorly educated young people do not foresee success in their lives. At the moment, fortunately, only a minority of them support radical, neo-Nazi parties. In this situation, it is imperative to display the Nazi past and its consequences. It is imperative to encourage viewers to stand up against violations of human rights.

When the Arbeitskreis Landsynagoge Roth began its work in 1996, Herbert Roth was the only survivor with whom we had contact. In 1998 nearly all the Jewish survivors from Roth took part in the solemn reopening of the synagogue, some of them accompanied by children and grandchildren. Many of us now stay in frequent contact with each other and have become close friends, even with members of the second and third generations. Members of the Arbeitskreis have been invited to the United States. For me, this connection is the most wonderful fruit of our work.

The surviving Jews of Roth and their families have gained confidence and are able to return to the place in which they were persecuted, from which they were violently expelled, and where no one stopped the Nazis from killing their beloved relatives and friends. I am very grateful for this new confidence and for the willingness of these Jews to reconcile with a new generation of Germans. I am grateful that we have had the opportunity to learn from the survivors themselves, and not only from archival material and the elderly inhabitants of the village. And I am happy that we can help the second and third generations find their roots and understand more about their family history.

Rabbi Robert Sternberg, Executive Director, Hatikvah Holocaust Education Center, Springfield, MA:

More than sixty years have passed since the last Nazi concentration camps were liberated. Today's school children are the last generation to have the possibility of meeting a Holocaust survivor and hearing personal testimony. Holocaust educators are now preparing for a time in the not-too-distant future when they will have to rely on other ways of making the Holocaust real and relevant.

Exhibits can be catalysts in the work to teach people to stand up and oppose acts of hatred, discrimination, and threats to civil rights. I have heard some people prejudge Holocaust exhibitions, worrying that they will come away saddened, depressed, and overwhelmed with feelings of hopelessness. "*A Reason to Remember*" intentionally addresses this concern by drawing attention to those things that empower visitors and give them a sense of purpose. One student from Springfield College who visited the exhibit in 2005 said, "*I really appreciate how this presentation was put together in a hopeful and personally touching manner. I have visited Holocaust museums before. Usually I leave the exhibit with nightmares, horrified, and almost with guilt for how people were treated. But I left here with hope and understanding of how this history has a powerful effect on our present day and future . . .*"

The Holocaust is fundamentally a study of human choice and human responsibility. "*A Reason to Remember*" and its accompanying curriculum explore the choices made by the victims of Nazi oppression as well as by those not targeted as victims. It also explores the consequences of such choices, in the past and today.

As the events of the Holocaust recede into the annals of history, its lessons for humanity will be the challenge of every new generation. By prompting us to reflect carefully upon the choices we make, visitors to Holocaust exhibits can become empowered to understand the critical role each of us plays in building and sustaining a safe, secure society.

Conclusion
By Deborah Roth-Howe

My hope, my prayer, is that visitors to "*A Reason to Remember*" will leave the exhibit understanding that the Holocaust was the story of Toni Roth, of Ilse Höchster, of Hugo Stern, Cilly Nathan, Joseph and Heinz Bergenstein and all their family members. The exhibit does not allow for abstraction. The people were real, their lives complicated and active, and their deaths illustrated in precise detail. The details illustrate the unfolding of a genocide and highlight the many places where that timeline could have been interrupted had people actively opposed the edicts which contradicted the teachings of every religion known to humankind. It is the story of ordinary people—ordinary people targeted as victims. It is also the story of ordinary people inflamed by Nazi doctrine, who responded by acting upon the basest possible instincts or by passively submitting to a doctrine they did not endorse but were too fearful to oppose. If these insights can be derived from viewing this and similar exhibits, and engaging in other such efforts, we can hope that the current generation will understand the critical need to speak up, protest loudly, and resist passivity if, when, and wherever such ugly doctrine raises its head once again. These are the insights and commitments that unite all those whose lives were directly or indirectly touched by the Holocaust: students in Germany and students in the United States, children of victims and children of perpetrators, descendants of bystanders and descendants of resistors, all of us.

Deborah Roth-Howe is a social worker and early childhood consultant living in western Massachusetts. She is co-author of the exhibit "*A Reason to Remember:* Roth, Germany 1933–1942" which documents the story of the demise of the small Jewish community of Roth, Germany. She is also author of "Wrestling with Legacy: An International, Cross-Generational Response to the Holocaust," published in *Smith College Studies in Social Work* 77:2/3 (2007): 7–24.

Herbert L. Roth was born in Roth, Germany in 1923. He fled Nazi persecution and immigrated to Chicago, IL, where he now lives as a retired business executive. He has researched and documented the history of Jewish life in the Hessen region of Germany.

Gabrielle Schmitt is an art teacher residing in Roth, Germany. She is a Founding Member of the Arbeitskreis Landsynagoge Roth and continues to design educational programs in the village to help preserve the memory and history of the village's former Jewish residents.

Annegret Wenz-Haubfleish is an archivist in Marburg, Germany. She is a Founding Member of the Arbeitskreis Landsynagoge Roth, and was instrumental in preserving the Jewish history of the village of Roth, Germany.

Rabbi Robert Sternberg is Executive Director of the Hatikvah Holocaust Education Center in Springfield, MA. An experienced teacher in the field of Holocaust studies, he designs workshops and curricula to assist educators in effectively teaching the lessons of the Holocaust.

Notes

1 Peter O. Chotjewitz, *Die mit Tränen säen* (Munich: Verlag Autoren-Edition, 1980).
2 Sven Lindquist, *Gräv där du står* (Stockholm: Bonniers, 1978).

Further Reading

"*A Reason to Remember*" Exhibition: www.hatikvah-center.org

6
Storytelling in SisterSong and the Voices of Feminism Project

LORETTA J. ROSS

As an African American feminist, I come from a verbal, storytelling culture with deep roots. For me, storytelling is about survival. Storytelling is how we passed on knowledge and culture, values and behaviors. The storyteller might be the griot or the grandmother. Both told us stories of our past, our present, and our future. Storytelling is how we saved our lives when reading was forbidden, knowledge was hidden, and cultural continuity was shattered. We weaved together the threads of our collective experiences to create quilts of iconic stories of triumphs, of failures, of dreams, and of realities. But most of all, the stories were about possibilities. Through stories we could *imagine*, arguably the most powerful word in any language. Through our imaginations, our stories defied our oppressions and offered both spiritual solace and practical advice to survive a hostile world and build communities in which we could thrive. Through stories and storytelling we could examine and explore the meanings in our lives.

Storytelling has been vital to my life's work and my political practices. I remember telling the story thirty years ago about how I had been kidnapped and raped as a child and why that experience led me to work at the country's first rape crisis center founded in 1972. Those stories of violations we shared in quavering voices with other scared women ignited a global movement to end violence against women. We may have more formally called it "consciousness-raising," but in essence we were telling each other stories to reclaim ourselves and our humanity.

We created a feminist culture with these stories, not through narratives of logic and structure, but by creating verbal snapshots of the lived experiences of women. We didn't have to all tell the same story in order to resonate with each other. Each story was unique but the act of telling our stories created strong bonds among diverse women who worked together to change our realities. Each story generated echoes of experiences we could all relate to our lives.

We could imagine a world in which women lived in freedom from violence, and we set about building rape crisis centers and domestic violence shelters not only to help women who had been violated, but also to project a vision of what a world without violence could look like for women.

My work today is with the SisterSong Women of Color Reproductive

Health Collective. Even our name represents a story. Ten years ago in 1997, sixteen women of color working on reproductive health issues came together to share our stories about how hard it is to do reproductive health work in our communities, poised as we are between the predominantly white feminist movement and our own ethnic communities and not entirely trusted or respected by either. Some of us worked as midwives; others worked for abortion rights, while others worked in HIV/AIDS or with immigrant or Indigenous women. Even though we were Native American, Latina, Asian American, and African American women relating our specific experiences in our own communities, it wasn't long before Juanita Williams pointed out that we were "singing the same song" but we weren't singing it in harmony. That's where the name SisterSong originated: from the commitment of diverse women of color to work together—metaphorically singing the same song—to build a reproductive justice movement that could create better lives for ourselves, our families and our communities. Our motto became, "we do collectively what we cannot do individually."

The foundational philosophy that glued us together is called "self-help" in which we powerfully use words in an active, inventive way to share the realities of our lives. We chose to use self-help because previous attempts to work together as women of color floundered because we did not have a process with which we could have difficult dialogues with each other. When we founded SisterSong as the fifth attempt to build a national coalition of women of color reproductive health organizations, we knew we needed a formal commitment to a process that would allow us to work together in healthy, healing, and holistic ways that would not be sabotaged by our internalized oppressions.

Through self-help we're perfecting the art of telling our stories so that we can connect with ourselves and other women to build a movement to save our lives. Self-help storytelling is not about solving each other's problems, but instead about creating a supportive, listening environment in which each woman has the loving attention to find the answers she needs in her own way and in her own time.

The phrase self-help has meant so many different things to people, it bears explaining how I'm using it. Self-help as developed by the National Black Women's Health Project and the National Latina Health Organization is a strategy for women to actively pursue our wellness—physically, spiritually, emotionally, and mentally—by supporting each other in addressing health concerns in our lives and those of our communities.

Self-help was born out of need. The way that racism, sexism, homophobia, classism, and heterosexism have influenced our lives creates interlocking systems of oppression that affect us. Self-help affirms our experiences as women of color and supports us as we become aware of and engage in resistance to the oppressive systems we face in our reality. As Lisa Diane White says, "Self-help allows us to take control of our lives and support each other to do the same."

An important aspect is owning our stories, and determining if, when, why, and how they are shared. As women of color we feel that others often tell our stories *for us* in a colonizing way, denying us the right not only to tell our own stories but to decide what the stories mean. Anthropologists study us; economists objectify us; historians dismiss us. But as women of color, we know we have never been passive victims in our stories, but we have been agents of our own destinies.

Because of this history of colonization and erasure, women of color are not often found authoring history texts about our participation in the reproductive rights movement. Until we wrote our book, *Undivided Rights: Women of Color Organize for Reproductive Justice*[1] in 2004 there had been no one source that documented the history of women of color in the reproductive rights movement. Into this context, in 2002, the Voices of Feminism Project of the Sophia Smith Collection (SSC) at Smith College in Northampton, MA came to interview me through an oral history project and invite me to add my papers to their archives. Here was another way of using stories to change everything.

Oral histories are an important method for documenting and preserving the valuable contributions women of color have made to the reproductive justice movement. As activists we are often too busy serving our communities and sustaining our organizations to stop and think about the preservation of our historical records and stories about the lives of the women who have made a difference building our movement.

The Sophia Smith Collection is the oldest women's history archive in the country. Its collections are especially strong in the areas of women's rights and women's liberation, birth control, U.S. women's international work, and peace. The primary sources document women's activities and ideas from the colonial era to the present, from anti-slavery and socialism to present-day struggles around welfare rights and sexual autonomy. Movements for social change, particularly those that emphasize feminist activity and thought, are the central focus of the collections. SSC launched the Voices of Feminism Project in 2002 with support from Wilma Mankiller, Gloria Steinem, and the Ford Foundation to preserve oral histories of approximately fifty women who have made important contributions to the feminist movement. The oral histories are videotaped and transcribed so that the images and the words of the women are forever archived.

I was approached by the Sophia Smith Collection because they became aware of gaps in their archives. They pride themselves on being the best archives in the country for feminist history, particularly within the reproductive rights movement, but they noticed that the archives were missing the stories and histories of women of color. While they were interviewing me, I just idly asked the question, "Who are the other women of color you are collecting?" They replied that they hadn't quite figured that out yet. I went from being the target of their collection to being a participant in helping them collect! Because I'd been in the movement, I had a pretty good, if subjective, idea who the movers and the shakers of the movement have been. To date I've done about ten oral histories of different women of color in the reproductive rights movement and have helped collect their papers and add them to the archives.

Because the documented history of the reproductive rights movement does not sufficiently represent the contributions of women of color, the Voices of Feminism Project seeks to correct this imbalance by ensuring that the stories and the records of women of color leaders and their organizations are preserved at the SSC. The purpose of the project is to add historical knowledge of women's movements, but especially to investigate historical and historiographical silences. Whose stories have been left out? What experiences are difficult to discuss and how should they be approached?

The archive intentionally does not collect what we call the "celebrity women"—women whose stories are more likely to be preserved because they are already in the public spotlight. Instead, we go after the women who made a difference but who aren't generally known to the public. I certainly would put myself in that category. That's what makes the collection particularly special—we are not going after the people with huge name recognition; we're going after the people who other feminists would say are important. We are making a political statement by collecting the papers and the stories of women who history would probably not remember if we didn't make special effort to ensure they were included.

This is a revolutionary act—for previously unheard voices to achieve permanent life in the archives. In the future, no writer who does her homework can claim that she can't find the stories of women of color who did this work. Any omission then will be the result of other issues, not the result of the absence of material. This development changes history.

For each of the fifty women in the oral history project, we do a videotaped oral history, which is archived along with her memorabilia or papers. For instance, in my archive, there's quite a bit of material from my early writings: personal and professional writing; posters from different movements and campaigns.

Archiving our histories in this way is intentional and strategic. Naturally, the biographer gives form to her subject through her own writer's lens. The beauty of oral history as a methodology for collecting stories is that what we receive is always in the narrator's own words. In this case, oral histories provide information about people or social groups whose written history is either missing or distorted. Oral histories can be a vehicle for activists to speak for themselves, to be the active agents in telling their own stories. They provide the opportunity for activists to trump the colonizing impulses of anthropological and historical research. Oral histories challenge and investigate existing power structures and sometimes reveal a wealth of information not available from formal, written sources.

Oral histories help people narrate their own lives, and in our project, create recordings of the voices that don't fit into the traditional historical discourses which too often omit women of color—and other women, too.

The actual experience of "being archived" can be surreal. This was certainly the case for me. The staff from the Sophia Smith Collection came to my house and packed up thirty-seven boxes of my life and took them off to Massachusetts. We shipped out all my early history—including family photos— to a strange, faraway place, leaving me with a sense of loss and also a sense that the best part of my life might already be over. As the Smith staff packed the thirty-seven boxes, the SisterSong staff watched not only *my* history, but *their* history walk out the door. They said with urgency, almost panic, "Now, wait a moment, wait a moment. How are we going to have access to this? We can't go up to Smith College and rifle through their archives. We'd have better access to it if we kept all these records here in Atlanta." I had to counter them with the reality that these materials were not actually so terribly accessible anyway, hidden up in my attic. I argued that all that stuff was surely more accessible at Smith. And then we saw the trade-off, being able to make our work and stories more broadly accessible to researchers and others, while at the same time relinquishing geographical control of all that life-material. The Sophia Smith Collection is available through the web, so anybody with a computer has access. The archive also sponsors scholarships and grants for people who need access to the collections.

There's a considerable expense in processing a personal collection for an archive, limiting the number of women whose oral histories and papers the project can include. Of course a great deal of staff time is required to sift through all the papers, to document them, to record oral histories . . . and then there is the issue, how many inches of shelf space are available. For each woman whose papers are in the Sophia Smith Collection, the archive has probably spent between fifty and one hundred thousand dollars on processing the material, which means that only a well-funded institution like Smith could do this work.

It's not uncommon for people to ask me why I didn't send my collection to a historically black women's college. It is such an expensive process that I discourage anybody from giving their collection to an institution that doesn't have the resources to handle it in a responsible way. It is not that these institutions are irresponsible, but the whole process is so costly. I think that the staff at Smith expects an outlay of four million dollars to collect and process the papers of fifty women.

The Sophia Smith Collection facilitates women owning our own stories at the same time as it broadens public access to women's voices. The Voices of Feminism project team had very detailed planning meetings at which we discussed the concept and process of ownership from a feminist point of view. We emerged explicitly respectful of the fact that we were preservationists and conveyors, but we weren't the originators of the stories, nor were we the owners. In practice, this means that, after we take an oral history, we provide a transcript. Then the narrator gets a chance to edit the transcript. Just as it is important for the activists to talk about the events of their lives, it is equally important for activists to be the authorities regarding the documentation and meanings of those events, so that meanings are not defined or assigned by someone else.

Through this oral history project, women themselves have the opportunity to provide their own contexts. I recently conducted an interview with Betita Martinez. Betita Martinez, a Mexican American woman, was born in the 1930s, and her activist career began during World War II. She started out working at the U.N., so in her oral history she was able to talk about the meaning of her activism and her activist role in relation to the war. In perpetuity, Betita's story will be available in her own voice, a voice that future historians must pay close attention to.

This process of determining our own meanings will change the perception of what is important and what history is. History is still imagined by most people as the story of Big Men and Big Events. Feminist oral history is about shifting the lens and looking not only at people and events and movements that are important to women, but at how those subjects illuminate society as a whole, beyond the traditional accounts. Omissions distort history, as noted historian Gerda Lerner observes. Omissions of the perspectives and accounts of women of color distort the entire history of the reproductive rights movement, and the wider social movement histories in which we are embedded.

The histories we are assembling also provide space for these women to share information that they would not include in a written account. A project participant may talk about the history of sexual violence in her life, or speak about her family relationships or her frustrations with other women, or give details about occasions when she experienced human rights violations. We consider it very important that the stories of women in the archives are always dynamic, in that they are connected to the stories of other women, and to broader activist movements.

Living in this era in which storytelling is so important and valued, I see a paradox unfolding. Over the last couple of decades, we've seen the development of a whole storytelling industry, with some odd results. I was in a communications seminar recently where a white man was lecturing a group of women about the importance of storytelling, totally oblivious to the irony of telling a group of women about storytelling. When storytelling, after all, built the women's movement! We are the masters of storytelling.

In some ways, it is a familiar feeling: our organic knowledge is being co-opted, boxed, and then resold back to us. The business community has recognized the importance of storytelling to organizational culture and profit-making. A whole cadre of "storytelling experts" is being paid quite handsomely to go around and tell us what we already know: storytelling matters.

For so long, our culture has claimed that, if it wasn't written, if you can't document it, "it" had little or no value. But now, all kinds of people, including The Powerful, are valorizing the oral tradition as a resource of immense value, making it officially important. We knew storytelling was important all along.

The fact that elder feminist women now have the power to archive history will have a significant impact on women in the movement right now and in the future. One of the things I've noticed as an activist, as an organizer, and now as an oral historian is that people don't know whose shoulders they stand on, particularly as women of color and particularly as young feminists. The information just doesn't seem to be easily available for newer people coming into the movement. If this information were available, these activists would be able to start where their predecessors left off, instead of reinventing the wheel all over again.

In SisterSong, we work with the power of using personal stories as a way for women to reclaim themselves and their humanity. Associating ourselves with archival status and achieving a place in history through this feminist process allows us to hold on to that same humanity. In the Sophia Smith Voices of Feminism Project, we are no longer objects of study. We have become subjects, with considerable control. In both venues, we assert ourselves as the authorities of our own lives.

Loretta J. Ross is the National Coordinator of the SisterSong Women of Color Reproductive Health Collective. She was the Founder and Executive Director of the National Center for Human Rights Education (NCHRE) in Atlanta, Georgia from 1996 to 2004. She was one of the first African American women to direct a rape crisis center in the 1970s. She holds an honorary Doctorate of Civil Law awarded in 2003 from Arcadia University. She is pursuing a Ph.D. in Women's Studies at Emory University in Atlanta. She is a mother, grandmother, and a great-grandmother.

Note

1   J. Silliman, M.G. Fried, L. Ross and E. Gutiérrez, *Undivided Rights: Women of Color Organize for Reproductive Justice* (Boston: South End Press, 2004).

Further Reading

SisterSong: www.sistersong.net

II

"This Needs Urgent Attention"

Stories in the Service of Protecting, Defending, Building Audience and Allies

7

"Our Stories, Told By Us"

The Neighborhood Story Project in
New Orleans

RACHEL BREUNLIN, ABRAM HIMELSTEIN, AND
ASHLEY NELSON

In the Beginning

Abram:

I was teaching writing at John McDonogh Senior High, just down the street from where I live. I use the word "teaching" loosely, as mostly what I was doing was failing to teach and collecting a paycheck to participate in a crime against children. John Mac was deeply dysfunctional, too chaotic to permit much in the way of school education.

I went home sour every day, and then I'd see my students in the streets, and know what the denial of education meant for the possibilities available to them.

Rachel was teaching at the school as well, and it went better for her, but it was still far from the level of teaching we wanted—a writing program where the kids owned the stories, and there was redemption for our neighborhoods and school. Because, to be honest, the stories coming out of the school were a beast: shootings, fights, and 80 percent not passing the exams required for graduation.

Rachel:

My friend, Ms. Ida Mae, was one of the janitors at the school. The queen of the Creole Wild West Mardi Gras Indian tribe, she worked all year to build a beautiful suit to wear on Mardi Gras morning. I hated to see how students deliberately threw trash on the ground for her to pick up. When I encouraged them to take some pride in their school, they denied responsibility, "It's her job." If they saw her only as someone who picked up their garbage, it was partly because the school didn't encourage anyone to be seen as a well-rounded person—a part of churches, clubs, and other organizations like Mardi Gras Indians, who might have been artists, musicians, or dancers outside of their time at school. Nor did it encourage an acknowledgment of emotion—

how struggling families, the stress of avoiding violence, becoming a parent, and having other adult responsibilites well before you got a diploma could affect school work. As one of our writers explains it, "Things was moving fast. Your maturity level was high. You seem older than you appear. Older and more knowledgable people will draw you for good and for bad." There was an incredible gap between the students' life experiences and these educational institutions.

Although there were many committed teachers at the school, there was a lot of distrust between the staff and the students. Every year, students were gunned down in the streets by other youth without an official acknowledgment from the school except for the ten-foot chain link fence laced with barbed wire, metal detectors, and uniform checks every morning. Parents and grandparents recalled days when they could sleep with their front doors open, when your neighbor would "bid you the time of day." They complained, "Kids these days, they ain't got *no* respect." Without faith in a system, many of

Ms. Ida Mae, Queen of the Creole Wild West; Rachel Breunlin

our students moved into the underground economy of drug dealing where they set their own rules. Before I lived in the Seventh Ward, before I heard gunshots at night and learned the next morning that another boy from John Mac had been shot around the corner from me, I was more sympathetic to this economic argument. Afterwards, it just wasn't good enough to just understand where the problem was coming from.

Young people were already speaking about the problems in raps, freestyles, poems, and graffiti. They were carrying caskets and wearing memorial t-shirts for fallen friends. Still, they were isolated from the larger dialogues. As a city, we didn't know each other's stories. I was lucky to have a small group of students and a fairly open curriculum. They taught me a lot about New Orleans—the difference between street smarts and school smarts—and I struggled with why it seemed "never the two shall meet." I put together small publications. I watched students who did really well in my class spiral and get kicked out of school. I watched public housing being torn down, rivalries between different areas of the city—known as wards—escalate into violence.

I experienced the joy of watching students feel the power of their own words, even as they grumbled about revisions. It was the first time many of my students had been required to write more than a couple of pages. Yet every time I felt like I was making progress, I'd be slapped with another setback. The school was over-enrolled. My last year as a writing teacher, there were more than fifteen floating teachers—i.e., without their own classroom—and the administration had changed for the fourth time in as many years. My classes were relegated to the storage room of the library.

Ashley:

I've always enjoyed writing. I wrote little poems and songs as a kid and soon found out that writing is one thing I am good at. I decided to stick with it. I attended John McDonogh Senior High where a good education is a myth. It didn't bother me. I was just happy for the free ride in high school—what teen wouldn't be? During my 10th grade free ride, I met Ms. Rachel, who was the creative-writing teacher in a closet of a classroom in the back of the library.

She had six of the worst kids in the school, but she did her thing—she taught us, ya know. We were always having interesting discussions and writing about things that were on our minds. Ms. Rachel let us get loose. We could write freely and not worry about what was written until it was done. She pushed us. If she knew we could write two pages, she made us write four. She told us we could do it in a class with no air conditioning, no books, and trash and graffiti everywhere. We believed her, so we wrote.

Abram:

I started talking to Rachel about what a real writing program would be like, and how to get students and their families involved. She had these books she had been producing in her classes, and they looked excellent, and her kids were seriously proud of them. The idea began to percolate: writing books about things that meant something to the students. I wanted to have them take ownership of the work, not to feel like it was for school work, so came up with the idea of paying them a thousand dollars—an advance on the royalties that would be due to them if the books sold more than a thousand copies. A lot of the issues driving students away from school were economic: Desire for after-school jobs or hustles. Writing has always been work to me, and I've always demanded a paycheck for my efforts, so I wanted to honor the work the writers would be doing. Plus it made a good comeback: when one of the writers would complain about how hard the work was, I'd say, "That's why you get paid."

Rachel:

Abram told me the story of his great-grandfather—a Jewish immigrant who ended up being a circus photographer and then settling in Clarksdale, Mississippi—who wrote autobiographies that weren't necessarily good, but nonetheless demystified the process of writing for the entire family. Abram had grown up believing he could make books and already had two to his name. He wanted the Neighborhood Story Project (NSP), as a book-making program, to do the same.

   With a background in urban and applied anthropology, I was excited that the project would be a bridge between the classroom and the neighborhoods where the students lived. Rather than looking at the deficits in our students and communities, I wanted to build on the strengths. I wanted young people to learn the deeper histories of their communities, see the connections between their own experiences and others, and be able to share their perspectives with them. There has been a lot of talk of schools being open to the community, but I was at the point where I thought the school should take a few steps into the neighborhoods as well. After all, there was nothing nicer than walking home from school and hearing my students call out, "Hey, Ms. Rachel!" Theory and potential practice aside, I was burnt out of teaching without having secure, full-time work. I wanted to wish Abram good luck, but then I thought of Ashley—all her anger and analysis and poetry—and said I'd do it.

Abram:

We started trying to make it real. The Literacy Alliance of Greater New Orleans was interested in the idea of having teenagers write books for the whole community, and they took me on as an Americorp position. Neighbors and friends stepped up and contributed what they could, and mid-year the University of New Orleans agreed to pay Rachel's salary.

   The school was overbooked and didn't have space for the writing project, so we rented an apartment across the street, and were given a table. We brought our favorite books from home and stocked the bookshelf. And then we went recruiting.

Ashley:

My 11th grade year, Ms. Rachel came to me and asked would I be interested in a writing project. I asked what kind and she explained the idea of the NSP. I thought, "A thousand dollars and I get to leave school? I'm all in."

Abram:

With seven students on board, we hosted a family dinner party at Rachel's house. With the students and their parents, we talked about the commitment—said we needed to build trust early on because there would be some hard moments. The students talked about their neighborhoods, and the parents shared stories and advice.

In the classroom, the first two months were spent becoming serious writers and serious readers. We wrote poems, kept journals, read good books, and talked about what made for good writing. We read *Our America: Life and Death on the South Side of Chicago*, and *The House on Mango Street.*[1] Rachel talked about the difference between the right and left side of the brain, and letting ideas percolate. We took field trips to places that would theoretically inspire writing. We started talking about ways to make the books interesting: struggle, plot, dialogue, and description.

And we got experts; photographers, writers, journalists started hearing about the project, and came in to do guest lectures, to teach the skills that Rachel and I didn't have, to give the writers a break from the long days.

Ashley:

Our assignment was to write a book about our block, but that was hard because I came from a housing project where we were all one community. Everybody hung everywhere. I couldn't just write about Orleans Avenue, for example, because it's not the only part that was happening in Lafitte. I told the class, "I'm gonna write about the whole project." It was also hard to know what story to start with because I didn't know what I wanted to show with writing a book. I had to find out what I wanted to tell people through the stories.

We began reading books similar to what we were going to publish, which helped me find my writing voice, but I still didn't have my inspiration. Most days I went to class, I didn't even feel like writing. I had so many other things on my mind that writing was too much to deal with: trying to balance school, a part-time job, plus I was writing a whole book—I didn't think I could manage. At one time I told Abram, "Man, I quit." He responded, "No, you don't." And there went the conversation. I was back to writing.

Rachel:

In November we started fieldwork. While most of the neighborhoods the students would be working in were predominantly African American, there were some areas where there was more diversity. Part of the goal of the project was to hear from people you normally wouldn't get to know, and to "defamiliarize" what you already think you do. As Zora Neale Hurston writes in *Mules and Men*, culture can be hard to see because it fits "like a tight chemise. I couldn't see it for wearing it . . . I had to have the spy-glass of Anthropology to look through at that."[2]

Teaching interview skills is a lot about interpersonal dynamics. How do you make someone feel comfortable with the interview? How do you ask for more details without seeming pushy or invasive? How do you narrow in on what is really important to the person you are interviewing? We had an all-day retreat at my house to discuss methodology and the ethics of doing fieldwork. We talked about stepping back from our everyday lives and explored the notion of cultural relativity and being open-minded to other people's stories.

We wrote practice questions and spent time interviewing each other before the students went out on their own. Their first round was with family members. The interviews lasted about five minutes—most were rapid fire and vague. The students were frustrated and Abram and I knew we needed to reassess the process. We were getting a chance to record stories that normally didn't leave the neighborhood, and we wanted to honor their experiences by making sure the students had enough mentorship and guidance to do good work. We decided to accompany them.

With this decision, we shifted how we viewed our work. It was no longer the students with one foot in the classroom and one foot in the neighborhoods—we were now hanging out on porches and front stoops, talking about bookmaking, and helping students to record their communities' stories. Kesha Jackson and I strategized with her grandmother, Mrs. Robinson, on who she should interview. Mrs. Robinson called her friends to see if they wouldn't mind talking—the next day, we were sitting at the Palm Tavern hearing Ms. Celie tell stories about the family's business.

Abram went with Sam and Arlet Wylie, brother and sister who lived above a corner store on St. Claude Avenue, to interview neighbors ranging from the white circus punks who lived next door to the drug dealers on the corner. Here Arlet reflects on the guys who used to hang out on her block:

> We never went outside—staying to ourselves was the best thing for us, or so my mom thought. She didn't want us conversating with the riffraff, or "street trash," as she called them. "Thugs" was also another word she used frequently.
>
> Our block of St. Claude is known as a hustle spot. A lot of people see these young teenage boys who hang outside as having no lives, no jobs,

no morals, and no family values. I thought so, too, until I got to be a teenager and started hanging outside on my balcony.

Throughout the rest of the book, both Arlet and Sam explore this world they were cautioned to stay away from in an effort to let people know "the stereotypes are not all true."

Ashley:

My first interview was with my grandma, who I've lived with on and off over the years. We talked about the closeness of Lafitte and it reminded me of the day my mama died. It gave me the idea for the first story I really cared about: "Help from the Strangest Places." It was about the day of my mama's funeral and how the community came over to lend their support. Writing this story helped me figure out what direction I wanted to take my book and that was showing the togetherness of the community I come from.

Rachel:

A dialectic quickly developed between the interviews and stories—interviews led to more stories and vice versa.

Ashley interviewing Charmaine; Rachel Breunlin

Abram:

And so the books began to come into being. There were crises and break-throughs weekly. Some days we argued, some days we wrote away from the hard parts of our lives. But most days we did it, we interviewed, took pictures, wrote down the stories that we kept hidden from most of the world.

Ashley:

It was hard trusting readers to understand and not judge. I was scared, but the Neighbourhood Story Project (NSP) family made writing this book amazing. We laughed at the funny stories and cried during the bad ones. What made it great was you could write anything and it was appreciated.

Abram:

We got the stories and interviews ready to be read. And then we let people read the drafts, and the books became more real. Each book had a committee of readers: a family member, a fellow teenager, and someone from the city who wanted to be a part of the Neighborhood Story Project. We would read the draft, and then talk about the book, where it was confusing, or needed more, or would endanger the writer or the neighbors. As we let people read the writing, and know the stories, people, including us, started believing that the books were already books, just waiting to be printed. And having people read the work put the fire under us.

Rachel:

At this stage, we were weaving together the interviews from the neighborhoods and the stories of the students' lives, and continuously talking about how to balance the honesty of a writer and the ethics of a fieldworker. We wanted to honor both sides of the project. Kesha wrote a story about growing up with a mother on drugs and the loneliness she felt living with her grandmother while her mom was in a rehab program:

> There were times when I was left inside alone and hungry. There were days when I would wake up without my mom and nights I didn't sleep. I had to sit there and think of places where I thought she would go, and I would call and they would always say that she just left or wasn't there when I knew that she was right there.

After a few months, Kesha took a trip to visit her mom, Pam, bringing along a tape recorder and list of questions, partly derived from her own writing.

K: So when you used to be gone, and I used to be calling for you, how did you feel?

P: It used to hurt, you know, because I never wanted to send you through any hard feelings or—I never, I made a promise when you was born and I let the promise go—and this is bringing back a lot of feelings [crying] . . .
K: It's OK. Sometimes when I used to call you, you used to be right there.
P: Mmhm.
K: Most of the time.

When Kesha came back to class the next day, she had gained the confidence to tell her story—in all its complexity—without worrying that it would jeopardize her relationship with her mom. Thinking about women's role as caretakers led her to structure the rest of her book around this theme.

Arlet and Sam wrote their book together. They balanced their different perspectives on family and community by writing complementary stories and doing a long interview with their mom together. Here, Arlet asks her mom, Emelda, about this process:

A: What is it like for us to be working on this book?
E: When I think about them, and I think about the book, it's just overwhelming pride that I feel. I hope that it makes them feel better about themselves. Maybe you don't feel so frustrated because now somebody knows your story and somebody knows your struggle. And it's inspiring because you're still standing. And you did not have to resort to some of the stuff that other people say they resorted to that lived in similar situations.

Abram:

During the spring semester, we did workshops on how to talk to the media. Ebony Bolding and I led the lesson, her talking about losing a year of school after a reporter twisted her words around while covering a story about a school shooting, me recounting a scene from the movie *Bull Durham* where the experienced player coaches the rookie on how to handle the media. The basic idea was that we wanted to shape the news, not be shaped by it. We spent time figuring out what we wanted our message to be, and then practiced staying on message no matter what kinds of questions the reporters asked us.

Rachel:

Of course, we were seen as a kind of media as well, and people's preconceived ideas about being interviewed—developed from police reports, social service workers, and reporters without any accountability to the community—influenced whether they wanted to talk to the students.

Ashley:

Consequently, the fieldwork wasn't always easy and welcoming. Sometimes people acted negatively towards us and the tape recorders. Who can blame them? Getting slammed by the media is common where I am from.

Rachel:

In Ashley's neighborhood, a barber named Freeman demonstrated some of the problems we were up against, but also the large impact of deep community work. Freeman had been in the neighborhood for over fifty years and Ashley thought he'd be willing to do an interview. The first time she asked, he responded, "For how much money?" I explained it was for a school project and he looked skeptical. There were faded photographs of Malcolm X on his wall, a past with the Nation of Islam, and a general skepticism about why this white lady was working with Ashley. How did he know we wouldn't make money off these books? I explained our non-profit status—that the sale of the book would go into funding the program in the future—but said we understood his concerns.

A week later, he sat in the barber chair talking to Ashley, but said he wouldn't sign the release form until we showed him the transcript. When we returned an edited interview a few weeks later, he was holding court on Orleans Avenue with a number of older guys in the neighborhood. He took the interview and started reading out loud to a hushed crowd. When he finished, another wave of recollections moved through the crowd, while Freeman said, "This is good. This is better than I thought." When we asked about the release form, he said he wasn't ready: "I want to share it a little more with my think tank. Come back tomorrow." When we returned, he said the interview was over by his aunt—"a church-going woman. I wanted to make sure I got the family history right." It took a few more stops to pick up the release form, but in the process, the interview passed through multiple readings. The community had a say in how their stories were shaped, and it made a big difference to their confidence in the project.

In each neighborhood, we brought the stories back for editing. In almost every instance, the interview passed through a number of small revisions as family and friends looked them over and gave advice. I recall sitting in Walter's bar while the bartender looked over a rough draft of the chapter she was in. One of her regular customers said, "I never thought anybody'd do something like a book down here."

"That's Aline's granddaughter."

"I know. She's doing *good.*"

Books Come Out

Abram:

I don't know how to talk about that night. Too many people in one room, the air conditioners failed, so we were all sweating. But here is the sentence that stays with me: Three hundred and fifty people, white and black, old and young, Christians and anarchists, in one room, on the same page, here to celebrate the publication of five books and six new authors. It felt like a functioning society, and that was the reward. The books were beyond what Rachel and I could have dreamed. More than yearbooks of a block (which would have been enough, Dayenu) the books had become literature.

We had envisioned block parties to celebrate the book releases, but the blocks couldn't wait and were at the citywide party. "This is my book," people said, and I've never felt better hearing it.

In the month before the storm we sold out of the first printing. Two thousand copies of the books, circulating around the city.

Ashley:

My book, along with all the others, shows our lives. They show our communities and they tell our stories. While writing this book, I released a lot of built-up energy. People needed to know about me, my family, and my neighborhood. In the project, all we really had was each other, but we remained happy. I told what I thought. I told the truth.

Rachel:

Since publication, each book has taken on a life of its own—traveling farther than we could have imagined into other high school classrooms, college curricula, juvenile detention centers, women's centers, independent bookstores around the country, and libraries. They have been excerpted in places like *Harper's Magazine* and *The Houston Chronicle*, and featured in other local and national press. Our students, as writers and agents of their own experiences, were shaping the way their communities were seen in New Orleans and around the country.

The biggest impact, however, was in the lives of our students, their families, and neighborhoods. The morning of the book release party, Kesha and I rented a car to drive across Lake Ponchartrain to pick up her mother, who had gotten special permission to come to the event from her rehab program. Kesha's book, *What Would the World Be Without Women? Stories from the Ninth Ward* was centered around the story of her mom. We wanted her mom to look through the final book before the event, so she could get comfortable with the finished product. Pam said, "I'm healing myself through Turning Points [the rehab center]. This is how Kesha's healing herself." Over the next few weeks, Pam sold over fifteen copies to other women in her program.

Before the storm, we were able to have three of the block parties. Each one had its own magic. The women who ran the Lafitte Residential Council, who were featured in Ashley's book, sponsored hers in the Sojourner Truth Community Center. The Wylies hosted their party at their new house, and Nine Times Social and Pleasure Club, featured in Kesha's book, surprised her with a second line parade during her block party in the Upper Ninth Ward. Neighbors, family members, and teachers danced through the streets with the books. As the evening came to a close, everyone autographed copies of the book. The sense of authorship extended beyond Kesha—it was her story, but it was theirs as well.

The Levees Fail

Rachel:

The week before the storm, the NSP was back at John Mac recruiting for the next wave of Neighborhood Story Project writers. The administration and teachers were excited about the books—planned on using them in their classes and encouraged other students to apply. Over forty students came out for the informational meeting.

We were also organizing Ebony's block party in the Sixth Ward for that weekend. Her mom, who worked in the cafeteria where Ebony went to

Kesha's block party; Rachel Breunlin

elementary school, had been promoting the event and many of Ebony's former teachers and classmates were planning to come out for the party. They also wanted Ebony to do a special reading at their school. I picked her up on Friday night to make sure she liked the music on the jukebox and said, "We just need to keep an eye on this storm."

Ashley:

I was preparing for Ebony's block party that Saturday. I heard her mama was cooking all kinds of good food—chicken from Man Chu's, dirty rice and red beans. I called Ms. Rachel to make plans to get there. She tells me it's cancelled because there is a storm coming. This is how I found out about Katrina. I thought it was just a normal Saturday. I had no idea that it would be my last time in New Orleans and have it feel like home.

Abram:

There aren't words to talk about how we felt when the levees broke. The next few days were some of the most intense in our lives. One by one the text messages came in, a little more floating and hopeful. And then we went home to bury and salvage. All of the writers were safe, all of the neighborhoods gone.

Rebuilding

Rachel:

For a long time, all we could think about was what we had lost. As we reconnected with people in the Neighborhood Story Project network, they were not only thankful to have the books, but to have gone through the process of participating in them. Mark Damico, one of the neighbors interviewed in Jana Dennis's book on Midcity, said that while many of his friends felt like they had lost neighborhoods they never really understood, his block of Palmyra Street was close knit, in large part because of Jana's book. In exile, the writers used the books to explain the New Orleans they knew to new classmates and neighbors.

John Mac—like the majority of New Orleans Public Schools—didn't reopen the year after the storm, and we began to look for other avenues to help people tell their stories until we could get back to the school. Nine Times Social and Pleasure Club members, inspired by Kesha's book, decided to write a book of their own. On Monday nights for more than eight months, we hosted writing workshops in our homes and interviews all over the city to tell the story of the Desire Public Housing Development and the creation of one of the first second line clubs in the Ninth Ward. The project brought club members back together who were just beginning to rebuild their lives in the city, and gave them a chance to document the people and places important to the story of their benevolent association. Their book, *Coming Out the Door for the Ninth Ward*, came out on November 17, 2006, two days before their parade.

Abram:

That Friday, fourteen months after Katrina, we celebrated what we still had. We had this new book, on its way to becoming a bestseller in New Orleans, and we had each other. There were 600 of us in a church hall—including the other NSP writers and their families. We started with prayer and readings from the book, middled with food cooked by Nine Times, and ended with dancing in preparation for Sunday's second line.

On Sunday, November 19, 2006, Nine Times gave the Ninth Ward its first second line since the flood. The process of making a destroyed city a home again is a slow one, especially with so many of us all over the map. People came in from all over the Diaspora to participate in the Nine Times parade. The Neighborhood Story Project hosted a "stop" along the parade route and the Wylies, back home again, helped us sell copies of *Coming Out the Door*.

There is no blueprint for rebuilding a city and a culture. We've all been trying to figure out how to respond. The guys from Nine Times, together, have given one of my favorite responses to the displacement and loss: Their book spans the distances and recounts our history. Their parades draw us near.

Ashley:

I came back to New Orleans to finish school and to continue working with the Neighborhood Story Project. But I also came home to be a part of the help because I believe just by being here we're pulling our home together again. Since I graduated, I've been going to Delgado Community College, teaching writing classes with the NSP, and working at Pizza Hut and a youth program called Rethink. Just by being here and participating makes it a little more like New Orleans—the New Orleans I wrote about.

Rachel Breunlin is the co-director of the Neighborhood Story Project and an instructor in the anthropology department at University of New Orleans. Her most recent article (with Helen Regis), published in *American Anthropologist*, was "Putting the Ninth Ward on the Map: Race, Place, and Transformation in Desire, New Orleans".

Abram Himelstein is the co-director of the Neighborhood Story Project and the author of numerous books, including *Tales of a Punk Rock Nothing* (with Jamie Schweser; New Month from the Dirty South, 1998) and *What the Hell Am I Doing Here?: The 100 T-Shirt Project* (Garrett County Press, 2003). A publisher, writer, and public school teacher, he is currently rebuilding the NSP's writing program at John McDonogh Senior High.

Ashley Nelson, author of the Neighborhood Story Project's *The Combination*, has taught in writing programs such as the NSP, Young Authors/Young Aspirations, and New Orleans Outreach. She has also worked with Rethink, Kids Rethinking New Orleans' Schools. After a year of Americorps service with the NSP, she is now a student at Delgado Community College.

Notes

1   LeAlan Jones and Lloyd Newman, with David Isay, *Our America: Life and Death on the South Side of Chicago* (New York: Pocket Books, 1998); Sandra Cisneros, *The House on Mango Street* (London: Bloomsbury, 2004).
2   Zora Neale Hurston, *Mules and Men* (New York: Harper and Row, 1990).

Further Reading

The Neighborhood Story Project, a partnership between the University of New Orleans and the Literacy Alliance of Greater New Orleans, is a community documentary organization dedicated to creating important literature about our city. Through teaching writing and interviewing, publishing, and hosting readings, book releases, and block parties, we reweave the fabric of community.

The Neighborhood Story Project: www.neighborhoodstoryproject.org

8

A Story of a Suicide and Social Change in Contemporary China

SHARON R. WESOKY

Some times I can feel my grandmother definitely will be in a place gazing at me. She can feel me doing good things. She will support me. Therefore I feel even stronger in my own self.

—**Xie Lihua, editor of *Rural Women* magazine**

In the 1950s, Xie Lihua's maternal grandmother committed suicide because her husband took a second wife. The husband had turned away from Xie's grandmother because she had borne only daughters, and he wanted a son. Forty years later, in 1993, the dead woman's granddaughter became the founder and chief editor of *Rural Women Knowing All*, China's first magazine dedicated to rural women.

In the fall of 1996, at the offices of *Rural Women Knowing All*, Xie Lihua received a manuscript submission from a reader named Wang Lixia. The essay, "In the End, You Don't Know What You are Living for in the World," is about the suicide of a young and simple but "kindhearted, diligent, and virtuous" village woman in northeastern China's Hebei Province. Wang Lixia told one tragic story, a single case of the circumstances that give rise to a suicide rate in China double the rate in the United States. This one tragic story also presses the reader to consider why China is the only country in the world where more women kill themselves than men.

I am a political scientist in the U.S. specializing in China. Like many scholars, I have selected research topics that intersect and resonate with the scholarly *and* non-scholarly aspects of my life. So after an initial focus on intellectual dissent in China, I turned to the subject of peasant women in that country. Xie Lihua, the editor, stimulated and helped shape this new interest when I met her in London after a conference at Oxford on "Chinese Women Organizing." I was moved by Xie Lihua's passion for the Practical Skills Training School for Rural Women that she had recently established outside of Beijing. I was, of course, awkwardly aware, as a scholar and as a person from the United States, that rural women in China live—to use a geographical term for some pretty heavy lifting—at a vast distance from me, an upper-middle-class, privileged American.

This awkward distance pointed to the kind of dilemma many scholars face. Academics are "supposed" to be "objective," standing outside of our subjects to create impartial and detached accounts of the worlds that we are studying. It isn't supposed to matter, in the world of scholarship, whether your subjects are "like" or "unlike" you. Yet, who among us achieves this "objectivity," as we struggle to assign meanings to our studies? I have been thinking about resolving this dilemma by moving closer to—even incorporating—elements of storytelling in my work. I was drawn to think about storytelling in part because of its relation, in China, to what poet and critic Kenneth Rexroth called "magnanimity" among "Far Eastern" artists, a courageous "human-heartedness" that provides a rich and illuminating contrast to market-driven "covetousness," "rationality," "objectivity," and other traits demanded by the capitalist economy.[1]

For Xie Lihua, magnanimity through storytelling is an inherent part of the mission of *Rural Women Knowing All* magazine. In the early years of the reform era in the 1980s and early 1990s, Xie was a Beijing-based journalist at the *China Women's News*, the official newspaper of the state-affiliated All-China Women's Federation. She was particularly dedicated to activities, beyond the scope of Communist Party work, designed to stimulate greater gender consciousness and activism. Her own rural origins and her grandmother's suicide contributed to her interest in editing a rural women's magazine. When Xie established *Rural Women Knowing All* in 1993, many new women's organizations were cropping up as China prepared to host the United Nations Fourth World Conference on Women in 1995. Most of these new organizations were based in cities and focused on urban matters. *Rural Women Knowing All* was the first and only publication of its type, especially providing a voice both for and on behalf of China's vast female rural population. At just this time, Chinese women living in the countryside were experiencing both the benefits and the degradations of post-Mao urbanization and marketization processes.

From the beginning, Xie positioned *stories* as a vital feature of the magazine's content. In fact, the elite women who founded and have edited the magazine in Beijing have defined the publication's central mission as providing a venue for the actual voices—or stories—of rural women. Up to 60 percent of the magazine's content is contributed by its rural women readers.

The magazine, titled simply *Rural Women* since 2003, provides technical and moral advice for its readership, ranging from a high of a quarter-million in the late 1990s to about 70,000 now. The magazine's circulation has declined, in part, because it was originally circulated under the auspices of local Women's Federation chapters, so most readers then were local-level officials, not ordinary village women. Today outreach bypasses officials; 80 percent of the readership is peasant women.

As the readership has become more targeted, the concept of the print magazine has expanded, now encompassing various grassroots projects dealing with issues such as literacy, political participation, job skills training, and domestic violence. Xie notes that the projects of her non-governmental organization (NGO) and the magazine are mutually supporting. Keeping her original commitment to narrative strong, she says, "We use so many stories, so that our projects become even more practical."

Rural Women explicitly defines itself as a publication and organization that promotes rights and gender consciousness of rural women. It was one of the earliest venues to call attention to the disproportionately high suicide rate among rural Chinese women; in the late 1990s, China had 21 percent of the world's women but 56 percent of its female suicides.[2] In July of 1996 the magazine founded a column "Why Did She Choose the Road of Suicide?" that openly recounted the individual stories of rural women's suicides, starting with accounts from a township in prosperous eastern Jiangsu Province that in 1995 had nine women dead of suicide within three months.

These early accounts of suicide prompted readers to submit stories of suicides from their own villages. In this way, village women were giving voice and visibility to their dead neighbors and relatives, an otherwise silenced and forgotten population.

Wang Lixia's tale is one such story. It contains themes common to many other renditions of the same narrative. This story provides an opportunity for one woman to offer her perspectives on the suicide crisis for others to consider, a gesture that lends this woman a kind of powerful public presence. The story also becomes a public venue for collecting and reviewing the sources of the crisis and even for imagining potential solutions. Finally, the suicide story in *Rural Women* provides evidence of the potentially transcendent power of long-standing storytelling traditions in Chinese culture, a power that transforms stories from simple narrative into a mechanism for promoting social change.

Wang Lixia, "In the End, You Don't Know What You are Living for in the World," published in *Rural Women Knowing All,* November 1996

June 20 was a sunny day with a rosy, clear morning. After rain, the little village seemed all the more lively. On the main street three crowds gathered, two bands of villagers, all discussing whether this year will have a good harvest.

Suddenly, astonishing news spread from the crowd of chatting people. "A life from Dongshan Village, Yang Guoyuan's wife Xu Fengzhi (Phoenix Branch) took poison to commit suicide!" . . .

Xu Fengzhi at that time was 29 years old, an ordinary rural woman. The year she was 20, through introductions, she married Dongshan Village's Yang

Guoyuan. After their marriage, the couple's relationship was decent. The next year, she had a son Xiaohai. Although her education level was not high, Xu Fengzhi conducted herself kindheartedly, diligently, virtuously. In the Yang family she respected the elderly and loved the young, inside the home and out. On the land of the mountain she was a good hand, commended by the villagers.

The year that the little son, Xiaohai, was five years old, due to their constrained family livelihood, Yang Guoyuan accompanied a couple from their village, Huang Mou and his wife, to brickyards in the south to find work. Huang Mou's wife was only twenty-six or twenty-seven years old. She loved to dress up and had the gift of the gab. She had a generally frivolous reputation.

Even though Huang Mou's wife's nature and Fengzhi's nature were extremely different, the two women could get along with each other. Because Huang Mou's wife often came to chat with Xu Fengzhi, she also got along with and knew Fengzhi's husband, Yang Guoyuan, well.

However, the time came when Fengzhi's husband accompanied Huang Mou and his wife to the south. Fengzhi was very trusting. First, she was trusting because she knew that the husband, Huang Mou, and his wife were traveling together, and second, she absolutely did not feel that her husband could be the kind of man who would sow his wild oats.

Yet things went contrary to her wishes. Even before Yang Guoyuan had been at the brickyard in the south for two months, he lost his ability to endure all of Huang Mou's wife's efforts to seduce him. He was finally seduced into adultery . . . As a consequence, Yang Guoyuan not only used all the year's hard-earned money to subsidize Huang Mou's wife, but also, because of participating in gambling, in the end he owed an outside debt . . .

Xu Fengzhi's heart was in shreds. She absolutely did not think that she herself could come to this kind of present plight. She thought of divorce, but this idea was a passing one in her mind. "No matter what, I cannot take this step," she said to herself.

Fengzhi had never seen the wider world. She resembled so many women in the mountains. Her life's goal was to get married in the valley, then care for her husband, bear children, and have a happy life. Now, her husband's feelings had changed, but she always felt that her husband would have a day to repent. After all, they were husband and wife from early days, and he was her child's dear dad. Fengzhi lived her life apparently without unreasonable demands. She once said this to someone, "As a woman, if I cannot have my husband and child, what value does my life still have?"

In order to make Yang Guoyuan change his views, Fengzhi tried everything. Many times she implored him, shed tears, barred the way, scolded her husband. Even after he beat her, she still did not abandon hope in her heart. Every day she kept silent and did not make a sound in work. In and out of the home she was methodically in control. With all her heart, she waited on her blind mother-in-law. Every day, Fengzhi made the old woman rice and other dishes, bearing her life coming and going. She thought, "Heaven has eyes, and my husband can repent, certainly he can."

Yet Heaven by no means opened its eyes. Yang Guoyuan had secret feelings for Huang Mou's wife's body, and he was utterly indifferent toward everything that Xu Fengzhi did . . .

On the morning of June 19th, Xu Fengzhi specially made a dinner of delicious dishes. The meal was on the table, and she contained the tears rising from the past and hoped she could return her husband—to the husband–wife feelings of former days. But Yang Guoyuan was not at all willing to listen. He lifted and overturned the table with the meal on it, and then he left.

At this moment there happened to be a pouring rain outside the window, with thunder and lightning. Looking at the splinters of bowls and trays on the ground, Xu Fengzhi's heart was also certainly thoroughly broken.

After the rain passed, Yang Guoyuan came through the door of the house and discovered Xu Fengzhi already on the verge of death. Getting the news, many neighbors hurried together to save her. Unfortunately the poison entered her five viscera, and it was impossible to save Xu Fengzhi.

A precious life gone, an only 29-year-old life, to be paid for by whom? I grieved, for Xu Fengzhi, for so many rural women.

Xu Fengzhi's story points toward the dilemmas characteristic of rural women's lives in the post-Mao reform milieu. Economic difficulties cause villagers, especially husbands, to migrate alone in search of employment possibilities. This kind of population mobility is a factor in the proliferation of extramarital affairs. It also stimulates the desire to participate in the commodity economy, an urge that is associated with gambling both near to and far away from home. In general, the social dislocations of the reforms, and the moral confusions that accompany these dislocations, have contributed to rural women's high suicide rate.

Suicides like Fengzhi's have become commonplace in the countryside and seem like an especially tragic modern phenomenon. But there are historical precursors of rural women's suicides and the stories about them. The conventional image of the young Chinese woman in society depicts her married away from her natal village and forced to live the second of the "Three Obediences" that structure her life: first, when young, she obeys her father; then she obeys her husband in her prime; and finally she is obedient to her son when elderly. She must also traditionally embody the Four Virtues of morality, propriety, modesty, and diligence.

Historically, stories provided a way that Chinese women could resist these injunctions. "Bridal laments" offered a way for women to recite their complaints. Sometimes these recitals even included suicide threats as a way of achieving some measure of redress for grievances and a vehicle for achieving some latitude and possibly even power. The "lamentation culture" of Chinese peasant women[3] has for centuries provided a context for creating stories about injustice. This culture was carried forward during the revolutionary period of the 1940s and 1950s, through the genre of "speaking bitterness," in which peasants and workers were encouraged by the Communist Party to reveal the ways they were deprived under China's past forms of rule. "Speaking bitterness" provided legitimacy to the new People's Republic of China as the people compared the problems of the *ancien régime* with the glories of the future. In the contemporary environment, personal storytelling about life's misfortunes on talk radio has become commonplace and widespread across China, with shows about sex and relationships being popular and increasingly acceptable.[4]

The ubiquity of sorrowful storytelling genres may promote even greater acceptability for the kinds of narratives that Wang Lixia produced about the death of Xu Fengzhi, and for the generally confessional nature of the magazine *Rural Women Knowing All*. In general, the magazine imagines and promotes a warm, companionable relationship between readers, journalists, and editors. It often features articles seeking to diminish the distance, both geographical and experiential, between its urban editorial office and its rural subscribers.

Rural Women also makes connections between stories and activism; it uses stories as a way of raising consciousness and pleading for transformation in the condition of China's rural women. Xie Lihua notes that what makes her organization distinct is that "We want women to change themselves. Many NGOs do projects and pay attention to projects. We pay attention to projects' effects on people." In many cases, project ideas come from magazine readers themselves. As with the suicide column, a number of the magazine's columns are designed to be reader-contributed. Plus, the magazine requires all of its editors to spend at least forty work days per year in the countryside themselves to remain connected to the rural areas.

Xie Lihua notes that one important mission of *Rural Women* is to oppose a common discourse (one even promoted from time to time by the Women's Federation) that rural women have "low quality" (*suzhi di*). Instead the magazine claims that rural women should and can have confidence in themselves. It publishes articles letting rural women know that all they are lacking is *opportunities*. By providing a venue for rural women's stories, the magazine allows these women to speak to each other and diminishes their otherwise isolated status. It also legitimizes the idea that rural women have control over their destinies. In a sense, the magazine creates a virtual community for rural women, aiming to encourage readers to think of themselves as powerful, individually and collectively.

In Wang Lixia's manuscript, the author not only narrates the suicide tale of Xu Fengzhi, but she also goes on to assume the powerful role of cultural critic, offering an analysis of the case, as well as suggestions for how to alleviate the suicide problem in China's countryside.

From studying the sources of Xu Fengzhi's death, we can discover many psychological factors commonly possessed by married rural women. First, in the heart there is only the loved person. Outside this, there is no world. Then, from what we have said here, men mostly go out to work. The women stay behind to work in the home. Their days are repeated again and again, the years are repeated again and again. The women are consumed by being busy in the little valley, and they are basically unable to see the outside world. Tilling the land and raising pigs are their enterprises, their husband and children are their life's hope. When chatting with me, sisters always love to say: "Is there any meaning in life?" "Why after all am I living?" But you can then say, "Not everyone therefore will commit suicide. So why this one?" There is a saying, "If finally your husband is good to you, then in this lifetime you can also be a good person." If your husband is good, then this is life's strong point. Once the husband has another love, the life of a woman seems to have lost all its value.

When all Xu Fengzhi's great effort could not redeem the situation, then she selected the road of suicide. The words of a song can represent this kind of psychology: "In the end, you don't know what you are living for in the world." Although there are other people who don't think of living like this, in the end it is difficult to break through the bitter bamboo fence of the rural home's little courtyard. As we investigate the causes of suicide, the key issues are always poverty, backwardness, and insufficient access to culture.

Urban women also have work, have their own enterprises, in addition to their husbands and children. If the urban family falls on hard times, there still is the woman's work, supporting the meaning of her life. So the woman's mental world is less likely to collapse, taking her down the road to suicide.

And yet in our kind of poor, closed-off, little mountain village, rural women basically do not have the possibility of searching for their own mental care. They cannot seek their own work outside of taking care of their families. So they feel mentally empty and worried. Keeping a good home and passing a good life becomes their life's earnest demand.

I think that in order to stop these kinds of events, that is, rural women's inclination for suicide, we must treat the origins of the problem.

One. Raise rural women's cultural level, let their minds be broadened, so that they know that besides their husband and children, their life also has even more roads that can give them choices, so that they know their life's value.

Two. Give rural women employment opportunities, let them put their own abilities to good use. At the same time, they also can get in touch with every kind and description of people and things in the kaleidoscopic world, to see it more widely, and not necessarily consider suicide when encountering difficulties.

The above is my little, immature opinion. My purpose is to wish to tell the countless rural sisters: no matter what setbacks you encounter, still treasure your life. After the rain, the sky will clear, and the bright sun will always appear!

Unlike bridal laments and "speaking bitterness," the stories (and the analysis) like this one from *Rural Women Knowing All*, mean to promote subjectivity and social change on both individual and societal levels—and especially to contribute to the immense project of creating civil society in China. Bridal laments provided a setting for women to complain about their situation, but were only briefly useful as an expression of grievances; women did not intend them to produce long-term resolution of oppressive conditions. Authorities created "speaking bitterness" as a way to highlight the evils of a pre-existing social order but primarily as part of a strategy to legitimate the new state apparatus—a project that allowed very little individual agency. *Rural Women Knowing All*, on the other hand, seeks to make a venue not only for narrating women's lives but also for changing these lives. In this spirit, Wang Lixia tells the story of Xu Fengzhi and then she offers explanations and suggestions for how the suicide crisis might be alleviated.

When *Rural Women* expanded, becoming a service-providing non-governmental organization, it took on the project of suicide prevention groups at the village level, and now the stories of these projects have also become part of the magazine's repertoire of tales to recount. Much has changed in rural China in the decade since the magazine instituted its suicide column. For instance, far greater percentages of rural residents have migrated to cities, although more often women remain behind in the villages. Greater Party-State attention to rural problems has led to greater legitimacy for projects like those instituted by *Rural Women* magazine.

One such project has been instituted in 36 Rollers Village, also in Hebei Province. The founder of a grassroots women's organization connected to *Rural Women*, Xu Fengqin, wrote the chronicle of this village in a recent issue of the magazine.

Xu Fengqin, "Hebei's Qinglong County: The New Life of the Women of 36 Rollers Village," published in *Rural Women*, February 2007

In the past, when people mentioned 36 Rollers Village, there was no one who didn't shake their head. It is famous in the whole county as a backwards village. It can be described like this: "Its thinking is outmoded, its spirit is empty, its actions are ignorant, its economy is backward." For so many years, the people of 36 Rollers Village tenaciously stuck to traditional concepts, women relied on their husbands and were not able to be economically independent . . . Before the year 2000, the typical picture was of nine people attempting suicide per year, among them six people dying.

It can be said that by undertaking a suicide intervention project, 36 Rollers Village changed its identity . . .

In order to correctly carry out a suicide intervention project, the Rural Women's Health Promotion Association continuously established new methods:

First of all, we organized 23 volunteers to go down to the village to perform . . . In the 36 Rollers Village school, family courtyards, and streets the volunteers performed for the village women. Seeing their performance, the women of 36 Rollers Village were shocked to their very beings. They felt, "We also should change our ways of life." . . . There were seven or eight rural women who came out of their homes and started to participate in cultural recreation activities. But they encountered the attacks of slanderous village gossip, so after two days, these efforts died prematurely . . . Next, the county Rural Women's Health Promotion Association invited old volunteers from the university to go to the villages to tutor the rural women in forming song teams . . . On October 1, 2006, they organized the "Rural Women Celebrating the 57th National Day Friendly Song Competition." This activity swiftly engaged the women's abilities to present cultural entertainments. Local television stations and newspapers all reported on the graceful bearing of the rural women of 36 Rollers Village. Through this activity, the rural women also found their own value.

The village committee saw that the suicide intervention project was entering people's hearts very deeply. So they bought four sets of sound systems for four cultural entertainment teams. The villagers also provided funds to buy color televisions. At this point, 36 Rollers Village found a new vitality. The people in the village began to look more spiritually alive.

The suicide intervention project has succeeded in 36 Rollers Village. There have been no new suicides there since the program began. Many report that the intervention project has also improved the overall quality of life for everyone in the village. This is just one example of how *Rural Women* magazine has drawn on the power of stories as a vehicle for social change. This power draws strands from traditional narrative forms like bridal laments and "speaking bitterness" and weaves these with contemporary impulses toward establishing civil society. Today the result is grassroots social action. Perhaps this development harkens back to the "human heartedness" evoked by Kenneth Rexroth, the "magnanimity" and "courage" that is an inherent part of traditional Chinese storytelling.

Reading mainstream Western media accounts of China these days, this generosity of spirit seems in short supply. Corruption, venality, rampant consumerism, and environmental degradation are the dominant trends apparent in a rapidly developing China. Yet "human heartedness" exists as well, efforts to promote social justice and fairness and even to maintain humanity amidst the dislocations of breakneck marketization and urbanization.

Sharon R. Wesoky is Associate Professor and Chair of Political Science at Allegheny College in Meadville, Pennsylvania and the author of *Chinese Feminism Faces Globalization* (Routledge, 2002). She has been visiting China since 1991 and for the past eight years has been a frequent visitor and volunteer at Rural Women, an NGO promoting rural women's rights and interests.

Notes

1   Kenneth Rexroth, "The Chinese Classic Novel in Translation," in *Bird in the Bush: Obvious Essays* (New York: New Directions, 1959).
2   Teresa Poole, " 'People Just Take Their Lives Lightly,' " *The Independent*, May 14, 1997, p. 10.
3   Anne E. McLaren, "The Grievance Rhetoric of Chinese Women: From Lamentation to Revolution," *Intersections: Gender, History and Culture in the Asian Context*, 4 (September 2000): paragraph 18. Available online at: http://wwwsshe.murdoch.edu.au/intersections/issue4/mclaren.html, accessed July 24, 2007.
4   One such show was "Words on the Night Breeze," recounted in Xinran, *The Good Women of China: Hidden Voices* (New York: Anchor Books, 2002).

Further Reading

English language website of *Rural Women*: www.nongjianv.org/web/english/index.html

9
Depo Diaries and the Power of Stories

ETOBSSIE WAKO AND CARA PAGE

Depo Diaries: A National Storytelling Project came out of our need to understand our own experiences with the adverse effects of birth control. We needed to highlight the ways that the medical community and others enforce systemic and coercive reproductive practices, relying on racist, ableist, heterosexist, and classist assumptions. Over generations, these assumptions continue to marginalize the health needs and quality of care of poor women, women of color, queer women, and women with disabilities. The Committee on Women, Population, and the Environment (CWPE) has been working for over fifteen years against policies that target certain women as the root cause of all global social ills. CWPE has been working against policies that subject certain women to unethical testing of contraceptives, involuntary sterilization, and reproductive control. We seek to promote women's rights to safe, voluntary birth control and abortion, and we strive for a reorientation of contraceptive technology that is safe, non-invasive, affordable, and woman-controlled. In addition, CWPE is committed to the principle that self-determination for all women can only come by addressing the intersections of oppressions and the impacts of these oppressions on our emotional, physical, and spiritual well-being.

In the early 1900s under the guise of promoting "good breeding" and "building a better race" of Americans, or what was known as "eugenics," a number of state laws and programs targeted certain women for sterilization, including Native American women, African American women, Latina women, poor women, and women with mental and developmental disabilities. By mid-century, when most official, abusive sterilization practices had been dismantled (if not wholly abandoned or discredited), or had been taken over by regulated private practices less easily monitored, government-funded public health clinics began distributing systemic hormonal birth controls which often had adverse, long-term effects on women and girls.

Late in the twentieth century, in 1992, the Food and Drug Administration (FDA) approved Depo-Provera, a synthetic hormonal contraceptive. Women's health activists mounted campaigns against the approval because they were

101

concerned about evidence that Depo caused severe depression, breast cancer, cervical cancer, higher HIV/AIDS susceptibility, excessive bleeding, weight change, and osteoporosis, among other health impacts. These activists were also concerned that Depo would probably be mass-marketed to clinics and doctors as an easy and cost-effective product to administer to females in poor communities and communities of color. Indeed, studies have determined that this is how health professionals—including many who likely believe that women in these communities ought to practice "population control"—have used Depo-Provera.

Vision for the Stories

At the INCITE! Color of Violence III Conference in New Orleans, Louisiana in the Spring of 2005, CWPE led a workshop called "The Tactics of C.R.A.C.K. & Other Methods of Eugenics & Population Control." The workshop defined certain birth control practices as strategies and acts of violence against women of color. Approximately thirty women of African, Asian, Middle Eastern, and Latina descent attended the workshop. Almost all of the women had either used Depo-Provera or had family members who were using it. Many of the women reported that no one had warned them about the full range of possible long-term effects of Depo-Provera, but many told about the results they had seen and felt. For example, women from rural, African American, southern communities noted that three generations of women in their families had been using Depo and had experienced serious side effects.

As women began to tell their stories in the workshop, it turned out that almost everyone had experienced an adverse side effect, but each woman had chosen to keep quiet—and isolated—about these matters in her life because of communal and religious taboos regarding sex and sexuality. Many women discussed feeling shame about their own bodies. Each woman thought there was something wrong only with herself. Most never linked their depression, their weight gain, or their extreme hair loss to the birth control they were using.

The workshop was intended to be a way of sharing information and generating some strategic planning about how to respond to—and dismantle—twenty-first-century eugenics. But the event took on a life of its own, becoming a transformative experience in which the participants told their own stories of Depo in a context of personal and political liberation. One woman after another told her story about and against reproductive injustice. We learned from this powerful process that using a model of storytelling to demand change and build public education around the dangers of such commonly known birth controls as Depo-Provera needed to come from the stories of our lived experiences.

Speaking Out of Isolation

Since the Depo Diaries initiative began in 2006, we have received stories from across the world. Some stories praise the convenience and privacy of

Depo-Provera. But most speak about the pain and isolation women experience while using the hormonal contraceptive. The narratives differ drastically from one another but at the same time, they are deeply connected by the ways that the writers express their experiences of disempowerment and the helplessness that follows. The stories also share this theme: many within the healthcare system seem ready to wholly disregard the physical, mental, and spiritual welfare of Depo users. Women report that navigating the healthcare systems has felt treacherous and dangerous, a voyage marked by hostility, dismissal, and a general contempt for their voices and experiences. The Depo Diaries initiative challenges this culture of enforced silence. It is built on the idea that when these women tell their stories, when all the stories are collected, a new power is born in that accumulation of narratives and in that collective voice. These stories take us out of isolation and grant us an opportunity to promote systemic change for our well-being and for the sustainability of our communities.

From Ontario, Canada

I originally asked for my tubes to be tied; however, the doctor went on and on about how I was too young for that. I was twenty-nine and had two children and was a single mom. I thought I was quite capable of deciding if I wanted more children or not, but the doctor kept arguing with me and told me how great Depo-Provera was. In the doctor's office I went to, the doctor always took the vial containing the Depo out of its box and neither the box nor the pamphlet with the side affects was given to me. Later that changed when I started asking to keep the boxes.

At first, the negative side effects were not noticeable. I totally lost my period and spotted at any time. The longer I used Depo, the more the side effects came out. First was the vaginal dryness and decrease in libido which caused much friction between my partner and me (no pun intended). Then I just started getting more and more tired, the longer I was on it, but the doctor dismissed this. He said I was a single mom with young children and that I was getting older (but not old enough to choose to have my tubes tied!).

Then I started forgetting things, getting irritable, getting shakes, etc. Soon, I had experienced about 80 percent of the negative side effects I read about on a particular site bashing Depo. I feel Depo triggered my thyroid disease although this illness is in my family. Once my thyroid resolved itself, I stupidly went back on Depo. I kept going back to the doctor and telling her that I felt like my thyroid was acting up again, and she kept testing it and saying it was fine. After a year of this, she started looking at me like I was crazy and offered me depression meds. I felt helpless. She thought I was going crazy, and I couldn't convince her that I was not.

After seeing that anti-Depo website and all the complaints, I was very relieved. I started crying so hard, I could hardly read the more than 300 complaints. After that I stopped using Depo. Immediately I began to feel better. The headaches went away. Irritability went away. My sex drive came back. My period came back. However!!!! I still have never felt like I got back to the way I used to feel before Depo even though I have not been using it for over a year.

The two things that feel like they have never resolved themselves are first, that I have problems remembering things (for example, sometimes it takes me ten minutes to remember how to spell a simple word) and second, I am always tired, although not as tired as I felt on Depo.

Anyway, thanks for listening. I really hope they do something to warn people about the side effects because my experience was awful. And one more thing! I asked over and over again to be monitored by the doctor, in the same way that women are when they take the birth control pill, and my doctor's office kept acting like they were too busy, and it wasn't necessary. I had one half-assed pap test done the whole time I was on Depo, and that was only because I demanded it. I would change doctor's offices immediately if I could, but there is a shortage in Brampton, where I live. People even have to take their newborns to walk-in clinics, and they get a different doctor every time for their well-baby check-ups. I guess a bad doctor is better than no doctor, but I wish I could sue them for the Depo thing!

From Alabama

I was prescribed Depo by a health clinic in Alabama when I was fifteen because, they said, it would help with my terrible periods. The only side effect I was told about was that I may not have a period. I used Depo for over ten years. Now, over a year after I stopped taking Depo, I suffer from terrible migraines, depression, weight gain, IBS, fibromyalgia, loss of libido. My periods have not returned without help, and I have many more problems. This drug is toxic and should be taken off the market. I was only a child when I was put on this drug, and now I am all messed up. I have been suffering with stomach problems for the past year and have not been able to find a source of the problem. I know it is from Depo.

From Newport News, VA

My ob/gyn prescribed Depo for me after the birth of my son. I gained forty pounds between the first shot and the second shot. While I was on it, mostly I thought it was wonderful. I had no periods and seemingly no other side effects, other than the weight gain. But actually, I started having migraine headaches, and I never had them before the shot. Also, from the time I got the first shot till I got off the shot, every pap I had was abnormal. Also, after receiving the first shot, the doctor told me I was basically on my way to cervical cancer. The same ob/gyn who prescribed Depo told me I should stop it because it was aggravating the condition.

Six months after I stopped the shots, my paps became normal. But I had a myriad of other problems I never had before taking Depo. I had painful ovulations. Painful and heavy cycles. Basically, I was having the entire period in a matter of hours. After this happened two cycles in a row, the doc urged me to go back on the shot since it stopped my cycle. I did. I was on it for a year. In that year, I was constantly sick, had constant pelvic pain, sex became very painful, and my paps were back to being abnormal again. I wanted off the shot, but I was scared. I went off the shot and immediately started birth control pills, hoping to get the cycle regulated so it wouldn't be like before. It didn't help. I ended up having a full vaginal hysterectomy in August 2002.

Location Unknown

I am twenty-seven years old and have been on Depo for over five years. Two weeks after my last shot, my body literally began falling apart overnight. I have tumors on my liver and cysts on my kidneys, osteoporosis, heart palpitations, vomit constantly, hiatal hernia, chest pains, shortness of breath, rapid heart rate, insomnia, muscle and bone pain, numbness on one side of my body. I am going through menopause, have blood in my stools, and much more! I literally woke up with all these ailments. I was perfectly healthy before. After no support from the medical community, I finally found tens of thousands of women on websites experiencing these same side effects. I also found websites that contained lists of these possible side effects so that I could present it to an emergency room person and get the tests done that I needed. I am currently undergoing breast cancer detection and cervical cancer testing as well. Again, I am only twenty-seven years old, but I feel as if I am eighty. Help me give women a voice. There is no freedom of choice if there is not an awareness of potential risks. The only warning I was given was that I would probably gain five pounds.

Feel free to ask me any questions. I am about to start doing everything I can to get awareness out. I may be only one person, but I am very "spirited" and very angry that a greedy pharmaceutical company has taken away my quality of life, and potentially life itself. I am equally upset at the damage it has caused to the tens of thousands of women who are writing about their "Depo-Provera horror stories" on the web. In some cases, the damage is not reversible. These are teenagers who are now sterile, who have cancer and osteoporosis. I will use my last breath to help women become aware of the dangers and get this drug off the market. We should have freedom of choice and that means knowing the facts.

Collective Voice and Power

In telling our stories, we are speaking about our pain, our resilience, and our self-determination. We are taking back our lives by naming how our bodies are viewed and treated inside the medical industrial complex. This storytelling initiative gives women an opportunity to highlight their negative experiences against the mass marketing and mass prescription of Depo-Provera. Through telling our stories, we are claiming our right to high-quality birth control and health care, generally. The Depo storytelling initiative has become an opportunity to participate in the creative process of story sharing, personal healing, empowerment, and community building. This kind of research creates a more accurate picture of the range and kinds of side effects women are experiencing while using Depo-Provera. It also makes it possible for us to expose the ways that women's bodies are still targeted for "population control." We believe that in order to create gynecological, reproductive, and other forms of basic safety and security for women, we must make these practices visible and, in the process, transform our isolation into collective action for reproductive freedom.

Beyond telling our stories we are highlighting leaders in reproductive justice. The Depo Diaries storytelling initiative has been instrumental in identifying groups and individuals working to overcome reproductive oppression. We have a vested interest in continuing to map and document networks and community initiatives that are effectively intervening against coercive practices by producing public education, providing accessible and creative ways to research and disseminate information, and other transformative approaches.

We are currently working on a DVD about women's experiences in coercive reproductive practices, and have developed a booklet which examines contraceptive technologies through a critical feminist and reproductive justice analysis. From information available on our webpage (www.cwpe.org) to community workshops and conferences, we are expanding the traditional discourse of reproductive health to incorporate the voices of marginalized communities and to offer a critical viewpoint that opposes these oppressive and population-based practices. We also recognize that there is a critical need to map stories of trans and queer women, indigenous women, women with disabilities, and immigrant and refugee women. We need to understand their particular stories of coercion and unethical testing, justified by historical pathologizing and the domination of bodies and communities. Through the work of Depo Diaries, we call on all of these communities for their acute knowledge about the experiences of women with healthcare systems—state, public, and private—to contribute to the work against all abusive practices.

Etobssie Wako is a women's health advocate whose work is grounded in expanding the existing parameters of health care to incorporate women's rights globally. She is interested in exploring the intersectionality of class, race, and gender as it applies to health programs, education, and services. She believes in the power of the personal narrative as a means to transcend oppressive practices and systems and promote just communities.

Cara Page is the former National Director of the Committee on Women, Population, and the Environment (CWPE). She is a queer performance artist and activist of color who has organized for queer rights, youth rights, economic and reproductive justice, and has worked to end violence and population control for over twenty years. She is the founder of Deeper Waters (a consulting company for healing and liberatory practices) and Kindred: A Southern Healing Arts Cooperative.

Further Reading

Please send testimonials and/or stories of your experiences of Depo-Provera and/or other adverse effects of birth control or stories of coercive reproductive practices to: depodiaries@cwpe.org

Please contact us for further information or inquiries of trainings and workshops on using stories as tools for liberatory practice against violence and population control at: powerofstories@cwpe.org

Visit the Committee on Women, Population, and the Environment's official website for current research, actions, and campaigns against population control: www.cwpe.org

Population & Development Program of Hampshire College: http://popdev.hampshire.edu

10
Immigrant Stories in the Hudson Valley

JO SALAS

Audience, teller, and actors at Immigrant Stories Playback Theatre performance; Elissa Davidson

Jorge:	Every story you hear is inside of you. When you leave home, you never know what's going to happen, you don't know if you're going to make it, you don't know if you're going to see someone again. There could be a happy ending. There could be no ending.
Manuela:	I want to tell everyone that we all came here to work, but not to hurt anybody. We came here for a better life for our families.

The Immigrant Stories Project

The Immigrant Stories Project is an ongoing series of interactive, bilingual theater performances with audiences of immigrants from Mexico, Colombia, Puerto Rico, Peru, Argentina, Ecuador, Belize, Paraguay, Guatemala, and the Dominican Republic. All live in the Mid-Hudson Valley of New York, a semi-rural region that has seen successive waves of immigration since the first Dutch and Huguenot settlers in the 1600s. Like many of their predecessors, recent immigrants have come here in desperation and hope, fleeing poverty that is a tragic outcome of history and politics in which the United States has played a significant part—most recently, with the impact of the North American Free Trade Agreement (NAFTA) which has led to millions of farmers losing their land. With no way of supporting their families, it is inevitable that many people look toward the great wealth and apparent opportunities just across the border.

Olivia:	I came here to help my family in Mexico. In my country it was difficult, no work, nothing we could do. I came eighteen years ago. This country gives me a lot and I appreciate it.
Cesar:	I wanted to come here so that I could help the ones who stayed behind.

The Playback Theatre format (used in many other contexts as well) invites audience members to tell personal stories which actors and musicians transform into theater on the spot. It is essentially a dialogue through action—one story sparks another, directly or indirectly. The process is collaborative and co-creative: each "teller" comes to the stage to tell the story in conversation with the "conductor" or emcee, then watches as the story is enacted, giving a final comment at the end. An atmosphere of exploration and discovery develops as voices are heard and responded to in spontaneous theater. The actors, like the tellers, step into unscripted and uncharted territory with each story.

My theater company, Hudson River Playback Theatre (HRPT), conceived the Immigrant Stories Project in discussion with administrators at the local Head Start center which provides support services for a growing number of immigrant families with children in the program. The administrators spoke of the extreme stresses that face many immigrants in our area: language barriers; poverty; isolation; distance from family of origin; the anxiety of living without legal immigration status; discrimination. As fellow community members and as an ensemble concerned with social justice, we proposed offering performances as an opportunity for public voice and as a forum in which participants could bear witness to their experience. Aware of the prevalence of stereotypes and untruths in the media, the government, and popular belief, we also hoped to foster respect and understanding on the part of non-immigrants who might attend.

Our offer was fueled by the desire to reach out to people in our midst who live in hardship, and to create change through stories. We were not at that time strongly connected to the immigrant community, nor are we ourselves Latino—which challenged us to educate ourselves, build relationships, and find Latino performers to join us. (In spite of developments on these fronts we continue to face such challenges, including the immediate awkwardness of writing this account without an immigrant co-author.)

With the help of Head Start staff and with funding from a local foundation, we organized twenty shows at all seven Head Start centers in Dutchess County, in playrooms, community rooms, or school gyms. Audience size ranged from ten to thirty-five. On the "stage"—not an actual stage but an open space in front of rows of folding chairs—we set up three chairs, one for the conductor, one for the translator, and one for the teller who would come to tell her story, returning to her seat in the audience after watching it enacted. Tellers told their stories in either Spanish or English, sometimes both (our team included a native Spanish speaker to translate at each show). The actors used both languages if they could (two are bilingual), as well as music, movement, and metaphor to bring the stories to life.

Non-immigrant parents and staff came to almost all the performances, listening intently and offering their own responses to the stories. Staff provided food so that people could eat and chat together before and afterwards.

Telling Stories

Arriving for a show for the first time, people seemed a bit shy, a bit puzzled; and then when we explained why we were there and how this kind of theater works, they became engaged. Sometimes, especially with larger and Latino-only audiences, the stories flowed. Other times there were long pauses as people decided if they wanted to speak up. Audience members laughed with recognition at some of the stories and enactments, like the time someone yelled out "Abran las fronteras!" (Open the border!) when we asked what Americans could do to make things easier for them. Often they wept over a story of danger or loss. It did not seem, as it sometimes does with other adult audiences unfamiliar with playback, that they were wondering how to categorize this unfamiliar kind of performance. Instead, they met us directly on the terms we offered: if you want to speak, we are here to listen, and we'll do our best to reflect the meanings that are important to you. Their openness was refreshing and artistically liberating for us.

The tellers told of the complexity of their experience—the difficult choice to come, the constant weighing of whether it was worth it or not. For many immigrants the journey here is highly dangerous, even traumatic. For those who manage to get visas the expense and effort are considerable, requiring financial sacrifice and sometimes the heartbreaking decision to leave behind a child, an aging parent, or a professional identity. Once here, life is not easy, with the formidable challenges of language, low-paying jobs, anxiety about legal status, and prejudice. The routine, dispiriting suspiciousness that immigrants have traditionally encountered has been exacerbated in the post-9/11 era by attempts by the president and some Congress members to foment fear about immigration, with grim consequences for undocumented immigrants. Most immigrants suffer at being far away from their extended families, especially at times of illness or death. On the other hand, people spoke frequently of their satisfaction and gratitude in overcoming obstacles and bringing dreams to fruition—in particular, the dream of education for their children.

The following fragments from different shows were each followed by improvised action and music, some brief and dance-like while others became longer scenes with characters and dialogue:

Maya: I left everything behind that I had worked so hard for, to come here with my husband. I now work as a cleaner. It is hard work, and it is not the work I want to be doing. I'm always thinking about the work that I did in my country, as a special ed teacher, and I hope some day to return to that kind of work.

Pablo: We were six of us crossing. During the entire night we could not do it because it was very controlled. We were waiting for dawn and were going to try it during the day, according to what the man who was helping us told us. Some policemen were watching us from a mountain, and they told us, "Come on up!" And we told them "No, you come down!" We weren't going to go up and if the policemen came down, what would happen to us?

Fidela: When we get here the first problem is the language. All the jobs require you speak English. And we don't know how to talk with our children's teachers at school.

Renata: I want to say that everything that happened to me back then was worth it. I'm happily married, I have my three kids, and I'm happy. At first I wanted to work in a nursing home. I went to school to become a certified nursing assistant and then I worked in a nursing home for eleven years. About six years ago I started my business. My children are teenagers. I hope they're learning from me what I learned from my parents.

Barbara: My husband has to work at least twelve hours a day in two different jobs. He's had to endure a lot of humiliation from his bosses. I've tried to look for work in a lot of different places, but unfortunately I can't get a job because of the language.

Julia: My son applied to all the universities. I'll never ever forget when he received the letter saying he was accepted. We are so happy now that he's actually in college. It's because of my husband, who worked so hard.

Serafina: I am sad because I don't see my family. Years pass without seeing them. When my father died I couldn't go.

In a Playback show, stories are received with full, respectful attention and minimal interruption, and then enacted with artistry. Tellers in all contexts frequently respond to this unusual atmosphere by telling something from their lives that is of great significance to them. The invoking of a heightened, aesthetic ritual allows stories of considerable sensitivity and pain to be told safely. Immigrant tellers spoke very openly of painful or tender memories. Other audience members, watching stories that often paralleled their own experiences, appeared riveted. We could not escape the sense that these stories constituted a new myth of immigration, as yet unintegrated into the layered national mythology of immigration, but readily recognized and embraced by the immigrant audiences.

Who were Serafina and Pablo and the other speakers telling their stories *to*? It's possible that they were addressing us, the visiting performers, as representatives of the powerful majority-culture world which, in their experience, is often uncomprehending, ignorant, and contemptuous. It is also possible, and likely, that to some degree the tellers were addressing non-immigrant parents and staff for the same reason, although the range of content of the stories did not seem to depend on whether there were non-immigrants in the audience or not.

From what some participants have told us in later conversations, they were also telling their stories to each other, to their fellow-immigrants, friends, and family members—making use of Playback Theatre's form of public storytelling with its inherent extension of resonance and meaning, which renders it quite different from private, conversational storytelling.

Humans are storytelling beings: we make sense of our individual and collective experience by the stories we tell. So we can assume that in this sense the tellers were also telling their stories to themselves. Personal storytelling is also, for any of us, an act of claiming identity and affirming meaning by saying, "This happened to me, this is what I lived and witnessed."

Border-Crossing Stories

Stories of crossing the border, intensely emotional in the telling and enacting, emerged in almost every one of the Head Start shows and continue to do so in the varied settings where we now perform. We do not specifically invite stories on this topic—our questions to the audience are deliberately open-ended and non-prescriptive throughout the show. In some situations we even try to divert border-crossing stories, when we are not sure of who is in the audience and if it is safe to divulge a teller's undocumented entry to the U.S. The tellers' paramount urgency to tell these stories speaks of the extreme trauma they have undergone: risking life, risking violence, enduring forced separation from loved ones including children, who sometimes have to be smuggled in separately. Some tell of beloved friends or relatives who've been lost in the attempt to cross:

> *Consuelo:* My brother called us when he was almost at the border. The following day the people waiting for him called to tell us he hadn't shown up. He was lost. To this day we don't know where he is or if he is dead or alive. He was my real brother, my only real sibling. For me it was very horrible not knowing. I keep thinking that I see him, but it's just people who look like him, the way they walk and their mannerisms.

Here is part of a story told by Lucia, who escaped to the U.S. as a young teenager after being raped and becoming pregnant. Her husband and younger children were in the audience. She spoke in English, occasionally asking the translator for help.

> When I was waiting in the line to cross the border, I felt so terrible. I was one of three women with all those men, and you see the helicopters above you. We had to run and then cross the river, and pay those men, and if you don't pay those men, they force you to stay. We had to cross over farms with dogs barking and men with guns. I held my breath so I could hear if anyone was behind me. I ran and ran and tried not to breathe so no one would hear me. When at last we finished crossing I was the only woman who made it across. I went for two days without

eating and I was so hungry. Looking back, I know it was because I was pregnant. Finally some men came and picked us up. They brought us two hot dogs for each person and a bottle of water, and oh god, this is what I wanted! I ate everything with one bite.

They put us in a place with a lot of other people, no shower, just tortillas to eat, and we waited there, and then my brother called. They gave me clean clothes and put me on an airplane. When I got here a taxi was waiting. It was like a dream. When I finally saw my brother, I felt so happy, I hugged him and he hugged me. I started to explain everything. I almost told him what happened with the boy in Mexico, but I was so afraid. I didn't tell anybody.

Lucia's long story was one of the most dramatic and moving I've ever heard in over thirty years of doing Playback Theatre. She seemed determined to tell it, in spite of being overwhelmed by emotion at various points. Her small daughter came to comfort her, seeing her mother's tears. The actors said later that as this delicate and detailed story unfolded they were worried about remembering all its parts, but in fact they captured it beautifully in action. Lucia nodded and smiled after it was over, still tearful but apparently content.

Almost a year after this show I asked Lucia what it had been like to tell the story, and how she has felt since then about having told it.

"I didn't plan to tell my story—it was suddenly just there," said Lucia, remembering. "There was much more that I could have told, but I didn't want to take more time. My husband was there. I hadn't told him what had happened to me—about how I came here. We don't tell each other everything. After that evening he was very quiet for about a week. Then he told me he was happy I'd told the story, he was very proud of me, and he loved me . . . I felt good that I'd told the story and I still feel good. I feel relieved now about those things that I told. The untold parts are still painful. After my children grow up I'd like to write the whole story so they can understand."

Other tellers of border-crossing stories have indicated a similar relief, consistent with the findings of trauma research that those who have undergone trauma feel a compulsion to tell their story, and that this telling is essential for healing to take place.

Making a Book

From the very first show audience members expressed the desire for their stories to be heard in the wider community, which encouraged us to move ahead with the idea of a photo-illustrated book of transcribed stories. We audio-taped most of the performances. A photographer attended three shows and came with me to take photos at the homes of two families.

As we worked on the book I met with several groups of immigrant parents to find out what hopes, concerns, and suggestions they might have about it.

I brought an early draft to each meeting and they passed it around with interest. Their comments emphasized, above all, their passionate desire to let non-immigrants know who they are and why they are here. Looking up from the pages in her hand, one woman said, softly and intently, "We want them to know that we are not bad people," a poignant indication of the dismissive and disrespectful attitude that she meets.

She and other parents also saw the book as a valuable means of letting their own children and their far-away families know what they have gone through. Another woman, with nods of agreement from others, stressed that the book should include success stories. They did not express concern about being identified by the stories or photos. (In the published book, *Half of My Heart/La Mitad de Mi Corazón*,[1] all names have been changed and photos are positioned separately from stories told by the individuals they depict. Written permission was given by people whose photos appear.)

With non-immigrant readers in mind we included a section called "Myths and Facts," drawn with permission from the National Immigration Forum and challenging some of the ubiquitous untruths that bolster anti-immigrant sentiments.

I visited Renata who had told a story about coming here as a young, undocumented immigrant twenty years ago. I wanted to show her the written version of what she'd told, in Spanish and English. "I'm proud of my story," Renata said after looking it over. "Please use it, and the photos. You don't even need to change my name."

We sat for a while in the small restaurant that she owns while she talked heatedly about the ignorance she often encounters. She mentioned an Anglo customer who'd recently traveled to Mexico as a tourist. "It's so beautiful there!" the woman had gushed. "Why did you want to come here?"

"I told her that I came here for the same reason that she came back here herself when her own dollars finally ran out—because this is where the money is."

Renata's anger was shared by others I spoke to and informed their desire to make the book available to non-immigrants. We all hoped that readers would respond the way non-immigrant audience members typically responded during the shows, with increased understanding and respect:

Valerie: I came to a greater understanding of what immigrant life is like. It's really touched my heart and it's given me some ideas of things I can do for this community as an American, and as a deacon in my church.

Gail: A lot of time people don't have a chance to hear these stories—it's good to have a chance to see these stories, and it's very emotional for me.

Building a Network

The asymmetry of carrying out this project as a non-Latino ensemble has been a drawback and has no doubt felt awkward to the immigrant participants as well. We have tried to address this question in various ways. By now, the third year of the project, a growing number of immigrants are becoming involved as performers, consultants, and creative collaborators. Local Spanish-language journalists have taken an interest in the project. Several Hispanic[2] community leaders offer support, networking, and advice.

One of the first to be involved beyond attending shows and telling a story was Adriana, a Head Start parent from Colombia. Adriana assisted with the production of the book by transcribing stories told in Spanish and then writing an introduction:

> Collaborating in this project has touched my personal life because I find myself far from my parents, my family, my best friends, and my "other half," my daughter Natalia, who is in my country . . . These stories touch soul and heart and they give me a lot of strength and courage to keep going forward and fulfill all my goals.

Once the book was published we began to include readings in performances, as a warm-up to stories from our new audiences. Adriana became a reader, as have several other participants in both the original and subsequent series of shows. Liliana, a Peruvian immigrant and Head Start center director, read stories in a show, as well as consulting with me on a number of aspects of the project. Leticia, a young woman from Mexico, came to a show and told her story about crossing the border. Six months later, at the second show in that venue, she told a story about recently getting her green card, describing her pride and satisfaction but also her deep sorrow at the fate of recent deportees. At the third she was on stage with us as a paid performer, reading a story from the book.

The current phase of the project includes a collaboration with the Youth Arts Group of a local advocacy and support organization, Rural and Migrant Ministry. YAG, as it is called, is composed of Hispanic and African American teenagers who use the arts to promote social justice. Two-thirds of them are the bilingual children of immigrants. They learned to do Playback Theatre in a series of training workshops and they now join us as actors in performances. Playback Theatre as a technique has become part of YAG's repertoire of skills: they feel empowered to use it in their own work, separate from our project.

There is much further to go in building a broader and stronger network with the local immigrant community. For myself, being white and non-Spanish-speaking, it is not always easy to make initial contact with key community members. The other HRPT members and I share a commitment to acquiring language skills, building relationships, and continuing to educate ourselves about the complex and changing realities of immigration.

The Future

As the project has evolved we have recognized both the need and the opportunity to ally the work more directly with the quest for immigrants' rights. The shows themselves are a form of activism: telling one's story in public space is a crucial step in claiming recognition and justice, and having one's story heard and comprehended by majority-culture members is another. We hope to go further. We are now in dialogue with immigrant rights activists about linking the project with other local initiatives. We are also exploring how to bring the impact of the stories to much larger audiences without endangering undocumented tellers, perhaps by creating a scripted piece based on their stories, with the participation of immigrant collaborators and performers.

The Immigrant Stories Project has deeply affected us, the members of Hudson River Playback Theatre, as individuals and as an organization. Like the non-immigrants in our audiences, we have been changed by meeting our immigrant neighbors and hearing their stories. We hope that the path forward is one that we walk together.

All names have been changed except for the three women mentioned in "Building a Network."

Jo Salas is the artistic director of Hudson River Playback Theatre, which has performed in theaters, schools, and other settings since 1990. She is the author of *Improvising Real Life: Personal Story in Playback Theatre* (3rd ed. Tusitala Publishing, 1999) and *Do My Story, Sing My Song: Music Therapy and Playback Theatre with Troubled Children* (Tusitala Publishing, 2007).

Note

1   *Half of My Heart/La Mitad de Mi Corazón: True Stories Told by Immigrants in Dutchess* The County, New York/Historias verídicas contadas por immigrantes del condado de Dutchess, New York. Edited by Jo Salas and Leslie Gauna with photos by Elissa I. Davidson (New York: Tusitala Publishing, 2007).
2   The author's use of the terms Hispanic and Latino reflects the immigrant community's usage of both words.

Further Reading

Hudson River Playback Theatre: www.hudsonriverplayback.org

11

Our Stories, Their Decisions
Voter Education Project

NATASHA FREIDUS

Laura Felix scans a diaper for her digital story; Natasha Freidus

Finally somebody's going to listen to what I've been thinking about!

It's important for the government to see our stories and to know that people like us can vote! That way they'll be behind us.

In Tucson, Arizona, a GED (General Equivalency Diploma) class huddles around the television. A Medicare card, gas bills, a photo of a young man in a hospital bed flash on the screen, images conveying a story familiar to the fifteen low-income adults who make up the audience. As Steve, the narrator, tells how he was cut off Arizona's Medicaid program despite his heart condition, despite the fact that his job at WalMart won't provide benefits for another five months, the nods increase in intensity. Steve ends his piece with a simple yet powerful question for his audience, "The choices the government makes effect us, how can we choose to affect them?" Stories breed stories, and as the facilitator turns off the VCR, students clamor to discuss their own frustrations with health insurance, the questions posed by Steve, and the value of voting.

This chapter will discuss the power and purpose of digital storytelling through a case study of "Our Stories, Their Decisions," a national voter education effort bringing home the personal impact of government decisions through story. Steve's story was just one of eight on the compilation DVD *Our Stories, Their Decisions*. These stories addressed experiences at the welfare office, with the public schools, at the housing authority—all places where larger decisions impact people on a daily basis. *Our Stories, Their Decisions* was shown across the country in the fall preceding the 2004 elections, helping traditional non-voters make the connection between government decision-making, the impact of those decisions, and the power of the vote. Our discussion will explore the *process*, a grassroots media workshop where individuals have authorial control over the script, imagery, and editing of their videos; the *product*, powerful first-person narratives that can be shown on DVD, VHS, CD, or the internet; and the *promotion*, the ways in which these stories are shared, distributed, and become part of larger organizing efforts for social justice.

Digital Storytelling for Active Citizenship

In community technology centers, youth programs, and makeshift portable labs throughout the country, individuals are searching through photo-albums, editing audio, and listening deeply to one another's stories. Weaving together voice, images, video, and music into brief personal videos, organizations use digital storytelling to document, reproduce, and communicate the stories of their lived experiences.

Since the birth of digital storytelling in the early nineties, disenfranchised groups have recognized the potential of this methodology as a tool to allow communities to speak for themselves. In the past few years, community digital storytelling has become part of labor organizing, domestic violence prevention, immigrant rights work, and a myriad of other issues. Despite the traditional challenges of breaking silence, and the newer challenges posed by technology, social justice efforts are finding ways to re-energize campaigns through this new medium.

In the year prior to the 2004 elections, groups representing disenfranchised voters were scurrying for new ways to foster voter engagement. While overall voter turnout has been at historical lows in recent years, low-income Americans, who are so directly affected by decisions made by elected officials, participate the least in elections.[1] *Our Stories, Their Decisions* was developed as part of the "Better Questions, Better Decisions Voter Education Initiative," a non-partisan, *skill-building* educational strategy engaging more low-income citizens as voters. In addition to an interactive workshop to help individuals understand the role of public decision-making in their lives, adult education students created a set of digital stories. In these stories, individuals:

- highlight the impact of government decisions on their lives
- demonstrate their strength and resiliency in navigating complex systems
- provide a "face" to issues including health care, immigration, education, drug treatment, and welfare
- raise critical questions around equity, justice, and civic participation.

The digital storytelling component of "Better Questions, Better Decisions" was based on the premise that the process of sharing, listening to, producing, and viewing stories can play a central role to deepen understanding of issues, create a sense of efficacy, and move people to action. We believed that stories could assist individuals in making connections between elected officials making decisions, and the day-to-day impact of these decisions. We anticipated that the stories we would document could serve as a powerful tool to resonate with other adults in the same situation. We also saw a need for the voice of people most impacted by government policy to be put out into the campaign dialogue—an authentic and refreshing alternative to candidates "using" the stories of "regular people" in stump speeches and campaign ads. And, while voter education campaigns were in full swing throughout the country, nowhere in these campaigns did low-income citizens have the opportunity to speak to one another.

The Process

In the tradition of digital storytelling, the workshop begins with a story circle. In this circle, participants share ideas and drafts for scripts, they pass treasured photos from hand to hand, and they brainstorm ideas for their media pieces. Oftentimes, participants are classmates, co-workers, and friends. Yet, more often than not, they have not heard one another's stories. In a culture where we've learned to keep our stories to ourselves, the story circle becomes a sacred space, a space where we hear portions and patterns of our lives reflected in the voices of others. One by one, each participant speaks . . .

When I came here I spoke only French, I took English classes to get my citizenship . . . I want to be a nurse assistant but I need to pass my GED first.

I'm worried that I'm not going to have enough money to pay my baby's medical bills . . .

When I was a child, I didn't say "I want to be a drug addict when I grow up . . ."

The story circle is not, however, group therapy. Its goal is to support the storyteller in the drafting and crafting of the story. Facilitators and participants provide feedback—repeating back images and phrases that stood out, suggesting details to add or to eliminate. Ultimately, however, the editing power remains in the hands of each storyteller. It isn't easy, yet most participants were clear on the importance of what they had to say, and had an eagerness to be heard. As one storyteller explained following the workshop, "*Even though it can be painful to remember our stories, it's important because it's a reminder of what we've been through, and that we know we can do it.*"

Our work with the storytellers began in New Hampshire, asking women in job-training programs to focus on their experiences with public institutions and the connection to voting. By posing prompts, we encouraged participants to brainstorm decisions made by public officials that impacted their lives. Many participants in digital storytelling workshops do not come to the workshop with a strong "sense of story." That sense is developed through activities, through affirmations from their peers, and from the discovery that others have experienced what they have gone through. For others, it is the visual element that makes their stories real, "*When you start, you don't know that you have a story, but then you look through your old photos and the pictures bring the story to life.*" In the "Our Stories, Their Decisions" workshop, participants searched for objects and images that could bring the stories to life. Laura, who tells a compelling story of her baby's health, brought in diapers to scan. Rene, whose story is about overcoming drug addiction, worried computer lab monitors momentarily with her Ziploc full of oregano.

In Arizona, it was these stories of drug abuse, health insurance, and immigration issues that were the prevalent issues facing low-income communities. Across the country, in New Hampshire, where recent welfare reform laws limited what constituted "work hours," welfare was top on the list. One participant, Kerri, told us, "*I wonder if the people who made the decisions for the forty required hours could come and live in my shoes for an hour. I wonder if they could do it. I wonder if they see these required hours as even being fair."* Kerri felt that her story was one common to many women in her position, doing their best to go back to school, work, and meet the new welfare stipulations. Angie, her classmate, used her experience on welfare to also question if the decision-makers had been through similar experiences. Both felt strongly that their peers needed to vote, to make sure that the needs and concerns of fellow welfare recipients were reflected in economic and social policies.

This workshop was focused on bringing real faces to the impact of government decisions. Participants, however, were not explicitly told to include a "voting message" in their stories. As workshop facilitators, we were looking for stories that could serve as prompts for dialogue around the impact of decision-making on non-voters. We wanted stories that could help others make connections between the people that make decisions for us, and the role that we can play in these decisions. Some participants chose to explicitly call on their audience to vote. *"There are some decisions in our lives that are made without our family being considered. They are made from Washington or state or local government, and that's why I vote. So I have a say in who is making those decisions for me. I want to know that they see my face and the faces of many people like me . . ."* Others chose to end their pieces with their own questions. *"It's very important for me that my baby and others have insurance. Having to think that my son could be without insurance next year I ask myself a lot of questions: Why do the people that have money get insurance, and people who have no money have less chances of being insured? Who are the people that make the decisions about who has insurance? Have they ever experienced what it is to struggle with a sick baby and not have the money to buy their medicines? . . . Shouldn't we think about our babies when we pick the people who make decisions for their health care?"* Still others called for a broader definition of civic action. *"I've been waiting for three years now to get permanent residency, I don't know how much longer I'll have to wait. There are a lot of people in my situation. Maybe they are afraid to use their voices. I cannot vote, yet, but I am not afraid to use my voice and work in the community . . . To the people who can vote, don't waste the opportunity to make a difference."* By providing storytellers with the space to define and articulate their own questions, messages, and experiences, stories ring with an authenticity that viewers could relate to. The collection came to represent the full range of engagement, frustration, bewilderment, and disengagement that disenfranchised citizens experience in elections and public decision-making.

The Product

At every digital storytelling workshop, a series of miracles occur. Final media pieces are constructed and finished out of ideas, scrapbooks, photo-albums. We completed the "Our Stories, Their Decisions" workshop, as always, with a screening of the new stories for the storytellers and workshop leaders—then incorporated all eight stories onto a DVD, VHS, and a website. The final pieces included two stories created in New Hampshire and six from Arizona.

Since the elections were looming large, post-production turnaround was quick, and DVD and VHS copies were duplicated, the website was disseminated, and within a few weeks of the workshop, adult educators throughout the states of New Hampshire and Arizona were showing copies of the stories in classrooms throughout the country. *Our Stories, Their Decisions* was intentionally designed for adult educators and other facilitators of low-income groups to view and select stories that resonated with their constituencies. A downloadable discussion guide accompanied the stories, encouraging facilitators to help viewers hone in on the decisions that were made in the stories:

Discussion Guide

a. *After viewing stories, please explain the following:* After these individuals learned about the impact of decisions and practiced their question formulation skills, these are the stories that they decided to tell. Which decisions stood out for you from these stories? *Review definition of decision again if necessary.*

b. All of us are impacted by government decisions one way or another. Do any of you have examples? Are there stories that you'd like to tell about decisions? *Each person takes a few minutes to think of their own story. Participants may write a story, draw pictures of a story, tell a story in a small group, to a partner, or directly to a large group.*

c. In some of the stories you just saw, the storytellers made a connection between these decisions that impact them and voting. Others asked questions about the government, and how elected officials make these decisions. What do you think? What connection do you see between voting and the story you just told?

These digital stories and discussion guide differed from traditional voting efforts by focusing in on the definition of a decision, and the stories that demonstrate the real impact of public decision-making. The process allowed participants to identify more clearly the power that their elected officials bring to their day-to-day lives, and consider what role they want to play in selecting individuals who will carry that power.

The Promotion

Our Stories, Their Decisions rested primarily on guerilla marketing and word of mouth. Within weeks of the product's release, we had requests for DVDs from adult education programs, immigrant organizing efforts, low-income housing advocacy groups, and other community organizations from across the country. Adult education teachers in particular were eager for new ways to approach voter education. "*We are constantly seeking more effective content for helping people make their own connections between their lives and the act of voting.*"[2]

Facilitators consistently reported back the depth of conversations prompted by the *Better Questions, Better Decisions* work. In an evaluative survey conducted by a JFK School of Government student, one-third of respondents wrote (without prompting) that voting is important after participating in a workshop. Students also indicated that they saw how politicians' decisions affect them, and that voting was a way of having a say. In a small group pre- and post-test survey, fourteen out of fifteen participants said that the training made them "more prepared" to vote and thirteen out of fifteen felt "more interested" in voting after the training (from the JFK student survey). Consistently, we found that as people viewed the stories created by peers, stories told in language they could relate to and faces they recognized, they developed critical-thinking and analytical skills.

Effective voter education must take place more than every four years. The use of *Our Stories, Their Decisions* has continued following the 2004 elections in Arizona and beyond for civic engagement. According to Pima College Adult Education Director of Civics, Ami Magisos:

> Teachers continue to share the digital stories with their classes as a starting point for students to consider how government decisions affect their lives and tell their own stories. Overall, the project has been an essential tool for us in our civic and elections education and training efforts.

These stories form part of a much broader effort to produce media by and for communities traditionally marginalized by mainstream channels. Stories breed stories, and we are collecting new stories that emerge from discussions, stories that continue to connect and educate non-voters, and stories that purport to convey their wisdom to those who make decisions for us. In the words of one Arizona storyteller:

> This project is so important because it's a way for our voices to be heard by our representatives or organizations that have power. Maybe it will give them the push so they can learn from our experiences.

Natasha Freidus is the founder and director of Creative Narrations, a multi-media consulting and training organization for social change. Natasha has taught workshops for diverse groups throughout the country and courses on multimedia narrative and media literacy at the Massachusetts Institute for Technology, University of Massachusetts, and University of Rovira and Virgili in Tarragona, Spain.

Notes

1 Better Questions, Better Decisions website: www.rightquestion.org/main
2 Committee Chair, Voter Education, Registration and Action Campaign, sponsored by the New England Literacy Resource Center.

Further Reading

Online Community for Digital Storytelling: http://StoriesForChange.net

12
Drawing Attention to Darfur

ANNIE SPARROW

The Darfur Conflict

Darfur. One of today's gravest man-made human rights and humanitarian crises. Named a genocide—the worst of all crimes—by the United States government, the world has stood by while Sudanese soldiers and militias have committed crimes against humanity, war crimes, and forced 3 million people to flee their homes. Yet this crisis is far from over. Begun in 2003 and now in its fourth year, the death toll continues to rise and 2.5 million survivors are stranded in sprawling, squalid refugee camps that themselves are under constant threat of attack and demolition.

Perhaps as many as 400,000 people have died, from slaughter and from the starvation and disease that followed. Despite the referral of Darfur to the International Criminal Court, the people of Darfur continue to suffer. People cannot return home, and the deliberate obstruction of humanitarian aid means many Darfurians are still dying. The enormity of the suffering demands the world's urgent attention. Yet Darfur is not accessible to the media, and unlike a tsunami or the Iraq invasion, a long, drawn-out crisis affecting Africans in a country a long way away doesn't give good television. So how is Darfur going to go down in history? Who are the people actually affected, and what happened to them? The challenge for humanitarians, human rights activists, community workers, and global citizens is how to draw attention to a concern, and find ways for the unaware to connect with this concern.

In March 2005, two people returned from the area with startling evidence of the crimes. An Australian pediatrician and a French lawyer were researching human rights abuses in Chad refugee camps, when they began to engage refugee children while interviewing their parents by giving them crayons, ink, and paper. Without any instruction or guidance, children as young as eight years of age sketched vivid scenes of the violence they had witnessed: the attacks by the militias, the aerial bombings, the rapes, the torching of entire villages, and the flight to Chad.

On May 1, 2005, two of these drawings of the crisis in Darfur were published in the *New York Times*. Since that date, those drawings and many others have spread across the globe, captivating the media, and drenching the public domain, fascinating people in all walks of life: aid workers, donors, bloggers, academics, students, film-makers, and policy-makers. These drawings have now been seen by hundreds of thousands of people, on television, in the press, and on the web, many of whom had never heard of Darfur before, much less the crimes against humanity perpetrated there over the last three years. No one could have foreseen such a wave of humanity. This is the story of how the products of a personal whim were fanned into a flame by an organization, becoming not only the most successful strategy of advocacy of that organization to date, but also the means of educating, connecting, and inspiring people to participate in the struggle for Darfur.

Isma's Drawing of her Darfur Experience

"And what is going on here?"
In response to my question, the endearing little girl, pointing at a mass of vivid colors she had just drawn on a sheet of paper, replied:
"My hut burning after being hit by a bomb."
"And this?" I asked, pointing at a man in green.
"A soldier from Sudan."
"And this?"—of a green vehicle with four wheels. "A tank," she said.
Finally, I asked about the upside-down figure.
"It's a woman. She is dead."
"Why is her face colored in red?"
"Oh, because she has been shot in the face," she answered.

Tanks, soldiers, bombs, and death. Isma is the eight-year-old author of this drawing. Like many of the thousands of children caught in the horror of the Darfur conflict, she has created her own visual vocabulary through which others can almost see what she witnessed, as if through her own eyes. Like many of the thousands of children caught in the horror of Darfur, she has, quite literally, placed on paper her personal witness of the crisis.

There are several dimensions to Isma's drawing. First, it is clear that Isma is deeply traumatized by what she has seen. Second, her drawing and the hundreds of others directly corroborate the atrocities that many agencies have documented in Darfur over the past four years, including the burning of villages, the shooting of civilians, and the sexual violence. Third, this drawing literally illustrates the complicity of the Sudanese government in the Darfur crisis, despite officials' repeated denials of non-involvement: the dead woman is dwarfed by a huge armored personnel carrier, and a Sudanese soldier in uniform.

Isma, age 8

A Genocide in Slow Motion

Since early 2003, the Sudanese government and the ethnic "Janjaweed" militias it arms have committed systematic, widespread, and intentional attacks on the civilian populations of Darfur, a region the size of France on Sudan's western border with Chad. It is one of the world's poorest and most inaccessible regions. The Janjaweed, a name meaning "devils on horseback," have deliberately targeted the Fur, Masalit, Zaghawa, and other ethnic tribes perceived to support the rebel insurgency. Government forces have overseen and directly participated in massacres, summary executions of civilians—including women and children—burnings of towns and villages, and the forcible depopulation of wide swathes of land long inhabited by these tribes.

Countless women and girls have been raped. Hundreds of villages have been bombed and burned. Water sources and food stocks have been destroyed, property and livestock looted. Schools and hospitals have been burnt to the ground. The Janjaweed militias, Muslim like the tribes they attack, have destroyed mosques, killed religious leaders, and desecrated Qurans belonging to their enemies. Villages abandoned out of fear have been destroyed, and even when the villages are left intact, most survivors are unwilling to return to start rebuilding their lives: "If we return," one refugee said, "we will be killed."

Estimates of the death toll from this destruction in Darfur vary. At least 130,000, and perhaps as many as 400,000 people have died from violence, as well as disease, starvation, and exposure due to the forced displacement. Although the slaughter has abated, the toll of death and displacement continues to rise. Those left homeless are still at risk: the 2 million living in camps inside Darfur are poorly protected, and women and girls are frequently the targets of sexual attacks when they venture from the camp to find firewood and food for their animals.

The Smallest Witnesses

In early 2005, two researchers from a human rights organization traveled to camps along the Chad–Sudan border housing refugee men, women, and children from Darfur. The purpose of the mission was to examine the consequences of sexual violence on refugees as part of the conflict, and assess the services and protection that were available.

During interviews with refugees, their children were given paper and crayons to draw whatever they wished. The first child we encountered, an eight-year-old named Mohammed, had never held a crayon or pencil before. That is not uncommon in a region where children are given chores such as shepherding from an early age. Indeed, although Mohammed could neither read nor write, he could count his sheep—twelve! So Mohammed gave the paper to his brothers. While we talked, they drew—without any instruction—pictures of Janjaweed on horseback and camel shooting civilians, Antonovs (military helicopters) dropping bombs on civilians and houses, an army tank firing on fleeing villagers. Looking at the drawings, Mohammed whispered, "I am still scared of the Janjaweed. I remember the guns and the planes." The last thing he said was "Darigi jugi"—I need to go home.

Over the following weeks of the research mission, these violent scenes were repeated in hundreds of drawings depicting the attacks by ground and by air. Children drew the Janjaweed overrunning and burning their villages and Sudanese forces attacking with Antonovs, MiG planes, and tanks. With great detail, children sketched the artillery and guns they had seen used, including Kalashnikovs, machine guns, bombs, and rockets. They also drew the attacks as they had seen them in action: huts and villages burning, the shooting of men, women, and children, and the rape of women and girls.

This "ethnic cleansing" was always meant to be out of the public view. There are virtually no publicly available photographs and little footage of Janjaweed militias or Sudanese soldiers attacking villages.

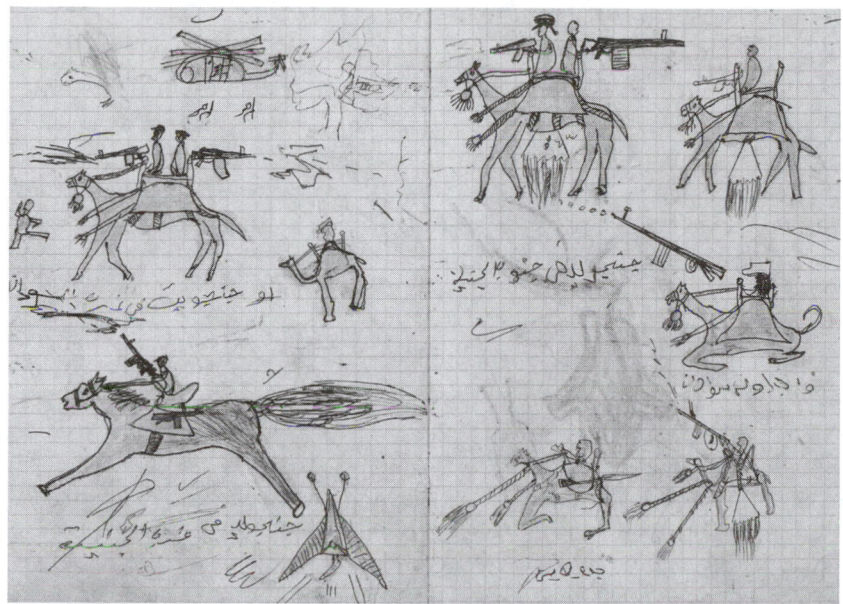

Abd al-Rahman, age 13

Thanks to the children, we now have outstanding graphic representations of the atrocities. We now know what a Janjaweed "in action" looks like. The drawings corroborate unerringly what we know of the crimes. Academically, it is fascinating. Emotionally, it is heartbreaking. From the point of view of humanitarian law, the drawings spontaneously construct a compelling case against the government of Sudan as the architects of this man-made crisis in Darfur, despite their repeated denials. These innocent depictions show us what the Sudanese government will not allow the media to film or photograph, in a way that is simultaneously instructing and heartbreaking. Moreover, these drawings are not confined to a few children, but were drawn by children who had fled from many villages and areas across Darfur. The drawings have a scale and sophistication that belies the government claims, and have a credibility that speaks for itself.

As they stand alone, each single drawing is shocking. As a whole, they form a collective and comprehensive damnation of the government of Sudan in the ethnic cleansing of Darfur. To hear and read the testimony of victims of atrocities is very powerful. To see such atrocities through the eyes of children, uncoached, and often uneducated, is compelling. Moreover, the graphical testimony showing war crimes and crimes against humanity by so many children is highly credible: it corroborates fact and provides certainty for those in the domestic and international community. A child as a witness of war engages the emotions of the public, and thus politicians and other stakeholders.

Telling Stories through a Visual Vocabulary

Some drawings speak for themselves. Others require the child's translation, which suddenly transforms a non-specific squiggle into a family fleeing from attack and rape, an open mouth into a scream, a cell phone into a desperate appeal for help, a red scribble into a fatal gunshot wound. Others are so sophisticated that the material of war may be accurately identified by military analysts, giving the drawings the added gravity of bearing witness against the government of Sudan as the true architects of this war.

The testimonies recounted by the adults are simultaneously drawn out by the children. For example, military helicopters are sent to survey the area to ensure no rebel groups are present in the targeted village. If clear, the signal is sent to the other forces and the attack begins. Rockets are shot targeting houses and civilians. Antonov planes drop bombs, villages are set on fire. Women are shot in the back, in the hand, in the face. Children are hunted by Janjaweed. Women and girls are taken away to be raped. Rape. Trying to see rape through the eyes of children, the mind recoils and rejects—and then we are forced to recognize the painfully obvious reality of a child witnessing a rape.

The different dimensions of these drawings allow them to be used on many levels:

1. The drawings accurately corroborate the atrocities that Human Rights Watch (HRW) and other agencies have comprehensively documented in Darfur over the last two years.
2. The drawings bear witness to the complicity of the Sudanese government as the architects of this conflict, as evidenced by the systematic sketches of attack helicopters, MiG fighter planes, and Antonovs, not only in the air but actually releasing bombs and firing rockets. In addition, the drawings depict tanks and armored personnel carriers. These are not weapons possessed by the Janjaweed, but represent part of the arsenal of the government of Sudan, purchased primarily from Russia.[1]
3. The drawings present a detailed illustration of the violation of the laws of war: of war crimes and crimes against humanity—such as the shooting of civilians, torching of civilian villages, and sexual violence. Indeed, they illustrate and inform not only the Darfur crisis, but other current conflicts and crimes of war.
4. They clearly represent an appeal for help and protection, as evidenced by the repetitive motif of cell phones and satellite phones, together with the explanation by the children.
5. Finally, they illustrate the psychological fallout of the crisis upon the children, who have now become accustomed to conflict as deadly and daily reality.

The Integrity of the Drawings

Many people have asked how the drawings came about. This is a fundamental question, as it relates why the drawings speak to so many people. There are other drawings of Darfur, for example, as well as drawings of many other conflict areas: Chechnya, Uganda, Iraq. Why have these ones carried so far? Why has there been so much press attached to these particular ones? On the web, there are hundreds of links, thousands of blogs, and hundreds of thousands of users of the drawings. Some of this is because the drawings show us what the media cannot. But I believe this also reflects the integrity and the credibility of the drawings.

In almost any third world environment, children are naturally very curious about foreigners: "Nazara, nazara!" they used to shout, looking at our white faces. Being the person that became the pediatrician, I love to engage with children. Perhaps I have "softie" written on my forehead in eighty different languages: wherever I go, children recognize me as a big kid poorly disguised as an adult, and within minutes we are playing chase, or hide and seek, or I just let them climb all over me, and sit in my lap. In Chad, engaging rapidly grew from saying "Ça va?" to shaking hands, to playing "chase" and other games. So, Olivier and I used to accumulate a small following very rapidly. When the time came to sit down with men and women, I had children crawling into my lap, eager to be involved, in any way. That was when I got out my scrapbooks and crayons, and let them draw away. For some, they had never drawn before. Others were very talented. I let them draw whatever they want. Not all draw pictures of violence—there are also animals, flowers, scenes of football and ordinary village life.

Children's drawings in war aren't new, yet the idea of drawing without an audience is an essential one. The importance of letting children draw exactly what they want, without any instruction, is often missed. Drawings which are done "for the folks back home," or even in an art therapy class, are already crafted with a message; and have lost the integrity which endows these drawings with such power. Moreover, they also possess enormous credibility when used to illustrate the complicity of the government of Sudan in this conflict.

As a younger doctor training for my pediatric exams, I used to ask children to draw for me while I was talking with their parents. This was a way to engage them (essential to stop them from being bored, throwing a tantrum, and tearing up the room), and to learn about their lives, their friends, their emotional health. It was also a great way to impress the examiners. Later on, working in an Australian detention center for asylum seekers, children drew pictures of flowers for me, trying to create beauty in a punitive, barren environment. Years later, working for a human rights organization, days before leaving for Chad to research the issue of sexual violence against Darfurian refugees, it struck me that I must take drawing materials with me, just in case I had the chance to engage with children. Little did I know!

The Laws of War

All parties to the armed conflict in Darfur are bound by the laws of war (also known as international humanitarian law). The laws of war can be found in the Geneva Conventions of 1949 and its two Additional Protocols of 1977. Sudan ratified the 1949 Conventions in 1957; most provisions of Additional Protocols I and II are recognized as customary law and must also be respected. The fighting in Darfur is considered a non-international (or internal) armed conflict. Article 3 common to the 1949 Conventions, which applies during internal armed conflicts, prohibits murder, torture, mutilation, hostage taking, and outrages upon personal dignity such as rape. When grave acts of violence are committed as part of a widespread and systematic attack on a civilian population, they are considered crimes against humanity.

All parties to the conflict in Sudan must also respect the laws of war on the methods and means of warfare. They must distinguish at all times between civilians and combatants, and between civilian property and military object-ives, and limit their attacks to combatants and military objectives. Attacks against civilians are prohibited, as are attacks on military targets that would cause indiscriminate or disproportionate harm to civilians. Also prohibited are acts or threats of violence intended to spread terror among the civilian popula-tion. The destruction of objects indispensable to the survival of the civilian population, such as food, agricultural areas for food production, crops, and wells or water points, is also unlawful.

The drawings explicitly show violations of the laws of war, as illustrated by extracts taken from the Geneva Conventions and its Protocols.

Attacks on Civilians

"The civilian population as such, as well as individual civilians, shall not be the object of attack. Acts or threats of violence the primary purpose of which is to spread terror among the civilian population are prohibited."

Sexual Violence

Civilians and captured combatants shall be protected against "outrages upon personal dignity, in particular humiliating and degrading treatment, rape, enforced prostitution and any form of indecent assault."

Rape and sexual violence against women and girls has been a prominent feature of the "ethnic cleansing" campaign carried out by government forces and militias, both during and following displacement in Darfur. Once dis-placed into camps in Darfur, or into refugee camps in Chad, women and girls continue to suffer sexual and gender-based violence. As discussed below,

Zania, age 8

rape and sexual violence have numerous social, economic, and medical consequences, including increasing the risk of contracting HIV/AIDS as a result of the violence.

Inhumane Treatment

Soldiers removed from combat "by sickness, wounds, detention, or any other cause shall be treated humanely" and shall be protected from "violence to life and person . . . cruel treatment and torture; . . . outrages upon personal dignity, in particular humiliating and degrading treatment."

Forcible Displacement

"The displacement of the civilian population shall not be ordered for reasons related to the conflict unless the security of the civilians involved or imperative military reasons so demand. Should such displacements have to be carried out, all possible measures shall be taken in order that the civilian population may be received under satisfactory conditions of shelter, hygiene, health, safety and nutrition . . . Civilians shall not be compelled to leave their own territory for reasons connected with the conflict."

Protection of Civilian Objects

"Civilian objects shall not be the object of attack or of reprisals . . . Attacks shall be limited strictly to military objectives. . . . In case of doubt whether an object which is normally dedicated to civilian purposes, such as a place of worship, a house or other dwelling or a school, is being used to make an effective contribution to military action, it shall be presumed not to be so used."

The art of war is nothing new. Crimes against humanity are nothing new, and children's drawings in times of war aren't new either. As graphic testimony of the ongoing atrocities committed in Darfur, though, they become a whole new art form. The drawings' ability to captivate the press and in doing so to generate public awareness on the Darfur crisis and successfully portray a credible picture of the reality of the crisis is a testimony to the appeal of the pictures. The drawings not only corroborate but are able to distill the essence of Darfur reports into drawings, thus rendering reports more intelligible and appealing to the public. They also provide a tool with which to illustrate

Doa, age 11/12

war crimes and crimes against humanity, so pertinent in today's culture of international and civil war.

How do you change the world? Emotion is key: all of us cry for the same reasons—pain, grief, heartache. No one could have expected that the drawings would insert themselves into the public domain with such effect, yet it's this translation of emotion into pictures that arouses the media attention. Nothing at HRW has ever matched the media appeal of these pictures. An idea implemented with integrity, with simplicity, that speaks. It's old, of course, to say that a picture tells a thousand words, but still true. These pictures illustrate all the words that can't be spoken, that aren't heard, of the millions of displaced. They speak for the dead as well as the living. They are living history. They are a cry for help that has echoed throughout the ether, perhaps the most significant tool for connection today. A visual vocabulary requiring little or no translation that captures hearts and minds, and may ultimately contribute to protection and peace in Darfur.

Pseudonyms are used for all children cited to preserve their privacy.

Annie Sparrow is an Australian critical care pediatrician turned public health physician, working in complex humanitarian emergencies across the globe. Her move into human rights followed a visit to Afghanistan under the Taliban regime. Since then she has worked in Haiti, Chad, Sudan, East Timor, and Somalia. She lives in Nairobi with her partner, a wild cat, and two owls.

Note

1   Source: *Defense & Foreign Affairs Handbook,*
    www.angelfire.com/ab/mazin/SudanAirForce.html

13

Insan Natak

Phoenix or Dodo in Lahore

MUHAMMAD MUSHTAQ

It was no earth-shaking event that took place in Kot Lakhpat in 1990. It was simply the materialization of an idealistic dream of four young people, three men and a woman, with university degrees and a vague notion to do good. By and by, the group would call itself The Insan Foundation.

Set on the high road to Ferozepur, Kot Lakhpat was, until the early 1960s, a sleepy little village that supplied vegetables to the kitchens of Lahore. With industrialization, the quiet town was ratcheted upscale, its new factories manned by mostly landless peasants who had been phased out by tractors and harvesters during Pakistan's so-called Green Revolution. Soon, under-privileged families lived in shanties cheek by jowl with the affluent Model Town of Lahore. In less than fifteen years, Kot Lakhpat grew into a vast, unplanned sprawl of warren-like homes with no infrastructure and poor amenities, including government schools that modeled themselves on dull, dreary, medieval institutions where rote learning and the rod were the norm.

No surprise then that truancy was common. If ignorant teachers were bad, parents did scarcely any better. Kot Lakhpat school dropouts, as young as seven or eight, worked as coolies in the fruit and vegetable market or selling plastic bags. Some apprenticed as motorcycle or car mechanics. A father handing his son over to one of the area's many auto shops customarily told the supervisor, "Take him, *ustad.* Turn him into a mechanic any way you can. His skin is yours; his bones mine." It was a license for maltreatment, for verbal and physical abuse, and even sexual molestation. What kept the harassed child in bondage was a daily allowance that he could take home: a paltry five rupees (less than ten cents in 1990) for up to twelve hours a day of work.

Such was the world of Kot Lakhpat in 1990 that four young people resolved to put to rights. Long years of General Muhammad Zia-ul-Haq's military dic-tatorship had ended, giving way to a new democratic order. Non-governmental organizations (NGOs) and other civil society groups took advantage of this newfound freedom to launch new initiatives for human and women's rights, education, and health. It was a time of hope and possibility.

The four young idealists of The Insan Foundation decided it would be a good start to survey Kot Lakhpat in order to ascertain the community's great-est need. They quickly discovered that education was what most parents craved for their children. In addition, they realized that a vast number of young boys made up the motor shop workforce throughout the area. Poverty obviously caused lack of education. Then came the awareness that providing the children with free primers and other stationery items would not get them interested in reading and writing and that teacher brutality and uninspired instruction drove them away from school.

Braving the uncouth arrogance of the workshop owners and relying on unconventional methods like handouts of confectionary and playing games in class, The Insan Foundation lured some twenty-five young boys to attend a daily two-hour school session located on the roof of a barber's shop and held at the unearthly hour of 5 a.m., so that the children would be free to go to work at eight.

Within months, a bond formed between the boys and the foundation. Here, for the first time, were older, educated friends with whom they could freely commune, friends who turned lessons into interesting activities. And for the members of The Insan Foundation, a new world also opened. Here were not dullards, but brilliant, inquisitive young minds, endlessly questioning the injustice of the system that held them captive. The boys aired their queries with amazing intensity, energy, and scope. Here were young minds that longed to be liberated. Soaring intellects shackled only by the ignorance that surrounded them.

Pakistan being a cricket-crazed country, naturally many wanted to grow up to be cricketers. And an overwhelming number wished one day to emulate heroes of the silver screen. Thus, part of each school session was given to thespian activity. At first it was loud, vulgar play-acting in the strictest tradition of Punjabi cinema that is miles from real life. The boys moved through unoriginal roles of swaggering hero to manipulative villain, following the plot of the latest release.

Yet it didn't take long to move from imitation to improvisation. The boys began to select their own roles and the dialogue, though still heavily borrowed from cinema, became more central to the young actors' own lives, addressing their real problems and concerns. As the drama grew closer to life, the boys dreamed of making their own feature film. With encouragement from The Insan Foundation, they devised a script that mixed three or four different Punjabi films with undercurrents from their own lives.

Films don't get made for free. The young actors of Kot Lakhpat learned to their disappointment that only a vast budget could produce the honky-tonk movies that filled their dreams. They put their heads together and, with encouragement, hit upon the notion of creating short skits. These would cost nothing and could be staged for local audiences. Instead of showing audiences what they already recognized from the movies, why not caricature a local personality, preferably one of the *ustad*s who the boys knew? After two months of dissecting and analyzing the characters they chose, then practicing their roles, the boys could pretty nearly be termed actors. One particular highly abusive *ustad* was chosen as a central protagonist.

Word of mouth broadcast the date and time of the performance. Among the traders, motor workshop owners, and sundry men in the audience was this exceptionally nasty motor mechanic. It was a crude production, without props, relying only on mime and dialogue. But it ended in a round of whole-hearted applause. And instead of taking umbrage, the caricatured man stood up to tell all present how ashamed he was of his behavior and even offered his assistance for the literacy class and his unstinting support to The Insan Foundation. It was a dawning: theater had much more influence than the group had imagined.

And so it was that the summer of 1991 saw the birth of Mistri Natak—Mechanics' Drama Group.

Meanwhile, The Insan Foundation did not lose its focus to provide literacy and was concentrating on increasing attendance at its early morning teaching sessions. Youngsters came and stayed for varying lengths of time, but two who remained were unusually sensitive souls: dark, energetic Irfan Ali, and plump, easygoing Mohammad Arif. They would become dedicated players in the story of Mistri Natak.

Eventually, the Mazdoor Markaz (Laborers' Centre) in Kot Lakhpat became the venue for the stage plays Mistri Natak was churning out every six to eight weeks. From creating overlong, tedious productions, the young actors learned to curb their impulses and shape intelligible story lines, focusing each play on one or two issues rather than trying to encompass every social problem they encountered. Because the cast was illiterate, dialogue was memorized. The Insan Foundation worked, so to speak, on an empty stomach. They were volunteers who met everyday expenses out of their own pockets. Thus the plays had no props, sound effects were made by mouth, and a youngster backstage maneuvered a slide projector for lighting.

By the end of 1993, Mistri Natak's work was getting a fair amount of attention among NGO circles. In 1994, The Insan Foundation received its first-ever funding and with money in the kitty, launched a novel initiative, turning street theater into train theater. After boarding a train from Lahore, the young actors traveled northward to Rawalpindi, Attock, and Peshawar, performing in crowded economy-class compartments. It was an idea spawned from the traditional *madari*, or juggler, who until the late 1960s entertained the public on the branch-line trains.

In 1995, a team from South Asia Partnership-Canada visited The Insan Foundation. The visit resulted in an exchange program via video between Canadian school children and the young actors of Mistri Natak.

With such attention, as 1996 rolled to its end, The Insan Foundation began toying with the idea of training its raw, award-winning thespians. The foundation had not originally been aware of the existence of parallel theater groups, or the possibility of learning from their greater experience. Now Insan contacted Lok Rehas—renowned for its issue-based plays—and asked them to provide a trainer. Sadly, while the heroes of Mistri Natak did indeed learn more of their craft, they did not enjoy the training workshops.

All the same, Mistri Natak raced along the fast track of success. The themes they introduced in their performances grew from personal experiences to larger issues concerning class, gender, education, peace, and more. Outsiders began to join the team of actors. And having thus come of age, Mistri Natak was renamed Insan Natak. The foundation was finding its financial feet; rehearsals could take place in an office rather than in parks or on street corners. Things were taking shape and heading toward ever more meaningful activity. Insan Natak had matured as a drama group with a clear-cut, anti-war, anti-child labor, and pro-human rights stance. It now had a repertoire of fifteen well-scripted plays and nearly 300 performances in venues ranging from streets and parks to trains and schools. Many of the original boys had moved on, but some kept in touch occasionally as visiting performers. Irfan Ali and Mohammad Arif, however, continued as permanent fixtures in the Insan Natak cosmos.

In 2000, the South Asia Partnership-Canada project ended, but by then Insan Natak's work had become known to a Canadian filmmaker interested in documenting the foundation's peace initiatives through street theater. Then just when Canadian children were scheduled to travel to Pakistan, the disaster of September 11, 2001 occurred. Amid new fears about security in the region, it was decided instead that Insan Natak's star duo, Irfan and Arif, would visit Canada.

On the Friday following 9/11, when militant mullahs hit Lahore's streets with messages of violence, The Insan Foundation Dove Day Peace Campaign sent Styrofoam dove cutouts inscribed with anti-war slogans aloft in gas-filled balloons. This hugely popular action continued every Friday for a year, while Irfan and Arif, as goodwill ambassadors, disabused Canadian children of the belief that Pakistanis were all turban-wearing killers.

For Irfan and Arif, who had never imagined they would ever leave their home, the trip was infinitely empowering. Their families, who had been concerned that they were wasting their lives in the theater, now realized how worthwhile it was. They were not only building bridges across chasms of prejudice, but they were men of substance now: instructors themselves. They had not gone to the West to wash dishes in cheap restaurants but to commune in equality with white people.

Insan Natak was now recognized by peace and human rights activists, and frequently called upon for performances and to enact the dove peace campaign. Following the 2003 standoff between Pakistan and India, Insan Natak traveled to India where the media lauded the troupe with interviews and photo-shoots. They returned with a feeling of fraternity for the people across the border. They'd taken their message of peace and love to Canada and India to great acclaim and they resolved now to make Insan Natak the best informal, issue-based theater in the world.

Yet if they were to grow, the team felt they must get technical theater training under an accomplished creative director. They met, then hired, a seasoned stage and television actor, a garrulous and gifted stage and television actor who had worked with Maheeda Gauhar, famed artistic director of Ajoka Theatre. Insan Natak believed it had engaged a man who understood the respect artists deserved and their spiritual and emotional needs. He made it known that it was a great honor to be invited to become the theater's creative director and led them to believe that he had no ulterior motives other than to do his bit to make Pakistan a better place. What he did not specify was his aim to shape Insan Natak into a self-sustaining professional troupe.

At The Insan Foundation, responsibility and authority had always been delegated. This policy was followed by Insan Natak as well. While themes for plays came from the players themselves, they were discussed with the foundation and once agreed upon, scripting and rehearsals took place without interference. The new creative director was similarly given a free hand to train his team as he thought best. As a first step, it was agreed that training should be moved out of the office to a separate space. An expensive portable stage was purchased, the first of its kind in Pakistan. A full-complement of lighting equipment was purchased.

Among the core group were Arif and Irfan, as well as Sitara Bano, who had joined The Insan Foundation in 1997, when it initiated its Child Rights Education and Literacy Program. An extraordinarily devoted teacher, she was also active in Insan Natak. It is indicative of her skill as an artist that from street theater she moved on to work in a number of television plays. But her first and foremost commitment remained with issue-based theater.

Sitara, Irfan, and Arif were very close friends and questioned whether the new, expensive premises, the air-conditioning, and elaborate stage and lighting equipment might not be too much. What's more, they said, the new director had been stressing the great expense that The Insan Foundation had gone through to train them, so that if they erred, which they indeed did, they were not, he claimed, worthy of the investment. Before long, the new director, the very person who had spoken so often about the need to treat artists with tenderness and respect, had transformed into a brash, uncaring slave-driver. No excuses, not sickness or injury, were accepted. Yet the troupe found that the director was repeatedly away shooting television episodes and absent from rehearsals.

The complaints began piling up. The director's instruction technique was loud, rude, and unkind—a sad departure from the quiet, friendly ways of Insan Natak before him. Old members, whose advice had once been sought and accepted, were now told they knew nothing of stage and drama. The laurels and praise they'd won in Canada and India were rubbish. The director maintained that it was his job to shatter the shells of self-delusion that armored the actors and only when the individual reduced to dirt would the real performer within emerge. The actors must unlearn everything they'd acquired in the past decade. The boys had been pampered by The Insan Foundation and utterly spoiled. They were prima donnas, irresponsible, their egos bloated.

So much for self-esteem. The director had become another *ustad*. And because the foundation's policy had been one of decentralization, there was no place to take complaints. For the first time, the members of Insan Natak felt abandoned.

The time for painful lessons had come. The Insan Foundation's creative director had broken away from his mentor, Gauhar, in an unpleasant episode and now at last with Insan Natak, he was in a position to compete with her. He would enter his production in a theater festival, despite the foundation's reservations that the troupe might not yet be capable of challenging professional artists. The director assured them this would not be a problem. He would augment the group with professional actors, who would work, he said, gratis.

For good or for ill, entering the play in the festival placed Insan Natak among other professional theaters. More than a decade after it had staged its first skits, the group broke with its own tradition and money became pivotal to its activities. In fact, the professional actors hired by the director were being paid and it rankled among the old guard, who had never expected to be compensated for fulfilling their dreams.

Soon another Lahore-based NGO approached Insan Natak to train its performers in issue-based drama. But Insan's creative director balked. The funding was meager, he said. Why had actors' fees not been built into the budget? The age of free performances, he declared, had passed. The Insan Foundation's arguments that the very basis of their philosophy was being altered fell on deaf ears. So for the first time, alarm bells within the foundation started ringing.

Nevertheless, Insan Natak resolved to keep its commitments. They would continue the performance with commercial, albeit B-grade actors, but following several heated arguments, Arif and Irfan decided to drop out. In the event, the play was staged with great difficulty, but not before it was agreed that the old guard would also receive remuneration. With that, Insan Natak took its first giant leap into commercialism.

August 2005 brought another opportunity to take street theater to India. The creative director was overjoyed at the possibility of leading his group to a festival where his old mentor had performed to great public and media approbation. His was a one-side competition, and now he felt he could stand on the same pedestal as Maheeda Gauhar. But to make it successful, he had to bring Arif and Irfan back into the fold. Their anger was tempered by memories of the affection and appreciation they'd received in India the previous year. They agreed to go. Insan Natak's performances and the Dove Day action were again acclaimed, despite the tensions and backbiting that accompanied the troupe throughout its Indian sojourn.

At last, the foundation realized it was time to deal drastically with the situation. Insan Natak had completely lost sight of its focus. The lack of supervision, born of the belief that if left alone, things would take their logical course, partly stemmed from the notion that if things went badly, Insan Natak would only lose its commercial artists—and ultimately be better off for it. When cash flowed, it killed the spirit of volunteerism that guided the group. Things had moved so quickly, there had been no time for reflection.

A meeting was called. There would be no accusations, no apology seeking, no analysis of what went wrong. Members would express themselves and be asked whether they wished to stay with the group or not. If not, there was always the possibility of a new beginning, a return to 1990s model, with a new set of youngsters. Regardless, it was clear that a complete overhaul was called for.

A decade and a half from their tentative start in the workshops of Kot Lakhpat, The Insan Foundation convened to deliberate the fate of Insan Natak. The creative director was not invited so that the members could speak freely. Allegations flew and, at the end, each member of the troupe was asked if they wanted to stay or go. With exciting new opportunities looming—such as the internationally renowned Cairo International Festival for Experimental Theatre—the members of Insan Natak decided to quit. But the biggest bombshell was the refusal of Irfan and Arif to continue. These were the young men who had come on board as little boys with greasy hands and soiled clothes, who had moved far ahead of their peers. Surely they would have stayed after the others, with all their unwanted professional baggage, left to pursue lucrative careers. Yet they, too, opted out. Only Sitara Bano agreed to stay.

A month later, at a second meeting with the creative director, after all the predictable accusations were aired, Insan Natak quietly died.

We learn through our mistakes. The Insan Foundation had misjudged the effect of the commercialism that had taken hold and believed the core members of the theater group were immune to it. Staff and actors have always been treated as equals and consequently they looked to the foundation as a friend, and felt a sense of ownership over it. The original group could not come to terms with invading outsiders. Although the theater group collapsed, the rich experiences the foundation offers to underprivileged children continues with informal gatherings where they play games, paint and draw on whitewashed walls, relieved from the horrors of an unjust world and able to develop a little more fully.

The Insan Foundation sees the failure of Insan Natak as a new beginning. This time the pitfalls are known.

One March morning, Sitara Bano, walking to The Insan Foundation office, spotted a boy of eight or nine—the same age Irfan Ali had been when he appeared at those first early morning literacy classes. Sitara paused to watch as the boy rummaged through a rubbish bin with his sisters and thought how this child might set the foundation for a new Insan Natak. Sitara Bano approached him and asked what he was called.

"My name is Irfan," he said.

Muhammad Mushtaq, Masters in Philosophy, is a social and political activist, a strong believer in the value of peace, and a supporter of children and youth. He started The Insan Foundation in 1990 with the aim to work for children's rights. Under his leadership The Insan Foundation developed and flourished with a prominent name as an organization for children and youth. Today The Insan Foundation is undertaking several initiatives for peace and social harmony by involving children and youth in mainstream struggle.

Further Reading

Insan Foundation Pakistan: www.insanpk.org

14

Everyone Needs to Know

Five Stories about AIDS and Art in India

**NANDITA PALCHOUDHURI, DAVID GERE,
MONIMALA CHITRAKAR, SAMIRAN PANDA,
AND MITHU JANA**

Monimala Chitrakar, author and scrollpainter; Rosemary Candelario

Nandita's Story

A few years ago, I was trying to find a contemporary function for the *patuas'* skill bank. The *patuas* of West Bengal are unique multimedia artists who paint narrative scrolls accompanied by sung poetry. Many of the *patuas* (pronounced poh-to-ah) live in Naya, a small village about 150 kilometers from Kolkata, India. As a folk arts curator based in Kolkata, I had a long working relationship with them, but in the year 2000 I could see signs that their art form was beginning to die out, mostly because of television and because the old system of patronage had collapsed. Some of the best artists, who would have had large rural audiences in years past, were beginning to seek other forms of employment, in furniture making, the gem-cutting industry, or farming. I began to wonder if there might be some way of adapting their work to contemporary conditions, to retain the ancient practice as well as develop a sustainable source of income. At first, I was not able to find that fit.

Then, one night, I saw Karuna Singh of the American Consulate in Kolkata at a dinner and I asked her, "What is your next project?" And she said the consulate was doing an HIV communications fair. She explained they were collecting printed HIV material from all over India, so that people from the states could see what was happening in other regions. And somehow it just connected: Would it be possible for me to commission a scroll and put it in the fair? Karuna's boss, Steve Levinsky, agreed immediately. I told him it would cost 10,000 Indian rupees (about $250), because we'd need to do a workshop with specialists in order to come up with a narrative. Steve sanctioned that, but he cautioned that the project would have to be turned around in three weeks.

From Naya I chose a husband-and-wife team, Rani and Shamsundar Chitrakar, thinking that it would help to have a man's and a woman's perspective side by side. Karuna then connected us to Thoughtshop, an organization in Kolkata that specializes in HIV communication. This was important because my biggest fear was, How am I going to talk with the *patuas* about sex? Up until that time, my work with the *patuas* was all about the *Mahabharata* and the *Ramayana*, the two most famous Indian epics, never explicitly about sex. I had premonitions of their walking out, especially because they had Muslim sensibilities meshed into the Hindu. (A unique characteristic of the *patuas* is that they have both Muslim and Hindu names, maintaining the ability to function in either society, either religion.) I needn't have worried.

The young couple from Thoughtshop clinically explained HIV to us, including the major routes of transmission, via blood products, sharing needles, mother to child, and unprotected sex. They also explained how by using a condom you could prevent a person from becoming infected. I have to admit this was the first time I was hearing this information. People in my social circle had always thought AIDS was about very promiscuous people, about other people, not us. As a result, I realized very clearly from our sessions together that my misconceptions were the same as those of the *patuas*. I erroneously thought, for example, that AIDS began with a human being having sex with an animal in Africa, that it spread only from the gay community, only from the U.S., and so on. Also, I didn't know anything about transmission through sharing needles, or from mother to child. All this was a revelation.

Interestingly, the *patuas* were more open to the Thoughtshop training than I. For a few years already, local non-governmental organizations had been commissioning their scrolls for social communication purposes. For a fee, the *patuas* made scrolls that addressed malnutrition, how to prevent diarrhea, overcoming illiteracy, the evils of dowry deaths and female infanticide, and the importance of polio vaccination. To be clear, this was not because of any personal commitment to these issues—they would sing about the importance of educating girls and still get their daughters married at sixteen. But they were open to such commissions. This allowed them to take on the information about HIV very clinically, without making any value judgments about it. They were able to draw condoms, penises, people engaged in sex, as casually as if they were drawing images of the gods and goddesses in the Hindu pantheon. I thought they would be constrained by value judgments, but they weren't at all.

About two weeks after the training, Rani and Shamsundar came back with the first song. Three to four weeks after that—after the song had been corrected a bit by the trainers—Rani and Shamsundar finished the visuals, a mix of transmission and prevention information. When Rani sang and displayed that scroll, it was the highlight of the American Center exhibition. The health minister for the state of West Bengal sat and heard the whole song, and he thought it was definitely the way to go forward with HIV education in the rural areas. Rani was in all the newspapers and on television. Across the board, people understood instinctively that this was a useful tool to bridge the gaps of culture, language, and literacy that existed in rural pockets. Even though the *patuas* were talking about sex and medical issues, the images looked like the gods in their regular scrolls. They weren't creating any stress in their viewers, none at all. And this was a good thing.

And right here is where I just let it go. I had an incomplete idea of where to take it, and so I moved on to my next project. That is, until I heard what was happening in Naya with the rest of the *patuas*.

David's Story

In 2003 I was finishing up a book on dance artists in the U.S. who made a difference in the AIDS epidemic, and I thought I was through with AIDS. I had first gotten involved in AIDS activist projects in the late 1980s. I was living in San Francisco at the time, writing about the arts for various newspapers. A friend was diagnosed HIV positive. Several well-known choreographers got sick and died. I found myself writing the obituaries of young men on a regular basis. And then the artwork I was seeing and reviewing in Bay Area theaters seemed increasingly to deal with HIV. Even when the references were indirect, it seemed that HIV was hovering ominously behind every stage curtain. In an odd way, I realized later that I had been formed as an art viewer and as a writer in the crucible of AIDS. And I thought, maybe it's time to give AIDS a break.

But then, I started noticing newspaper articles about the AIDS situation in India, on the other side of the world. Twenty years earlier, just out of college myself, I had won a fellowship to live and work in a small college in south India. I had been back only once since that time. But suddenly I found myself poring over articles in the newspaper that likened the situation in India to the time I remembered so well from the late 1980s in San Francisco. The first cases of HIV had been detected in Chennai in 1986. If epidemiologists were correct, the rate of new infections was rising so quickly that India would soon become the country with the highest number of infections in the world. I began to wonder about the role Indian artists were playing in the epidemic, and so in 2004 I got myself a Fulbright fellowship and went off with my family to Bangalore, to see what I could see.

At the beginning I pursued the project with the dispassionate interest of the academic researcher. I culled through the library and searched the web. I called contacts. I tracked down artists in any medium who were seeking to intervene in the AIDS epidemic. One of the best contacts turned out to be Karuna Singh at the American Center in Kolkata, who made it a personal practice to gather information on HIV and the arts. Her list of names was long. She told me about Nandita Palchoudhuri, a folk arts curator who had commissioned a pair of artists to make scrolls about AIDS. I resolved to go meet them in their village.

One day in 2004 I ventured out to Naya in a rented car, a three-hour journey that extended from the near pandemonium of Kolkata's streets to placid villages and finally to serene stretches of verdant rice paddy. Aditi Nath Sarkar, a profound scholar who knew the *patuas* intimately, came along as guide and translator.

Our first stop was the simple home of Rani and Shamsundar Chitrakar, who graciously showed us the scrolls they had made for the American Center exhibition. Rani sang her scroll—a plaintive poem that accurately described how HIV is transmitted—and then allowed me to document it on film. We then walked down a narrow path to the home of one of the elders of the village, and to our surprise he had painted an HIV scroll as well. He offered to sing it for us. Aditi whispered the translation in my ear as the man sang. The text was shocking. AIDS came from Poland, he asserted. And here are the little pills you can take to cure you. (Currently, AIDS is manageable but incurable.)

As it turned out, every household in Naya seemed to have its own AIDS scroll, each more bizarre in content than the one that came before. These were such curiosities that a niche market had opened up for them, amongst Western tourists in particular. Of course, I reinforced those market forces by purchasing every scroll on HIV I could find, more than ten in the space of two hours, each more weirdly inaccurate than the one that came before.

A month later, Nandita, the folk arts curator, was visiting Bangalore and came over to meet me at home. I showed her the set of scrolls and she was nearly as shocked by their content as I had been. How did the little project at the American Center end up veering so far out of control? And was it her responsibility, or mine, to do something about it?

A few months later I decided to invite Rani and one of the younger and extremely talented scrollpainters, Monimala, to attend a workshop I was organizing in Kolkata. (No longer the dispassionate academic, I had embraced the role of the HIV activist by founding an organization called MAKE ART/ STOP AIDS.) Rani was already an old hand at HIV interventions, but Monimala was only just beginning.

Not surprisingly, Rani and Monimala looked intimidated when they first arrived at the workshop. The fancy hotel was daunting, and then they encountered more than sixty musicians, choreographers, puppeteers, videographers, actors, photographers, and visual designers who had already made a personal commitment to stop AIDS in India. In addition, there were fifteen international artists and scholars, from as far away as South Africa and Suriname, most of them seasoned activists. The two *patuas*, with Nandita as translator, gravitated to the corners of the room, as if to hide.

Gradually, though, they emerged from the shadows and began to take on a larger role, acting as the unofficial conscience of the gathering. They asked straightforward questions that others were afraid to ask. They wondered why the urban artists were so afraid to address sex in their work. And they acted as inside informants on village life, especially with regard to what would work and what wouldn't in the village where they themselves live.

On the final day, as we gathered to debrief with government officials, Monimala astonished me by raising her hand to demand a role for herself and her fellow *patuas* in the public health interventions being planned for West Bengal. As she spoke, she seemed both calm and bold. And I thought to myself, this is a person who is capable of changing the world.

Monimala's Story

I remember walking into the Oberoi Grand Hotel in Kolkata, with Rani and Nandita Di, and thinking how beautiful it was. I found the hotel fantastic. At the time, I was living in Naya with my husband and seven children in a small hut with a tin roof. At the hotel, Rani and I had our own room with a bathtub— we washed our sarees in it—with as much hot water as we wanted, and plush white towels to dry our hair. It was luxurious.

At the beginning of the MAKE ART/STOP AIDS workshop, Rani and I felt extremely shy. We loved the variety of people who were there, but it was embarrassing to talk about condoms and such in front of them. Rani had been trained by the Thoughtshop people some years before, but neither of us had ever talked about sex in a public venue. Nandita Di—that's how I refer to her, as if she were my older sister—translated for us. We kept quiet.

I was really very hesitant and not sure what we had gotten into. Nandita Di brought me so I came, without knowing the importance of the occasion.

There was a woman at the meeting named Asha, very pretty, and wearing a beautiful silk saree. At first I thought she was there as one of the organizers. But when I realized that she had HIV, I really got very worried. There was an instance when I was thirsty and took water from a bottle, and Rani told me that Asha had been drinking from the same bottle. I moved away from Asha and sat in a different place. I worried that if I sat near her, I would contract the illness. Rani and I decided that we shouldn't even be there.

I had made some scrolls about HIV, based on Rani's first one, but I did it to make money. My scroll said the correct things—that you can't get HIV from sitting with people, sharing a meal, sharing drink—but I didn't believe what I was saying. I was pretending. I was afraid. Even Rani was in the same condition.

Gradually, though, as I sat in the meetings, with Nandita Di softly explaining what people were saying, I came to feel differently. I realized that if Nandita Di and David, people I respect, could be giving so much time and energy to this, and not for any gain of their own, it must be very important. As I sat with everybody, the awkwardness slowly melted away. More and more educated people, not illiterates like us, were giving so much time and intensity to this. It must be very serious. I really didn't know what HIV was before. But now I was understanding that there might be a part that I and the other scrollpainters could play, in reaching people like me.

We *patuas* have a special way of communicating that urban styles don't. That was the whole idea when I first started working with Rani, to use the communicative potential of the scroll that wasn't available in other forms. This was confirmed to me when I watched the street theater performances at the MAKE ART/STOP AIDS workshop. If this were done in the villages near my home, I thought to myself, all the women and children would have gone away. It works in the city. City people are educated and have access to all kinds of communication, such as movies in English or Hindi. But the scroll has a different sort of quality, a very good inherent quality through which information can be understood and accepted. People like me only understand Bengali. When I sing and show the scroll, people are getting information in their own language, and in a way that they understand.

The idea for the *patuas'* intervention came to me on the last day. We sat in a big circle at the last session and were joined by Mr. Sureshkumar, the head of the West Bengal State AIDS Prevention and Control Society. Everyone was talking about what we had learned from our three days together, about the best ways for artists to help stop the AIDS epidemic. Over the course of the workshop, as we saw that everybody was conversing about these things in a normal way, and as we got more and more exposed, we began to relax and talk openly too. So I said to Mr. Sureshkumar, "Why don't you include us in your project? Why don't you hire us, the *patuas* of Naya, to sing our songs and teach our neighbors about HIV?"

Mr. Sureshkumar is a powerful person, so it wasn't easy to make this suggestion. At the beginning of the meetings I was nervous, but by the time I spoke up I was not nervous any more. I thought this was a moment I couldn't let pass. It would mean income for poor people like us. And if Asha can get this disease, maybe I or my children could too. So spreading information was something important to do. I was trying to make a point, but getting my thinking and attitude together took a lot of strength.

It took time, but little by little after that meeting in Kolkata we managed to create an intervention that we are now performing in villages in rural areas of West Bengal. Two *patuas*—one man and one woman—are joined by a pair of community health workers from SPARSHA, the Society for Positive Atmosphere and Related Support to HIV/AIDS. We go four times to each village, to sing poems about how HIV/AIDS is transmitted, how and why to use a condom, and what we call "positive living"—how to access medications, live peacefully and safely within your community, and have a good life. As part of the intervention I sing the story of Asha, the beautiful HIV-positive woman at the MAKE ART/STOP AIDS workshop. I tell how her husband died, how she was unfairly shunned, and how her family finally overcame the stigma of AIDS and took pity on her. Now Asha is married to another HIV-positive person and has a son with him, who is HIV negative. That amazes me.

In the end I had sympathy with Asha. After years of working closely with people who are infected with HIV I am now totally convinced that you can't get AIDS from sitting together or drinking from the same glass. I know this because I've experienced it myself.

What do I like best about performing the intervention? The money! That's true. But second best, what I really like is that we are going to the audience and performing for them where they live. People are surrounded by the sound we are presenting. It's not like performing in a theater. In addition, we are singing in a situation where men, women, mothers-in-law, fathers-in-law, children, all are listening at the same time to the song and to the conversations with the community health workers. It's very important that they are hearing us collectively. The husband can say to the wife, these are the issues. And the wife can say the same thing to the husband. They are being reached together. And we're not talking down to them.

I also wanted to say that the singing is important, but the talking is very important too. The whole thing works much better with the health workers there. The song contributes one part of the information, but the health workers can expand on that. They are looked up to like doctors. People have confidence in them. What the song does is a good beginning, but it's not enough. Besides, it really makes a difference when the people realize that one of the community health workers is a person living with HIV. And that we're all working together.

Samiran's Story

As a medical doctor I have always believed in the power of the arts to improve quality of life. My association with art forms dates back to my college days when, like college students everywhere, we would make performances addressing social inequalities. This was before 1986 when AIDS was first detected in India. In 1987, our virology professor would talk about AIDS in India, but all the slides used for teaching featured the faces of Americans or Africans.

Then, in 1992, I began working in Manipur, a northeastern state with a very tough HIV problem, associated with injecting drug use. HIV became part of my life because some of my friends in Manipur were HIV positive. In Manipur there is a theatrical tradition called *sumang leela*, in which men play female as well as male roles. Plays were made in this tradition to deal with the themes of the day. That was my first exposure, where I came to know about the strength of art forms to address HIV/AIDS.

In Manipur I was very lonely. People referred to my two rooms, which were attached to my office, as the haunted house. I had no family with me. My only friends were ex-intravenous drug users. However, I did have a TV. One day I switched it on and suddenly hit on a channel where I saw the American movie *Philadelphia*, and in the movie a person living with HIV (Tom Hanks) tried to shake the hand of his lawyer (Denzel Washington). The guy withdrew his hand. I realized then that all sorts of art forms—*sumang leela* in Manipur and a movie in Hollywood—could address AIDS issues. This was palpable for me. So when I learned about the MAKE ART/STOP AIDS project from Umesh Kakarania, an HIV-positive hemophiliac in Kolkata, the concept appealed to me. This scrollpainting intervention made sense to me as a good public health tool, in part because this art form is indigenous, culturally acceptable, and evokes a sincere interest in the community.

A considerable proportion of the funds India spent on AIDS education in the early years of the HIV epidemic was based on standard models of health communication, which didn't accomplish much in terms of addressing negative attitudes or changing risk practices. The typical posters, pamphlets, or leaflets just didn't do the trick. It's the *way* you do it, the medium you use, that changes behavior. One-on-one interaction, where people can clarify their doubts in a friendly environment, is key too. Art contributes to this with something that David has called the "amplifying effect." You get the information you need in a form you can hear and absorb. That's how this whole thing germinated in my mind, and that's how, as a medical doctor and researcher, I first got involved in the scrollpainters' project.

I came to Kolkata from Manipur in 1994, when very few healthcare workers were willing to touch and treat people living with HIV. Gradually, word went out that there was a doctor who talks and cares. I had a friend, Dr. Anupam Dutta Gupta, a physiatrist with the Kolkata chapter of the Hemophilia Society, through whom I met two very special hemophiliac men, Apurbo and Umesh, who were HIV positive. One evening Apurbo's friends came to me and said, "Can we have a talk with you?" It seems that Apurbo had shared his HIV status with them, after which, as they described it, "the sky broke loose." "We never imagined this would happen," they said. They used to smoke cigarettes together, passing them along from person to person, and they smoked on that eventful evening too when Apurbo shared the results of his blood test. "For a moment we were hesitant—did we do the right thing by sharing a cigarette with him?" one man explained. "But then we told ourselves, 'Oh, but we know that HIV doesn't get transmitted this way.' " From this experience they understood how discrimination against people with AIDS happens. It comes from irrational fear.

Building on this they said to me, "We don't want to stand only by Apurbo, but by all those like Apurbo who have contracted HIV." This brings to mind the Charlton Heston movie *Ben-Hur*, the scene where the lepers are kept in a valley, and a bucket full of bread is sent to them hanging from a rope. To me, people artificially created that circumstance, maybe out of fear of contracting the disease. You call it a community? That's nonsense, keeping people with disease in one place and healthy people in another. Did you ever ask those leprosy patients if they envisioned life that way? If you ask me, they still wanted to be with their mothers and fathers, their sisters and brothers, their friends. So that's how we started SPARSHA in 1998, as a coalition of people living with HIV/AIDS and their friends. Our slogan is "Be a part, not apart."

Very recently one of the MAKE ART/STOP AIDS project staff, Mousumi, who was on anti-retroviral treatment, started having fainting attacks and breathlessness. I diagnosed anemia and the treating physician at the hospital ordered a blood transfusion. Who served as the blood replacement donors? Surya and Ranjan, Mousumi's two youngest HIV-negative colleagues from SPARSHA. She was given four bottles of blood transfusion and came back to life. For me, that was a high point. For so long, HIV-negative people have treated positive people as if they were in the gutter. They must have done something bad. Now I see an act of generosity from two people who are known to be HIV negative, and they're not thinking that this is for someone whose days are counted—a justification I have heard a number of times from others for not doing anything for people living with HIV. Surya and Ranjan did not think about whether their friend was deserving or not. None of it matters except that someone needs help. That's exactly what SPARSHA is all about.

Mithu's Story

I didn't know about HIV/AIDS until my husband fell sick and I lost him to AIDS. That was 2002–03 when I was living in a village named Balokrouth under Daspur Police Station in the district of Paschim Medinipur in West Bengal. I really went through a very difficult time when he died, because in our culture when someone passes on you need to get the body cremated right away. But out of fear nobody would come to help us out with this last ritual. Nobody came. And then when the information went out that my husband had died of AIDS, my eldest daughter, who was ready for kindergarten, couldn't get admitted to school. Everyone said they needed to know first if she was carrying HIV.

I came to know about SPARSHA during that time, because the organization was working in a nearby village. A female counselor said, "Don't worry, we'll take care of you." And then I got my daughter tested and she was negative, so I got her admitted in school. At that same time, however, I came to know that I was infected with HIV, which was very difficult to hear. Soon after, I began working with SPARSHA as a community health worker and researcher, focusing on projects that deal with women and children. One day Samiran told me he wanted me to work on an arts-based project looking at the attitudes of community members to people living with HIV/AIDS, and I thought, Wow, that's something I could do, because I myself have experienced discrimination from the community at large. This was the scrollpainting project.

I knew about scrollpainting since my childhood days, because in my village the *patuas* would come and sing episodes from the *Ramayana* or *Mahabharata*, the two great epics of India, which are like the *Iliad* and *Odyssey*. When I first started working with the project, I knew that scrollpainters and their singing would attract people, which was good. But I also realized that talking face to face was equally important. I believe it's especially important that an HIV-positive person be part of the process.

When, as part of the intervention, I was giving my personal testimony about HIV/AIDS and was interacting with the people in the community around me, the response would often be, "You are HIV positive, so of course you would say it is OK to hug someone, to live with someone who has HIV." And then I would say, "Look here, it's not me alone. We in SPARSHA work in a mixed team. Here is a living example." This made an impression. This model of a person who is not infected with the virus working with a person who is living with the virus is very powerful.

My colleague Rupali, who is also a person living with HIV/AIDS, told her story in one village. And then the next time she visited, the children of the village recognized her and started to mimic her in a lighthearted way. "My name is Rupali, and I am living with HIV/AIDS." They laughed and ran away. We all thought that was wonderful, because it showed that they heard her story, and that they were thinking about what it would mean to live with HIV. They were learning to empathize. At SPARSHA we believe that empathy—some people call it "identification"—is key to the success of any AIDS intervention.

Recently I have been involved in analyzing the data from the villages where we worked, and what we've found is a dramatic decrease in stigmatizing attitudes. Before the intervention, almost all our interviewees said that people living with HIV should be ashamed or legally isolated. We asked if they would allow someone known to be infected with HIV to cook rice and other food in the kitchen, and they said no. After the intervention everything changed. Almost everyone said that people living with HIV should not be ashamed. Moreover, they said that they would keep their children in school alongside HIV-positive classmates. In scientific terms, these results were considered highly significant. The next step is actual behavior change, like getting people to use condoms when they have sex. In public health, this is the most difficult thing to do, but we're still trying.

In 2007 I presented the results of our intervention at a meeting in New Delhi, with the head of the National AIDS Control Organization and other important people in attendance. I never thought that I would be able to be in front of so many people and talk to them about my own experience of going through life, and also about the project we created. I felt really good because I helped in bringing awareness about HIV/AIDS to others. I never thought I would be able to do this.

This feels particularly significant because I am a woman. I believe that everybody has the right to information about HIV/AIDS, and that the right to protect themselves from HIV should be equal for men and women. This is essential for everyone, but especially for women in rural areas of India where they have only one partner—their husbands—but are still vulnerable to HIV. At one point in time I thought HIV information was not relevant to me, but it was. Everyone needs to know.

Nandita Palchoudhuri is a Calcutta-based curator working with Indian folk practices and traditional crafts. Her work creates cutting-edge functional applications for traditional skills, often by addressing a current social need. Her process is aimed at regenerating the craft while providing sustainable livelihood for highly skilled but often unemployed artisan groups.

David Gere is Director of MAKE ART/STOP AIDS, an international network of artists intervening in the AIDS epidemic. He also serves as Director of the Art | Global Health Center at the University of California, Los Angeles and is Co-chair and Associate Professor in the Department of World Arts and Cultures, where he teaches courses in AIDS/arts activism. His most recent book is *How to Make Dances in an Epidemic: Tracking Choreography in the Age of AIDS* (University of Wisconsin Press, 2004).

Monimala Chitrakar comes from a family of traditional scrollpainter-singers based in Naya, a tiny hamlet in the Pingla district of West Bengal. Her exceptional skills as an illustrator and storyteller through ballads have been showcased all over India as well as in the United States and New Zealand.

Samiran Panda is a physician-researcher trained in tropical medicine. He is currently working on an innovative, community-based model in the districts of West Bengal to reduce stigma around HIV/AIDS. His work among injecting drug users and their regular female sex partners laid the foundation for HIV intervention development in the Indian sub-continent.

Mithu Jana is a healthcare worker living with HIV. She works with the Society for Positive Atmosphere and Related Support to HIV/AIDS (SPARSHA) in Calcutta, India. She has two daughters, one of whom has HIV as well. Making people aware about HIV is the motto of her life. She also wants to ensure that those infected with the virus are not discriminated against.

III

"Weaving Freedom into New Tongues"

Stories in the Service of Challenging and Transforming Beliefs

15

The We That Sets Us Free

Imagining a World without Prisons

ALICE DO VALLE

WITH WOMEN FEATURED IN THE CD COMPILATION

THE WE THAT SETS US FREE

The We That Sets Us Free CD Cover. Designed by Design Action Collective. Background collage by Palmira Gutierrez

One day I woke up in prison
Searching for something as certain as the concrete against my palm
I am writing this poem to survive

I tie revolutions to kite strings
So when my daughters are raised to be kings
They can remember that the mind of a child is closest to God

I tie evolution to my wings
So when my daughters are caged they sing
Freedom into kingdoms, and remember
Feathers break concrete

See I am the We I dreamed of
We are the ones weaving
Freedom into new tongues . . .

Climbing Poe Tree*

Just because we are locked up doesn't mean that we don't still exist.
—Beverly Henry

In prison I don't have a name—they just know me by a number.
—Zundre Johnson

I had no awareness at all of the abuses of the prison system before I came here.
—Jane Dorotik

Beverly, a long-time anti-prison activist and peer health educator; Zundre, a mother of three separated from her children by a prison sentence; and Jane, a nurse, an optimist, a mother, and an animal lover, are imprisoned at the Central California Women's Facility (CCWF) and Valley State Prison for Women (VSPW)—the largest women's prison complex in the world located outside of Chowchilla, California. Along with other women inside, their activism and resistance were instrumental in making a CD that tells their stories, describes their experiences of captivity, investigates the realities of the current system, and lays out ideas for real safety and justice. Making the CD emerged as a form of resistance to the institution of the prison and as a protest against the silencing of people caged inside prisons. This is the story of that CD, *The We That Sets Us Free*, of those who created it, and of its effect on the world.

Breaking Out of Prison

Prisons have colonized hearts and minds. They have infiltrated our physical landscape, our media-saturated discourse, and our ideas about safety and justice. People in prison, the ones who directly bear the brunt of this obsession, are especially shut out of public discourse and public consciousness. They have no space to tell of the daily oppressions they experience. They have no space to articulate what liberation would look like. Their stories, experiences, and dreams are also caged.

In a culture obsessed with retribution, expulsion, and punishment, there is very little space for imagining a society beyond oppression and fear. It is curiously appropriate, then, that it is from inside prison, a space most managed, most oppressed, most silenced, that voices of resistance, imagination, and healing should break out.

These voices are articulated in a CD produced by Justice Now, an Oakland-based human rights organization that works with women in prison and the broader community to build a safe, compassionate world without prisons. *The We That Sets Us Free*—the result of a two-year collaboration among activists, artists, and musicians inside and outside of prison—is a compendium of testimonials, interviews, music, poetry, and spoken word, excerpts of which are included throughout this chapter.

> *You can see the pain in her eyes when she's feeling oppressed*
> *What is the system's mission—frontin' like they're trying to correct?*
> *Our lives with their silly corrections it feels like infection*
> *Seeping in my veins so I take rebellious direction*
>
> Stephanie*

As the U.S. imprisons more people than any other country in the world—both in absolute numbers and in rate of imprisonment—it is difficult to ignore the presence—and the expansion—of the prison system and of those who are under its control. In fact, omnipresent references to prisons, prisoners, and "criminal justice" in our cultural, social, and political landscape are used to reinforce the belief that certain people *should be* in prison and to justify our society's continued investment in these institutions as a way of promoting "justice" and "safety."

Despite the growing visibility of the prison system, imprisoned people are shut out of the visible field. Prison planners intentionally isolate institutions geographically from urban population centers where prisoners' families, advocates, and communities are located. Prison bureaucracy and the phone company monopolies have made it virtually impossible for families on fixed incomes to keep in touch. Prisoners have very little access to human rights advocates or to the media. In fact, California, among many states across the country, has enacted "media bans" that make it impossible for reporters to conduct face-to-face interviews with people in prison at their request.

Because of the invisibility and disenfranchisement of people in prison, particularly women (because of their vulnerability and their lower numbers compared to men), it is especially urgent that the stories and ideas of imprisoned women break into public consciousness. Indeed, it is because of their experiences of violence and imprisonment in particular that women can lead the way toward defining and realizing new forms of safety and justice.

> *I am a prison abolitionist because I want to live in a world . . . that doesn't organize itself around violence and punishment and confinement. I want to live in a world where we believe that every single person who's here is worth caring for, where we no longer throw people away.*
>
> Cassandra*

The process of making the CD—and the fact that the CD exists—has given a group of imprisoned women a space for articulating ideas freely and a space for dreaming aloud about a world that no longer relies on violence and imprisonment to "solve" contemporary failings in our society. For these women the CD project created a space for sharing personal experiences and structural analysis that challenge mainstream representations of incarcerated women. It is a space for singing; a space to rhythm; and an opportunity to take our rightful place as leaders in the movement for prison abolition.

The Making of *The We That Sets Us Free*

What does safety mean to you? How can people who are most impacted by oppression lead the struggle for liberation? How can cultural work help sustain this movement? In 2001, Justice Now staff began conducting interviews with women in prison, excerpts of which were featured at an art show in Oakland, California, organized by the Prison Activist Resource Center. The aim was to redefine concepts such as "justice," "safety," and "violence."

The idea for the CD came organically out of these conversations. We began recording at the end of 2002. When we brought up questions about the impact of prisons on women's lives and their communities, many of the women reacted with both cynicism and excitement. The questions worked to challenge the interviewers and interviewees in confronting and overcoming stale ideas about equality, justice, and safety. Only then could we imagine a world that did not rely on prisons. The process of recording created an opportunity for critical reflection and, over time, for leadership development.

Many of the women inside who were first approached with questions such as, "What makes you feel safe?" and "What would a world without prisons look like to you?" thought they were participating in a theoretical exercise. They were willing to explore, but many had reservations about its usefulness. Some women didn't think any of us—the ones on the inside or the ones on the outside—could really imagine a world without prisons.

> *I think we're so used to having a world so totally defined by prisons and*

'prisons as the answer to safety, prisons as the answer to everything' that to actually ask someone, it's kind of shocking to say, what would it be like if they didn't exist . . . I think whole possibilities for justice and human liberation would be opened up.

Donna*

"What do you mean, 'A world without prisons?' What does that mean to you?" Madalin Bloxson, a 51-year-old African American woman serving a life sentence, asked Justice Now's co-director Cynthia Chandler.

Madalin leaned back, looked at Cynthia, and said, "I wanted to meet you because when I first heard about this project, I thought, 'Who is this person? Is she out of her mind?' " Madalin wanted to know if Cynthia had personally suffered violence and, if so, how that experience had shaped her thinking about prisons.

They talked. Madalin's hard questions led to a pivotal conversation that led to many other hard questions. At first Madalin was cynical about the idea of a world without prisons. She thought this was an impractical, idealistic, and naive thought-experiment, and her cynicism never faded away completely. Madalin was clear about the powerful role prisons play in this society and how much money is being made via the prison-industrial complex. These insights reinforced Madalin's belief that prisons are permanent.

"I strongly believe that education is the key to internal freedom and soul survival," Madalin wrote to us, imposing and well spoken. She became involved in the CD and other projects but has never stopped asking the hard questions. She is currently a board member for Justice Now.

Through interactions and discussions, we recognized that many of us had been harmed, and in different ways. No one was denying the complexities of the issue. But we found ourselves engaged with these difficult questions, especially around abolition, as an exercise that allowed us to think outside of the prison "box."

How can we be safe in a world without prisons? Well, that seems like a really easy question. We can be safe in a world without prisons if we create a world in which our relationships to each other are based in mutuality and respect and care rather than evaluation and punishment and expulsion. So safety would be something that we would make by remaking society into something that was a collective endeavor rather than individual competition.

Ruth*

We approached the project with a commitment to work respectfully with those of us who the prison system had the greatest impact on. We were aware of the fine line between providing an opportunity for women inside to share ideas and experiences—and the objectification of those women. How to approach the women? How to ask for contributions? How to integrate everyone into not only the content but also the shape of this project?

The goal was to build a tapestry of personal narratives intertwined with—and against the background of—the political context and social conditions of those lives. How to do that while being as true as possible to each person's ideas and language? How to convey facts about a person's history and present condition, illustrating how these are grounded in experience? How could we all be mindful of the stereotyping tendency that reduces facts to labels and uses labels to dismiss a woman's experiences? We worked hard answering these questions carefully.

We decided on an essential principle: to pay close attention to the ways that all of us have internalized certain values despite ongoing efforts to decolonize our ideas and re-invent our experiences. Only with this kind of attention to ourselves and our own "received wisdom" would we be able to challenge culturally predominant stereotypes of people who survive violence, especially people in prison. Only then could we make the process of creating the CD, itself, a form of resistance against the institution of the prison and the silencing of people inside these institutions.

> *Of course I know there is a problem with my being black*
> *And yes I know that society feels that I am a minority and in everything I*
> * lack*
> *Well today that is not so*
> *In fact it never was but I am sure you already know*
>
> Hakim*

We developed another essential principle: we are allies but we are also enmeshed in a special kind of power dynamics as we make this CD. We must not lose sight of our outsider privileges. We ask the questions. We record the conversations that we will broadcast. We can go in and out of the prison gates. All this shapes the interactions between the women inside and the women from outside.

We learned to share our own experiences, show our respect, acknowledge the contributions of all of us—in order to build friendships across the barriers of privilege. Many of the women who participated in the making of the CD were already participants in other Justice Now projects; it wasn't so hard to see what we all had in common and to honor and respect our partners honestly.

Here is another principle, or maybe a core recognition: political and cultural participation is risky for people in prison. The simple fact of meeting with an advocate from the outside in a prison visiting room puts a prisoner in an especially vulnerable position, especially when prison officials believe that the lawyer or the legal advocate is outspoken. To be expressing political opinions and attesting to abuses suffered in prison while sitting in a sterile visiting room with staring guards is not an easy task. There is no doubt that all the women inside who participated in this project were courageous beyond measure. Women had a choice whether or not to communicate with advocates and how. They had to decide whether to give a name to their voices or not. Everyone was aware that Justice Now couldn't offer much protection. Some women turned down participation not because of conflicting politics but because of fear. Most participated despite the danger.

Over twenty-five women in prison actively engaged in the process of telling and collecting stories, circulating calls for submissions, enlisting the help of others, and most profoundly shaping and creating the CD. The process took over a year. All that time we communicated during prison visits, via collect calls, and through letters. Each contributor, in her own way, inspired us all to imagine new ways of living in the world.

Outside of prison, we collaborated with visual artists, musicians and poets, sound people, graphic designers, and other creative folks and activists who generously donated their time and expertise. Most of these contributors understood the vision of the project from the first moment they heard about it. Most of them jumped at the opportunity to participate. Outside artists shaped the project in so many ways—by making an illustration for the cover of the CD; by writing a song with lyrics that touch the soul; and by conducting a special interview. Contributors came from across the country, from the San Francisco Bay Area, Detroit, New York, and Tucson.

The process was challenging. But fortified by our principles, we tried to practice the kinds of relationships and collaborations we want for the world we are fighting to live in—a world based on collaboration and compassion, respect and equality, resource reallocation, diversity, and cultural integrity.

Transforming Ourselves and Our Movement

In the United States most people hold ideas about prisons that they do not examine. We have been conditioned not to ask questions or speculate about a different way, other solutions. We acquiesce, not because we don't have the capacity to question, but because it is not demanded of us, and sometimes if we question authority, the authorities say we're "unpatriotic," or "too radical," or impractical, or something worse. Our imaginations have been colonized by fear and violence. By now it's past time to strengthen our imaginations so that we can conceptualize a world with new possibilities for justice and safety. This "strengthening" work is the political project of the CD.

The CD was released at the opening plenary of the 2005 Incite conference "The Color of Violence III" in New Orleans—an anti-racist organizing event to resist violence against women of color. We believed the CD would spark real dialogue. We believed the CD would encourage people to rethink the way we live and especially rethink our dependency on prisons. We believed the CD would move our audience to action.

People must become activists because each of us is always affecting each other in our world in every relationship and in every situation. By the character of our presence, we profoundly affect each other and our sense of selves, of possibility, of our sense of hope, of the world we live in.

Jane*

Since our opening in New Orleans, activists on the outside have played the CD at various venues—local, national, and international—bringing the actual voices of women inside far beyond the prison. We've all learned that these presentations have become an effective vehicle for organizing. Listening to testimonials and stories straight from women survivors of state violence appears to be a powerful way to challenge what ordinary people believe about the root causes of the problems we face. The CD has been able to mobilize critical support and to fuel the movement for liberation. When people hear the CD, they want to make it available to others. They want to generate further connections and opportunities for sharing these stories.

"The first time I started listening to the CD, it actually moved me to tears. In large part, I think, because of the medium of the message: this is how real news comes to me, how real communication happens, communication that reaches the soul, not just the much-distracted ears. It comes hand-to-hand, with art and care, with time to meditate and let holistic connections and dreams sink in. Perhaps best of all, it comes not from a single reporter but from a choir of voices, compiled, connected, collaborating, and ever in the process of networking. It wasn't 'news' to me in the sense that I'd known to some degree about jail issues for a long time, but the clarity and directedness of the CD and your organizing felt like a new degree of movement to be aware of, a new way to share with others." This is what a listener from Ohio wrote to Justice Now.

"I have heard your CD and was touched by the songs. I feel that everything in the CD needs to be heard by tons of women," a seventeen-year-old girl from a group home in Oakland told us. After describing how she herself had survived violence in the streets, in her home, and in the criminal justice system, she celebrated she had been clean and sober for nineteen months. Also she promised to "inspire lots of young women with my words and your CD," when she left the group home in a few months.

This project has had an enormous impact on the way Justice Now staff relate to the people we have worked with. We are very clear that all of us are yearning for the same things—safety, justice, and liberation. The dialogue we began with the making of the CD is one that continues today.

"I want people to know that I am an artist and it's really lonely in here," was how Marie Bandrup described herself in an interview over the phone. Marie was very quiet and somewhat isolated from other women inside. The CD gave Marie a connection with people on the outside and an avenue to express herself artistically. Through this collaboration she grew out of her shell and has remained active, serving on Justice Now's Board of Directors, contributing to fundraising efforts, and providing continued leadership from the inside. With her activism she hopes to "inspire others and have those on the outside to see people inside through different eyes."

This was also the first major project that many women activists inside collaborated on with Justice Now. It was an opportunity for them to express their power through their own ideas, analysis, and experiences. Some women have continued working with Justice Now long after their participation on the CD.

> *I'm an activist against the prison system because as the prison system works now, I have seen so many ideas, lives and spirits just totally squashed by the bureaucracy, and by the total abuse and dehumanization that goes on within these walls. It's time we learn to stand up.*
>
> Misty*

"I wish that people [who listen to the CD] are moved into becoming activists and proactive, that there is a struggle [they] can contribute to," said Stephanie Collins about how she wanted her words in the CD to touch others. Stephanie, a 29-year-old black artist who has been imprisoned since she was 18, wrote a spoken word piece for the CD, but couldn't record it because she was in administrative segregation—a prison within a prison—during that time. "I hoped it would be enlightening for those who have no idea about what happens behind these walls," said Ms. Collins whose favorite love is writing. She hoped that "Peers would feel like they could do more, to have confidence and self esteem," referring to the transformative nature of the project.

"Do you know how proud I am to be part of such an important project? Knowing that my views can touch the hearts of others makes everything worth doing," Zundre Johnson wrote after being informed that the CD had come out and was being distributed.

"Thanks for allowing me to be a part of the project and allowing my voice to be heard. It means a lot to me because not many of us are heard due to the fact that we are behind prison walls," wrote Hakim, a 22-year-old, strong-minded, ambitious black lesbian serving a seven years-to-life sentence. Hakim believes that knowledge is power and that people deserve second chances. She wrote a poem especially for the CD. Since Hakim started working with Justice Now at age 19, she has participated in countless other projects, including writing and publishing an opinion piece in *Alternet* about the meaning of the 4th of July for her.

> *I think that a world without prisons is not a complicated thing to think about. We are putting people away. We are really saying, "What would a world without slavery look like?" We can't imagine it? Of course we can*

imagine it. I believe that if we created a situation and a world society where people are not hungry, where people are not going without, that we can find a way to live in happiness and peace truly with each other, and we won't even remember what it was like to have a world with prisons.

Elaine*

People will respond differently to the CD depending on their location. How much do they understand about the roots of our social problems? How sensitive are they to the rhetoric of political discourse in the United States? Listening to the CD may not make activists out of everybody. But listening has the powerful potential to challenge "received wisdom" and to blast away lethargy. The first step toward change is listening. The second step is learning. The process of creating the CD, and now the CD itself, contributes to waking up our imaginations and our capacity to listen. For all of us who contributed to making *The We That Sets Us Free*, bearing witness to stories of resistance has been transformative. Now we have a tool to help us all continue the work.

I am more than a revolutionary
I am more than just freedom's child
I am more than a visionary
So keep me safe now family
Don't let me stray
Don't let me fall

Piper*

Alice do Valle centered her work at Justice Now on bringing the voices of those most impacted by systems of oppression to public discourse. She currently lives in her hometown of Rio de Janeiro, Brazil. She wants to thank her friend and colleague Sarah H. Cross for her help with this chapter.

*In order of appearance:

Alixa Garcia and Naima Penniman make up a Heart Beat Soul Sister Artist Warrior duo called "**Climbing Poe Tree**." On a mission to re-envision and shape the world through evolutionary art that speaks truth to power, together they perform poetry, dance, create public art, and work with prisoners and young people through arts education.

Stephanie Collins is a 29-year-old black woman artist who has been imprisoned since she was 18. Stephanie's favorite love is writing.

Cassandra Shaylor is a co-founder and co-director of Justice Now and a Ph.D. candidate in the History of Consciousness Department at UC Santa Cruz where she is completing a dissertation on the intersections of race, gender, sexuality, and the prison industrial complex.

Donna Willmott is a former political prisoner who found her home at Legal Services for Prisoners with Children, where she works to promote the leadership of family members of prisoners who are struggling for their rights and the rights of their loved ones inside.

Ruth Wilson Gilmore is Associate Professor of Geography and American Studies & Ethnicity at the University of Southern California. She is a long-time political activist and currently works with the California Prison Moratorium Project and Critical Resistance. *Golden Gulag*, her book on California's prison expansion, is forthcoming.

Hakim is a 22-year-old, strong-minded, ambitious black lesbian serving a seven years-to-life sentence who believes that knowledge is power and that people deserve second chances.

Jane Dorotik—"I'm a nurse, an optimist, a mother, and an animal lover. I have worked all my life as a senior executive in healthcare settings. I had no awareness at all of the abuses of the prison system before I came here."

Misty Rojo believes you don't pity incarcerated women; instead, you question your own knowledge and belief in the society that has failed them and the system that has victimized them.

Elaine Brown became, in 1974, the first and only woman to lead the Black Panther Party. In her autobiographical memoir, *A Taste of Power: A Black Woman's Story* (Anchor, 1993), Brown recounts her life from the ghettos of North Philly to her leadership in one of the most important and militant civil rights groups in U.S. history.

Piper Anderson is a queer woman of color performance artist, writer, activist, and educator based in Brooklyn, NY. She is the National Outreach Coordinator for "We Got Issues!" produced by the Next Wave of Women & Power and Coordinator of the Lyrics on Lockdown.

Further Reading

Justice Now: www.justicenow.org

16

Hearing the Great Ancestors and "Women Living Under Muslim Laws"

AISHA LEE FOX SHAHEED

I would like to welcome you all to this session on feminism and the women's movement. As we all know, the women's movement started a couple of centuries ago with women's struggles in Europe and the West . . .

begins one speaker, only to be interrupted by a second speaker who protests:

Excuse me, I don't think that's true. I think women have been active in many parts of the world. How can you say that it's only in the West and Europe? We know women from different parts of the world were active . . .

The first speaker resumes: *Well yes, maybe women were active in different places, but I think we all know that in our parts of the world, and in our countries the ideas of the women's movement came to us from women in Europe and North America . . .*

Suddenly the lights go down, an image of a woman appears on a screen and a voice from elsewhere in the room calls out,

How can you have forgotten me . . .?

*   *   *

So begins a presentation of the *Great Ancestors*. The staged altercation above could occur at a round-table workshop, at the front of a lecture hall, or on a stage of a theater. The disembodied voice continues, "I am Umm-Salama" and launches into a narrativized account of her life in Baghdad in the eighth century. Recounting the story of her third marriage to Abbas, who would later become Caliph, she explains how she was the one who made the proposal, paid the amount for his dower, and then made him officially promise to be monogamous. As Umm-Salama completes her short narrative, a new image appears of an extremely self-satisfied looking woman wearing bright red shoes, from a Persian miniature. A new voice reads out the story of Aisha bint Talha who, in Mecca in the early 700s, not only married multiple times and was regarded as highly learned, but also refused to veil. To give a synopsis of these women's stories, each segment provides a narrativized account or a quotation from the woman herself, as drawn from the pages of history. Each minute-long "act" is accompanied by a suitable image or, as is especially the case from the twentieth century, a photograph of the woman in question. Each segment is read in under sixty seconds, drawing from people who lived and events occurring from the eighth century to the 1940s. Most of the women profiled were Muslim, though some were minorities in Muslim-majority regions and others may have identified as secular. Each one, however, operated in Muslim contexts, asserting rights for themselves and for others, establishing the foundations of female education, and engaging in solidarity actions with other women.

Feminism in the Muslim World Training Institutes

For years, Farida Shaheed, of the international feminist solidarity network Women Living Under Muslim Laws (WLUML) had been collecting fragments of histories relating to women operating in Muslim contexts who asserted their own rights and/or championed the rights of others. These seemingly disparate slivers of history came together for her during the planning of the second Feminism in the Muslim World Leadership Institute, jointly conducted by WLUML and the Center for Women's Global Leadership (CWGL) of Rutgers University. CWGL had been conducting feminist leadership work-shops since 1991, to which WLUML had encouraged their networkers to apply. Their joint institutes were held in Istanbul in September 1998 and again in Lagos in the autumn of 1999.

These intensive residential institutes, lasting two weeks each, were designed to strengthen the capacities and skills of younger women active in WLUML. Bringing together over twenty young women leaders from twenty Muslim countries and/or Muslim communities, the institutes aimed to help the parti-cipants strengthen their local projects, enhance their work within WLUML, and generally help groom a new generation of women's rights activists. Of the participants, some lived in a self-proclaimed "Islamic" state, others in a secular context. Some were part of the Muslim majority in their country (e.g., Malaysia), others belonged to a Muslim minority (e.g., India), and some were non-Muslims from places increasingly affected by religious-political forces.

Though the participants came from diverse backgrounds and had differing relationships with Islam as a spiritual and political force, a space was created for the sharing of experiences at a transnational level. It was widely acknowl-edged that the discourses of conservative Islamists have been intensifying in the past few decades and women have become caught between a narrow version of history and the ambiguities of a globalized world. Firstly, Muslim women are all too often represented by others and have limited access to positions providing control over accessing and distributing information. In addition, women in Muslim communities are generally depicted as static and oppressed and when their efforts are celebrated they often gloss over women's gender-based alliances which contributes to their activism. WLUML recognized the need to build upon the work of earlier historians and writers who had brought Muslim women's contributions to light in order to counter the dominant representations of women, emanating from conservative Muslim quarters as well as from the Western media. The desire to introduce contemporary activists to vibrant women from the past coincided with the broader objectives of the feminist leadership institutes.

The institutes had three underlying themes: connecting the local to the global; making the link between women's struggles and human rights; and connecting the past and present. One of many components of the second institute was the presentation of the *Great Ancestors*, which during its preparation became informally referred to as "the light-and-sound show." Conceived of as a training module, the *Great Ancestors* addresses each of the three underlying themes of the institutes. The international flavor of the presentation is perhaps its most striking aspect, and the inclusion of "Ancestors" from not only the Middle East and South Asia, but also sub-Saharan Africa, Central Asia, and the Far East, clearly demonstrates that women across the globe were actively participating in Muslim contexts. Though the specific religious and cultural traditions have varied widely in each region over time, the training module shows that women fighting for women's rights were not tied to a specific locale. Of particular interest were the transnational solidarity efforts women undertook in the past. Though there was not enough time in the script to allow for more than a passing mention, the companion volume of research discusses examples of these international links, such as a delegation of Egyptian feminists who attended a large conference in Rome in 1923, or R.A. Kartini of Indonesia who, at the turn of the twentieth century, shared intellectual correspondence with Dutch women.

The connections between women's rights and human rights was also a key theme of the institutes, but were expanded upon more in sessions other than in the *Great Ancestors*. In large part this is due to the fact that all the women discussed in the *Ancestors* were active before 1950 at which time the discourse of modern human rights was in its infancy insofar as it pertained to women's rights. Nonetheless, some of the women discussed in the module adamantly asserted their rights, often using the language of Islam, and many others had an implicitly rights-based approach to their activism. Many of the women we read about were actively engaged in social justice struggles, whether this was defined as fighting against colonial rule, working at a national political level, or fighting for the rights of religious minorities.

The theme of linking past and present struggles was key to the general discussion of a contemporary feminist leadership in Muslim communities, and many participants were surprised at the rich collection of activist predecessors they encountered. The historical nature of the *Great Ancestors* lends itself well to the issue of recognizing past achievments and learning lessons to apply to today's women's movements. Still, the presentation of the *Ancestors* makes it explicit that some issues which today may be seen as strategic priorities by both feminists and their critics, such as regulating sex outside of marriage, were not always points of contention. For example, in the eleventh and twelfth centuries in Spain, many well-known women writers of the elite classes were very frank about their lovers, through both their literature and their actions. Conversely, other issues were as contentious in the past as today, such as debates over veiling and a mother's right to custody of her children. Almost 100 years ago, Begum Sharifa Hamid Ali was encouraging marriage contracts (*nikahnama*) that included the many unactivated rights provided to women under Islam. Today, in the early twenty-first century, the marriage contract is still a site of contestation; activists in Afghanistan are currently trying to reform the national marriage contract (*nikahkhat*) to protect women's interests within the institution of marriage. In addition to showing the participants that women of the past contended with many of the issues we still address today, the module presented the listeners with versions of the past they may not otherwise have been familiar with. Standard historiographies, in all cultural traditions, have marginalized women and their contributions. Where some researchers, such as Fatima Mernissi and Leila Ahmed, have blazed the trails of Muslim women's history by uncovering and sharing stories of empowered women, the organizers of the feminist leadership institutes continued the tradition by sharing these stories with the participants. The intention was that this revisiting of women's histories could subsequently be reproduced by participants in their own communities thereby educating and inspiring others. It is not enough to say that the *Great Ancestors* sought to make history entertaining for the audience through narrativization and colorful images; by personalizing the women of the past, the presentation encouraged participants to draw connections with their own lives and use these considerations to shape their own futures.

Farida Shaheed and the other members of WLUML wanted to circulate the *Great Ancestors* widely so that these stories could be shared with many, inspiring others to research their own histories. Before the module could be distributed, however, it not only had to be finalized for print, but also needed a comprehensive list of the historical and contemporary references used. This was not only exercising a good publishing ethos: it ensured that those using the module could not be accused by their detractors of "making up" history. With citations in hand, the *Great Ancestors* can now be performed in any setting one may see fit, be it a workshop, a classroom, a theater, or beyond.

To facilitate reproduction of the presentation, the *Great Ancestors* was published as a set of two books. The first includes the script and all accompanying images in an easy-to-handle, spiral-bound format. The script can be photocopied for the readers and the images can either be photocopied onto overhead transparencies or scanned into a computer for use as a Power-Point presentation, depending on the equipment available to the organizers. The companion volume is presented as a historical reference, providing context and more in-depth information on every person and issue discussed in the script as well as numerous additional Ancestors not mentioned in the script, in addition to a complete bibliography of sources used. This publication of the *Great Ancestors* now allows these stories of courage and activism to be even more widely distributed and elaborated upon by all who use it.

As the process of historical research can never be fully exhausted, the *Great Ancestors* is inevitably a work-in-progress. WLUML is constantly learning more about the Ancestors already included along with new information about other women activists of the past. Tentative ideas for expanding the project include a second volume of the publication, providing more examples of women and their actions. Other methods of dissemination are being explored such as film, where the voices of these women and their narratives can be given a new vitality with the use of moving images and music. On the other hand, the current structure of the module gives suggestions on how to read the script and what images to use, but in practice there is a wide scope for creativity in the performance. We have encountered many interesting discussions arising from men reading the first-person narratives as "a Muslim woman."

Reclaiming History, Disseminating Information, Storytelling

There are three main objectives to the *Great Ancestors* project. The first is historical, namely the desire to recover marginalized life-stories of women from the past. As Moroccan sociologist Fatima Mernissi has argued, this historical project is one of urgency and responsibility, especially for those conducting feminist and/or post-colonial research: "*Muslim women in general . . . cannot count on anyone, scholar or not, 'involved' or 'neutral,' to read their history for them. Rereading it for themselves is entirely their responsibility and their duty. Our demand for the full and complete enjoyment of our universal human rights, here and now, requires us to take over our history, to reread it, and to reconstruct a wide-open Muslim past. This duty, moreover, can turn out to be no drab, disagreeable task, but rather a journey filled with delight.*"[1] The recovery of these women's lives was not as straightforward as seeking out small references in existing historical accounts. In the case of the extraordinary story of Bibi Zainab, who, in the nineteenth century launched a tightly organized and widespread armed women's militia in Iran first against the British monopoly over tobacco and then against injustice in general, the references to her life and work come to us through court records, complaining about her actions and those of her troops. We also know of her exploits through the folklore sung and told by women of Tabriz, who have kept Bibi Zainab's story alive. Consequently it is impossible to know the exact number of grain storehouses broken open to feed the poor nor can we relate how many women fighters were killed in action. Nonetheless, we do know that the collective actions of these women not only posed a challenge to the British and Iranian governments, but also left enough of an impression of justice and courage upon the citizenry for them to be kept alive in popular memory.

Having excavated information on women of the past, the second objective of the *Great Ancestors* project was to disseminate this information. Collating the material in a typically academic way, including the use of scholarly language and extensive referencing, would have resulted in just another textbook. While historical textbooks have their place, it is probably safe to assume that the majority of people do not read them, either due to lack of availability in English or the vernacular, or time constraints (especially amongst professional women), and limited literacy. To disseminate the words and actions of these inspirational Ancestors to the widest possible audience, we decided to narrativize their stories and contexts into entertaining nuggets. Whenever the actual words—written or spoken—by the women in question were available, we used them. Where the historical figures were merely mentioned in passing in broader chronicles, we personalized their tales through narrative, in order to restore flesh-and-blood vibrancy to their segments, underscoring that these were vibrant women, not characters.

The use of numerous voices to read the monologues, dialogue, and quotations captivates the listeners' attention. Not required to focus on a single voice, reminiscent of a didactic lecture, listeners instead hear five voices, ideally with different accents and intonations. Rather than having the information presented by a "voice-of-God" style of narration, as is common in a traditional documentary (both film and radio), having a small cast of readers ensures the audience process the information being read aloud through a series of characters with whom to identify. Many instances in the script use the first-person singular to heighten the intimacy between the speaker and the listener, as with the opening line when the voice representing Umm-Salama provocatively inquires of the audience, "How can you have forgotten me . . .?" Later in the series of narratives, with the account of Zuleikha Buransheva of a Soviet-controlled region of Central Asia, the listener is directly drawn into a confidential huddle through the words of her daughter who recounts:

> *After my mother, Zuleikha Buransheva, married in 1924, she found herself in a patriarchal Uzbek family, where she had all the responsibilities of a daughter-in-law . . . To end her slave-like existence, she left her husband, joined the Communist Party, and started working as a women's organizer in a silk-weaving cooperative, called an artel . . .* [2]

Finally, it was not enough to simply collect and narrativize the historical information on the lives of these women. It was necessary that contemporary women and men *hear* these stories; they arm the listener with the knowledge that women from Muslim backgrounds have a rich feminist history to be proud of and therefore serve as a potential source of self-empowerment. Especially in a global political climate that supports the portrayal of Muslim women as static, oppressed, and silent, it is nobody's responsibility but our own to correct these misconceptions. While it has become especially fashionable, particularly post-9/11, to write "about Muslim women" (and even though this may be done with the best of intentions) such projects are all too often sensationalistic accounts of the hardships suffered by women, such as polygamy and the veil. Furthermore, such hardships are seen to stem from Islam itself as a religious doctrine, without concomitant attention paid to the exploitation of religion for political goals. The *Great Ancestors* not only relates stories of independent and socially active Muslim women, but shows how many of these women were aware of such manipulations over a century ago. As stated by Bengali writer and educator Rokeya Hossain (1880–1932):

> *Whenever a woman has tried to raise her head, she has been brought down to her knees on the ground of either religious impiety or scriptural taboo . . . Men have always propagated such* [measures] *as edicts of God to keep us women in the dark . . .*[3]

Some women, such as the Javanese R.A. Kartini (1879–1904), were overtly critical of certain religiously sanctioned traditions, such as polygyny:

> *The Moslem law allows a man to have four wives at the same time. And though it be a thousand times over no sin according to the Moslem law and doctrine, I shall forever call it a sin . . .*[4]

Others, like Begum Sharifa Hamid Ali, of pre-Independence India, argued that some Islamic traditions were worth keeping. She drew up and circulated a model marriage contract which included the delegated right of divorce, a right she stated all women should have.

In the initial presentations of this material into the Feminism in the Muslim World Leadership Institute, the reactions of the participants testify to their astonishment at coming face to face with heroines from their own past who had hitherto been invisible to them:

> *The group as a whole felt empowered to be able to relate to powerful female figures and to identify potential role models who have emerged from their own cultures . . . Louisa Ait-Hamou from Algeria . . . initially felt she "did not believe in such an exercise," later told the group that, "I have just been re-connected with my history."*[5]

After the presentation, the participants in the institute related their own stories to each other of how they became interested in feminism, whether rooted in a negative experience in their childhood or in an inspiring woman in their own family. As studies with school children show, the telling of stories has the potential to foster a connection between the content of the tale and the individual lives of the listeners. The listeners identify with the voices and the stories they hear (and will identify with some segments more than others), and relate the content to their own personal or collective circumstances. Hearing the *Great Ancestors* in a collective setting is a more dynamic experience than the less interactive engagement of individual reading. Listeners are encouraged to ask questions about the material they have just heard and seen, to share other stories with the group, and ultimately to link these struggles of the past to their own current context. Not claiming to be definitive or all-inclusive, the script invites audiences to research other women of history, perhaps in their own regions or drawn from one's own area of expertise (medicine, law, literature, etc.).

The positive reaction to the *Great Ancestors* has been encouraging. The sheer volume and variety of people mentioned in the presentation ensures that through the narratives almost everyone learns about somebody new. Many are pleasantly surprised to learn that women were active so many centuries ago or that Muslim women were politically organized in areas such as sub-Saharan Africa. Listeners from non-Muslim communities have drawn parallels with their own histories. The Intercultural Grandmothers women's group of Saskatchewan, Canada told me that they were struck by the similarities between the *Great Ancestors* and the storytelling-as-therapy sessions they had organized in the local Métis and First Nations community. She described how the women attending these story-sharing circles told of their arduous experiences within the residential school system, a reality which is sanitized in traditional historical accounts. Being sidelined by the annals of recorded history was as acutely apparent in this community as in the cases of the women included in the *Great Ancestors*.

While the overall reception of the presentation has been largely positive, some criticisms arose when the script was performed in Farsi by a women's group in Iran. Participants noted the marked discrepancy between the age of the performers, many of whom were in their late teens and early twenties, and the content of certain first-person narratives which described much older women. Others voiced ideological criticisms from a secularist perspective, arguing that by representing these women within a framework of Muslim history the presentation privileged a religiously defined version of the past. The intent of the *Ancestors* is to show the diversity of these women's relationship to Islam. Some considerations had to be made in relation to religion; so as not to inflame orthodox sensibilities, the publication did not include any information considered too contentious in scriptural debates.

Political concerns such as these informed the selection process and shaped the vocabulary used to present these historical anecdotes. In recent years, oral tradition and storytelling have gained more acceptance as legitimate forms of presenting and preserving histories. Rather than "storytelling as history," however, the *Great Ancestors* offers "history as storytelling." Partly to bypass the stigma of written history as dull and laborious and partly to engage women—especially those operating in Muslim contexts—with their own histories, this project brings to life the voices, words, and images of women who have been relegated to the margins of traditional scholarship. No one else will recover these histories for us and without telling the stories of our foremothers to others we condemn them to be once again forgotten by history.[6]

Aisha Lee Fox Shaheed is a writer-researcher with a background in history, emphasizing gender, (post)colonialism, and historiography. She is an active networker for the transnational feminist solidarity network, Women Living Under Muslim Laws (WLUML). Her forthcoming publications include a chapter on the history of veiling in Muslim contexts and an analytical overview of the status of women and women's activism in Saudi Arabia.

Notes

1   Fatima Mernissi, *Hidden from History: The Forgotten Queens of Islam* (Lahore: ASR Publications, 1994), 116.

2   Farida Shaheed, *Great Ancestors: Women Asserting Rights in Muslim Contexts [Training Manual]* (Lahore: Shirkat gah, 2005), 114.

3   Rokeya Hossain, cited in Bharati Ray, *Early Feminists of Colonial India* (New Delhi: Oxford University Press, 2002), 63–4.

4   Raden Adjeng Kartini, cited in Kumari Jayawardena, *Feminism and Nationalism in the Third World*, 2nd ed. (Lahore: ASR, 1993), 61.

5   Anissa Hélie, *Feminism in the Muslim World Leadership Institutes: 1998 & 1999 Reports* (London: Center for Women's Global Leadership & Women Living Under Muslim Laws, 2000), 36.

6   The most recent Institute was held in Malaysia in 2007.

17

Creating a Forum
LGBTQ Youth and The Home Project *in Chicago*

MEGAN CARNEY

Zavier Hairsten (standing) and Amy Cornelius (seated); Michael Brasilow

How do we ask questions that don't divide?
How do we build bridges? I don't know.
How do we wake people up?
—Excerpt from *The Home Project*

I'm sitting in a bright, warm room at the Broadway Youth Center (BYC), a new drop-in center in Chicago for youth who are homeless and/or identify as lesbian, gay, bisexual, transgender, questioning, or queer (LGBTQ). The BYC, run by the Howard Brown Health Center, is a vibrant place where youth can get free health care, showers and clean clothes, compassionate counseling, and hot food. On this day, like every day, the place is bustling. I'm in a room with twenty adults who are settling in for a day of volunteer training.

My good friend, Joe, the manager of the BYC, asked me to gather a few youth to speak and I invited five remarkable youth leaders from About Face Youth Theatre, the program that I direct. They are sitting in a row as panelists at the front of the room. They are joking easily with the crowd and speaking about wanting adults to be "real" with them, to "just be yourself."

Then J., one of the youth leaders, someone I have grown very close to, tells a story. She came out to her parents over the holidays and told them that she had a girlfriend. The next night she woke up to hear her mother yelling the word "faggot" and she got scared, because she knew it was about her. This was not the first of the big fights and, tired of living in fear, J. was about to walk out for good when her dad convinced her to stay. The next morning, she went to the BYC to find out what her options might be if she left home.

The next speaker was a woman from the Night Ministry, a local organization that provides services and shelter to homeless youth and adults. She talked numbers:

There's an estimated 15,000 homeless youth each year in Chicago;
About 40% of them, approximately 6,000 of these youth identify as LGBT;
There are less than 100 beds in Chicago shelters designated for youth.
—Chicago Coalition for the Homeless

This is how theater projects start for me. I am going about my business when a question hauls back and punches me in the gut. Or maybe it's an idea that takes my breath away. Something rears up and demands my attention and in this moment I feel saddened by my friend's story, shocked by the numbers, and compelled to do something.

The question for me is "whose responsibility is this?" The idea that comes is to open up a public dialogue and performance about LGBTQ youth and homelessness and see what happens.

Home Base

About Face Theatre in Chicago was founded in 1995 to create plays representing gay and lesbian lives. In 1998, in the aftermath of Matthew Shepard's murder in Laramie, Wyoming and amidst national demonstrations against violence toward LGBTQ people, a team of artists, myself included, launched About Face Youth Theatre (AFYT) to give voice to emerging youth activists and investigate methods of creating new plays from oral histories. In the first year, a youth ensemble performed a five-week run of an original play, *First Breath*, and Chicago theater and activist communities rose up in support. The program quickly grew to include year-round leadership development and performance opportunities as well as touring shows. After six years the question emerged, how can AFYT remain relevant and vital in a pursuit of social justice? What's next? That's when I heard J.'s story.

The Home Project is a theatrical investigation of the issues around homelessness among LGBTQ youth and their allies. Developed through interviews, story circles, a theatrical laboratory process, multiple guest artists, and ongoing opportunities for civic dialogue, *The Home Project* yielded an original full-length play that premiered at Victory Gardens as part of About Face Theatre's 10th anniversary season in July 2006 and a touring show that is still in action.

The Home Project was created through multiple collaborations between artists, activists, social workers, philanthropists, and civic leaders. This group is diverse in sexual and gender identity, race, class, age, and ability and we value that diversity as a vital contribution to the work. As a director, playwright, and social activist, I'm interested in how relationships form through creative collaboration, in the ways we can include many voices in new play development, and how public performances can advance a social change movement. This chapter addresses some of the issues and events that emerged for me during the first phase of *The Home Project* process. I have included the voices of some of my collaborators, through their own writing or their co-authored text, throughout.

Project Design: Reflecting Values and Goals

Everything matters when people's true stories are involved. A lot of what I rely on as a "typical" theater production model gets me about halfway when it comes to making new plays in community collaborations. There is important work to be done in forming relationships with individuals and creating a production schedule that allows for multiple voices to be heard and various needs to be met throughout the process. For me, the measure of success includes how the work was made and who was in the room while we made it as well as the beauty and craft of the final artistic production and I believe it is possible to have it all.

Story Collection

I love sitting with people and listening to stories. I love how one person's story inspires another's, how people who think they have nothing to say suddenly find they can't shut up, and how much we can learn from and about each other through this simplest of acts. True stories provided the majority of the material for the script. Youth artists worked on how to use interview techniques of open and closed questions, building trust, and providing solid follow up. Together we determined which youth groups and individuals to reach out to around town and what types of stories we were seeking.

I kept reminding myself, and others, that the scope of our work was to investigate the issue of youth homelessness and raise awareness of our findings. As a theater company, we do not and never will have the resources to solve the problem of so many youth on the street, as hard as that is to admit. But by connecting with a partner organization that shared our goals, we thought we could have a larger impact on this issue. A partnership between AFYT and the Broadway Youth Center (BYC) that started years before was able to expand quickly in response to *The Home Project* idea. AFYT provided programming and a public forum for the issues while a BYC case manager attended every laboratory session, providing education and direct support for youth as well as necessary resources.

Lots of our story collecting took place at the BYC and being in that space allowed us to build relationships with many youth who were not able to commit to the rehearsal process and participate in the performances. The time we spent at the BYC also offered a glimpse of the complexity of the issues.

I met V. at the first workshop at the BYC. She had a very cool '80s style. She told me she had done a lot of theater in high school. It was near the end of the night and V. was about to read something she had just written about a bicycle and she was treating it like she thought it wasn't worth much. Then one of the case workers said, "Why don't you read that tree story from the other day? That was sort of about home." V. reached into her bag and pulled out a spiral-bound journal and read a story full of rich detail and strong images about the tree in her Gramma's front yard that she would run away to and disappear in when she was a child. It was a beautiful story. I told her how much I liked it and that I thought it would be a great addition for the show.

Weeks passed and V. didn't show up at the BYC. She had been staying in a local shelter, but now, no one knew where she was.

The next time I saw her, she had lost her bag with everything, including the journal with the tree story. As I told her she could always rewrite it for the show, I felt foolish. How could a play possibly matter to her? On her eighteenth birthday her mom told her she was tired of fighting and it was time for V. to pack her bags. How dare I ask for anything?

Weeks passed and the news came around that V. had moved to the suburbs to stay with her girlfriend's family. I let the story go.

Theatrical Laboratory

Twenty youth and six adults gathered five days a week for a month-long laboratory to explore the collected stories and prepare a workshop production to share with audiences.

Each meeting started with an exercise we call "The Candle." The group gathers in a circle and a candle is lit. As the candle is passed, each person verbally or silently "throws in" a distraction, which might be good or bad. Once the candle has made it around the circle, on the count of three, the candle, and our distractions, are extinguished. We return to the candle at the end of the session to take out something we value and will hold on to until we meet again. We came to rely on the candle as a way of entering the space and building community.

Many of the ensemble members had never been on stage before and so we integrated basic performance training for voice and body awareness into all of our meetings. We used a variety of techniques from improvisation, sculpting, gesture, and writing exercises that provided necessary skills while building movement vocabulary for the show. For example, if sculpting were used as a warm-up, it would then be applied to story material as a technique for adapting a scene for the stage.

I wanted the play to hold layers and complications that included not just the collected stories but also the ensemble's response to the stories and so we spent time talking about the gathered material as a way of finding intersections with our own lives. The diversity of the ensemble meant that sometimes the intersection was another story of homelessness and sometimes it was the realization that an individual had never really thought about homelessness before. The entire spectrum of responses had value and found their way into the script as narrative frames, as direct commentary, or as invented characters.

Writing exercises became an opportunity for more private reflection and resulted in ideas for new scenes or list poems that combined a line from each writer. "The Ideal World Dance" began as a writing exercise in response to the question, "What would an ideal world look like?" One line was selected from each writer and arranged into a poem. In performance, the spoken text was set to hip hop music with one person speaking the lyrics into a microphone while others performed a choreographed dance.

In a perfect world you could flirt with any cute guy you see and he'd be flattered and say thank you whether he's interested or not.

There would be no acne of any kind. There would be no viruses or deadly germs.

Loved ones would leave but always come back with presents in fancy paper.

No one would claim to love then turn + exclude + smash others down.

"Coming out" would not be an issue because you wouldn't have to be "in" in the first place.

You wouldn't be afraid to completely be yourself.

With humor and simplicity this excerpt demonstrates that basic rights and freedoms are often not available for LGBTQ youth. It was during this time that stories were pouring in, sometimes from surprising places.

*V. showed up at an ensemble meeting with her girlfriend looking healthy and happy. She couldn't do the show because of a new job, but she said, "Do you still want this?" She pulled out of her back pocket a small piece of paper ripped from a journal. At the top, in bold underlined letters, it read **GRAMMA'S TREE**. In blue ink, in the smallest writing I had ever seen, she had rewritten the story and offered it to the play.*

Up, way up in those branches, I felt like I could see everything . . . I found solace in those branches when someone died, when something changed, when I was hurt or alone or scared. Every child runs away at some point, to somewhere, usually not for very long. I ran away to the tree. I knew just how to sit in the branches, hugging the trunk, so anyone looking for me would have to stand directly below to see me. I knew the tree was listening. A year and a half after Gramma, Grampa passed away and my family sold the house. I lost my tree. One day, when I was still living at home, I asked my mom if we could drive over there.

In the story as the scene progresses, her mom drives her to the house where she encounters the new owner. She asks for permission to climb the tree, he hesitates, but agrees. In the play other actors join her in a dance with sound as she climbs.

All I felt was rough bark, strong branches, and happy memories. It was like everything good from my childhood was stored in the tree.

Civic Dialogue

Three youth who had previously participated in AFYT took on the role of the Youth Leadership Council. They engaged with an adult artist and facilitator to practice skills of posing open, provoking questions and leading large group discussions. This civic dialogue team practiced with the ensemble throughout the process and eventually designed a dialogue model for use with our workshop audiences. The questions and perspectives shared during the audience dialogues impacted our understanding of the show each night and will influence the ongoing development toward full production. Melanie, one of the youth facilitators, shared this account:

> When stories are shared, real people connect. In the post-show discussion, we created a space where social action begins, people in a room, where ... the spectators become actors themselves. When you know people's stories and feel the struggle in their journey, it's very difficult to deny the urge of wanting to connect with those stories and wanting to do something to support them.

Co-Authorship: Continuing to Listen

In the final week of our laboratory, it was time to start making firm decisions and I proposed to the group a running order of our multiple stories, songs, connective pieces. We ran through the show in this order and then sat to discuss my proposal. One story of a young man's journey, which we named "Traveler" had been challenging us more than the others. Our protagonist was unable to settle in any shelter or with his family and he was running out of time because at twenty-one years of age, he would no longer be eligible for certain state resources. Through the weeks, we had spent hours in conversation about our nomad's predicament and even more hours trying to embody the story for performance. We used image theater techniques from Boal to animate group sculptures in attempts to recreate the mysterious landmarks in the Traveler's journey. We also edited through nearly twenty pages of dense narrative in search of his theatrical voice.

On this day in our rehearsal process, as we discussed the order, one person reported feeling there was an awkward leap from the "Traveler" story into the "Ideal World" (described above). I agreed but argued that a sharp contrast was exactly what we need at that moment to build momentum and re-enforce the complexity of the issues. Then someone else spoke up and agreed with the sense of disconnect, then another and another and it was clear I held a minority opinion.

This was a challenging moment for me. I was worried about running out of time. We needed a decision fast so the show had time to gel before we got our first audience. But I also knew that we hadn't yet arrived at the best idea. It was true that I was tired and I had spent a good deal of time arranging the order. But it was also true that in my work with this ensemble so far, all of the perfect answers had resided somewhere within the group. The moment demanded that I set my director's ego aside and facilitate. I could almost feel the different hat settle on my head. "It sounds like we have different opinions about this. Let's figure it out." With the words barely out of my mouth, ideas came flying. We sat and talked until we were done and in the end, we were all in agreement.

We needed to interrupt our own play and share this complication with our audience.

We were telling very sensitive stories and were very careful not to dramatize them as sad, emotionally devastating events to be relived in the theater. We wanted to alert our audience to the injustices within the stories and leave questions unanswered so that we could have a lively discussion afterwards. Out of this motivation, we decided to directly address the audience in this moment of disjuncture in the play, drawing on Brecht's ideas of alienation, we approached the dilemma from a rational standpoint rather than relying on our emotional responses. We asked people to *think* rather than *feel* their way through the situation.

This is the end of the Traveler scene, after our protagonist has bounced from practically every social service agency in the city and exhausted all family connections.

Interviewer:	The Department of Human Services needs some form of ID to help you.
Traveler:	Don't have one.
Interviewer:	We can get started with a social security number.
Traveler:	Don't have one.
Interviewer:	Oh.

R. enters and listens.

Traveler:	What about the housing lists?
Interviewer:	All housing lists are full.
Traveler:	Of course. That's alright.
Interviewer:	But that doesn't give you any shelter to go to.
Traveler:	Yeah, well, people aren't meant to live in shelters.

The lights come up on the audience. R. addresses the audience.

R: We all want him to figure it out, don't we? We spent a lot of time talking about this as an ensemble because we were confused. Why couldn't he stop moving? ... But the thing is, shelters are scary places. You are physically at risk in a shelter. If you're queer or transgender, it's even worse ... the shelter can't guarantee your safety.

R., as interrupting narrator, goes on to explain Survival Skills 101—dumpster diving, tricking, squatting—the skills you learn on the street.

R: How do I know this? I've been homeless, I've been in shelters, on the streets. And I know I'm not the only one in here ... so, why is he still on the streets? It's the only way he can stay in control . . . Pride. It's the one thing people with a home think homeless people don't have, but it's the one thing homeless youth hold on to more than anything else.

R. spoke the ideas of the ensemble, and of his own experience, and filled in the gap.

Social Change: From the Inside Out

The Home Project methodology works to mobilize social change in two ways. Sharing stories builds trust and internal strength within the ensemble by inviting each person to step outside of his/her own experiences. There is also a magical alchemy that occurs with storytelling in that the more details the teller reveals, the more the listener identifies. Specificity triggers memories and images for the listener from their own experience. By the time the ensemble had adapted and embodied each other's stories, deep, familial bonds had formed among us and this infused the work with a sense of shared ownership. Is it too simple to propose that for the person with a home, homelessness no longer feels so removed; for the homeless person, their experience is valued and validated?

With the addition of the audience, social change is mobilized through participation in a public event. *The Home Project* does not offer a prescription for ending homelessness. Rather, in the face of despair and potential paralysis, *The Home Project* creates opportunities for individuals to take action. Perhaps Melanie says it best:

> Sometimes you don't know what kinds of statements you are making or the theory behind them until you see it played out, put into action, and accepted into a community. We as actors and activists found our own voices to end the silence and the civic dialogue after the show was a chance for the spectators to embrace the voices, connect with them, and find ways to take action and help in taking responsibility for the homeless youth in their community.

Taking responsibility can look like many things. One person might stop judging homeless people they pass on the street, another might write to their representative and start a local campaign, and someone else pulls out a checkbook. Each is a positive step forward.

On the last night, V. came to see the play. We were all nervous. Her story launched the play and now contained not only direct excerpts from her writing but a gestural dance. During the audience dialogue her story was mentioned and V. raised her hand and said proudly, "That's my story" and she stood while the audience applauded.

Some of the youth have stayed in touch with me through e-mail, some still work with About Face Theatre and the BYC. But I don't know where V. is now. I don't know where a lot of them are.

In the room, during the first phase of *The Home Project*, and then through the second year, with additional ensemble members and more audiences, as we made the play, then as the play was happening, and always when the audience joined in by standing up, sharing their outrage, their sorrow, a desire for change, I had the sense that change was happening. How do we measure the long-term impact of such an experience? I know that the process of making and the experience of seeing the show changed the lives of many individuals who have written me beautiful letters and e-mails. I know it changed mine. I am less afraid of homelessness and more angry about it. I am more open to the world I live in and I believe even more strongly in the power of the arts. For the people who need numbers, I don't have more impressive statistics to share. But I do know this. One young woman who is a bold and brave social worker in Chicago, a storyteller for *The Home Project*, just finished the business plan to roll out a foster care program for homeless youth who identify as LGBT. It would be the first ever. She says *The Home Project* helped build the momentum to get it done, to get other people on board. And she reminds me, big change, real change, takes time.

The Home Project premiered at Victory Gardens Theater in Chicago in July 2006. Scripts and touring shows are now available nationwide. Special thanks to Randall Jenson, Melanie Stinson, and Jessie Sanjurjo for personal contributions to this chapter.

Megan Carney is a founding director of About Face Youth Theatre where her work as a writer, director, and educator contributed to eight critically praised original plays. She continues to create plays and public art projects within community contexts around the country and can be reached at mcarney3@gmail.com

References and Further Reading

Boal, A. (1992). *Games for Actors and Non-Actors*. New York: Routledge.
Brecht, B. (1957). *Brecht on Theatre: the Development of an Aesthetic*. Frankfurt am Main: Suhrkamp Verlag.
About Face Youth Theatre: www.aboutfacetheatre.com
Broadway Youth Center: www.howardbrown.org
The Night Ministry: www.thenightministry.org

18
From Storytelling to Community Development
Jaghori, Afghanistan

WAHID OMAR

At the Afghan Academy, Chel Bughtu, District of Jaghori, Afghanistan; Wahid Omar

The way to Jaghori was a bumpy one. Twelve hours of snow-packed dirt roads through the rugged, spectacular Hindu Kush, into the heart of Afghanistan.

It was March 2005. A few days before, I'd boarded a plane in Denver, Colorado, where my home and life were finally established after my exile. In 1978, at 19, I fled from Afghanistan, just before the Soviet invasion. Now, I was president of Afghans4Tomorrow, a non-profit humanitarian organization based in the United States and involved with myriad projects to help in the reconstruction of a nation devastated by twenty-three years of war. My trip to Jaghori, a remote region located in the north of Ghazni Province, was intended to assess and observe literacy courses organized by local communities with the support of an American non-governmental organization, Future Generations.

Jaghori is populated by Hazaras, an ethnic group believed by some to be descendents of Genghis Khan, the thirteenth-century Mongol invader. The Hazaras have been persecuted for hundreds of years by Afghanistan's Pashtun majority and their suffering only worsened during the recent two decades of war. In his bestselling novel, *The Kite Runner*, Khaled Hosseini gives a harrowingly accurate description of the level of maltreatment the Hazara people have undergone.

Afghanistan's long wars—from 1978 to 2001—destroyed not only a country (with more than two million dead and twice as many displaced), but also transformed the age-old art of storytelling. Across the years, the arts were targeted by conservative groups such as the Taliban, who hounded and executed *rawis*—traditional storytellers—Sufis, poets, artists, and musicians, among others, thus nearly extinguishing Afghanistan's rich, irreplaceable artistic traditions. Storytelling, an ancient art form conveying fairy tales, folklore, legends, myths, and religious epics, has become a rare commodity and the *rawi* is almost extinct.

Yet the *need* to tell tales has not died and cannot be extinguished. Today, every Afghan has become a storyteller, and every Afghan has a story to tell. During long nights, at home or over tea in the *chaikhana*s, men and women recollect their experiences, often telling the same horror stories again and again with deep passion and persistence, demanding that listeners bear witness to those dark moments in history. The great stories of Afghanistan's past are not entirely forgotten, but war, terror, personal losses, and small victories have become new and additional themes of interaction between people. Throughout Afghanistan, the magical wonders of fairy tales seem to have been overwhelmed by narratives of the dreadful realities of war. Yet in the process of sharing their accounts, their mutual experiences, Afghans—tribes, villages, and families separated by bombs, landmines, and warlords—are unconsciously rebuilding communities and helping to heal profound psychological problems. Oral traditions have many functions, including as safety valves to relieve tensions caused by oppression and venting a society's animosities as well as expressing its aspirations.

We arrived at sunset in the beautiful village of Sange Mashi, in Jaghori, where we were greeted and fed by the villagers, with typical generosity. We discussed the area's problems and educational challenges with the village elders. Professional teachers refuse to relocate to such an isolated place. Seventh grade girls, therefore, are teaching the first graders. My objectives and those of Future Generations were to explore how best we could help these adolescent, self-made teachers.

My early experiences with storytellers around Afghanistan, as well as my instincts, led me to believe that a non-traditional storytelling approach could be an effective tool toward improving the lives and strengthening the confidence of these young female teachers. The next day, after discussing the matter with Dr. Carl Taylor, founder of Future Generations and co-author of the book *Just and Lasting Change*, I proposed using storytelling as a matrix not only to identify problems concerning the community but to resolve them.

Storytelling is not merely an antiquated art form. Worldwide, in its various manifestations, it is a normal part of modern life. Our everyday speech, our conversations with our neighbors and friends are all storytelling performances. Whether the stories are situational or told by professionals, I believed that there was surely a way to use stories to further community development.

In order to discover whether there was any opportunity to use storytelling for community development in Jaghori, we needed to interview our clients and set the ground. Our first assessment session for one of Future Generation's

Inside the classroom; Wahid Omar

literacy courses took place in the village of Deh Kona, with a population of about 1,500 and an average family size of ten. Eighteen female students, between the ages of fourteen and sixteen, were enrolled in Deh Kona's three-month-long literacy course. Most came from a village sixty miles away, accompanied by male relatives. The girls and their male relatives stayed in a makeshift educational center where they studied, ate, and slept.

Their teacher, Shirin Jan, was an eighth grader, only a little less shy than her students. She was about sixteen years of age and her students seemed to enjoy her presence. I started to question her students and one of them caught my attention. Adela, fourteen years old, dressed in colorful traditional dress, was small, black hazelnut eyed, and very swift. Our dialogue started this way:

How is the course going?
—It's going well.
Do you like studying?
—Yes.
What do you hope to accomplish at the end of your training?
—To go back to my village and to teach others about what I learned.
Being far from home for so long is not a problem?
—Yes, but we have no choice.
What do you study?
—We study how to read and we also study health skills.
Why do you study?
—No answer.
What do you do for hobbies?
—No answer.
What do you boys do for hobbies? (The question was addressed this time to their male relatives.)
—We play volley ball.
(Back to the girls.)
The cloth you are wearing, is it your own product?
—Our family bought them.
Your male relatives are playing volley ball for hobbies. What about you girls, what do you do?
—We tell stories and have fun telling them to each other.
What kind of stories?
—All kinds.
Are they stories you heard from your parents or grandparents?
—Some yes. We tell each other fairy tales and other stories.

Perhaps Adela was silent when I asked her why she was studying because she just didn't know what to answer. To her, the question was probably redundant because I had already asked her about what she was hoping to accomplish. At the end of her studies, she's going back to her village to help others, and that's what matters. The reality is that most of these young girls will go back to their village and will get married soon because of their age, and thus preserve their thousand years old tradition and culture.

Also, my question had been loaded with our Western vision and our ideas about equal opportunities for men and women and a better future for women. This vision for girls like Adela became especially fervent in the West, when the Taliban were ousted from power, even though our worries about women seem forgotten nowadays.

Adela's second silence, when I asked about her hobbies, was a "cultural silence." Adela probably felt that in asking about her hobbies, I was breaching good manners. After all, I was a stranger. My status required her to be silent in such a social encounter, until trust was established.

When Adela told me that girls told stories to each other in their free time, this pierced me like a sharp arrow, and I seized this excellent opportunity to inquire more about the nature of stories they told one another. I learned that the local families regularly told stories during or outside of their working time. This conversation and others led to a breakthrough project at the collective level in Jaghori changing the lives of an entire community.

The project, which I call The Dialogue, took shape as events unfolded. First, I proposed a literary contest to the girls. I was interested in beginning by encouraging these young teachers to think of themselves as important story-tellers. I asked them to write a fictional or non-fictional story, to recall a story of the past (such as a fairy tale, though not necessarily), or to create their own fictional narrative. The winner would receive a non-monetary prize, *The Poems of Hafiz*, but all the girls would receive some prize for writing. The criterion for winning first prize was to combine originality, creativity, and literacy, depending on the type of story. The girls were cautioned not to seek help from others and were asked to send their work to my office in Kabul, where a panel of three judges would determine the winner.

The twenty stories we received were mixtures of fairy tales, poems, and creative writing, all part of the oral tradition repertoire in Afghanistan. I was surprised by the level of literacy of these young contestants. It was way above the average in Afghanistan. They were able to write their stories, sometimes very eloquently, adding a touch of their own imaginations to recreate a once-told story. Apparently, the lack of arable land and the harsh weather in Jaghori provided a unique opportunity for these young girls to tell each other stories all year long. Ironically, persecution by the Pashtuns who forced these people to live in such a bleak, secluded area turned them into storytellers and writers armed with knowledge and education. These young girls were indeed "story-tellers." They could perform orally, and now it was clear, they could also write beautiful stories.

These beautiful stories often combined "the real" with fiction. The people of Jaghori, including these adolescent girls, had faced many forms of adversity, including the Taliban. Like millions of Afghans, they, too, were seeking ways to defeat the enemy. What better way than storytelling to identify yourself as the "hero," carrying a heavy burden through a daunting quest, to find a better day and a happy ending? What better way to overcome the persecution of an entire ethnic group, the Hazaras, than to identify yourself as a powerful hero? A good example is the story by one of our young contestants, in which a powerful money lender and warlord persecutes villagers and commits crimes. The true identity of the warlord is never revealed, but references like "police" and "governor" indicate the story is a real one, a recent event embedded in a fairy tale. The image of the traditional monster, dragon, and other beasts in fairy tales was replaced by the image of the warlord, reminding us about the sad realities of Afghanistan. The story is a constant struggle between a Hazara hero and a powerful warlord and his sons. This writer, like many of the young authors, wrote about injustice and racism in her stories. After many vicissitudes, the story ends with the defeat of the evil warlord and justice is done. Our young Hazara storyteller uses a critical discourse in her story in order to counteract the mainstream Pashtun and Tajik discourse that degrades and belittles her people.

For the young storywriters, storytelling also has the potential to relieve their boredom, as they live day to day, caught in the monotonous chores of the household. The story is a dream, a way to talk about that hero, that young prince, who will one day rescue them. These young girls identify themselves with the stunning princesses in the stories. They also imagine the hero who will rescue them in real life. For the young Hazara girls in Jaghori, this will be a rich Hazara boy coming back from exile. Since the region is so desolate, a combination of wars and economic hardship forced young Hazara boys to live as refugees in Iran and Pakistan for many years. Hope for a better future and a proper suitor is one of the motivations for these juvenile storytellers, as they continue the tradition of crafting heroic tales.

As I read the young teachers' stories, I was struck by one in particular, in which real and disturbing events were inserted into a fairy tale. In this story, a poor woodcutter lives with his wife, who is mute. They both work very hard only to receive meager incomes with which they must feed their children and support a widow in their village. After many praises and lengthy declarations about the role of charity in an Islamic society, God magically changes their fate and restores the woman's speech. The woodcutter is also rewarded and becomes very rich. The couple lives happily ever after.

As I was about to put the story aside, I noticed that there was more. Curiously, a third page, which was not really a postscript, appeared where our young author had shifted the story, now praising education and enumerating the benefits of knowledge. With no transition at all, she was now telling her own story, an old technique in traditional literature, inserting something "real" into the arena of the "story." The girl wrote about her make-shift school, her classmates, and the teacher. She complained that the teacher called the students names. She expressed her sadness to be called "donkey," "sheep," and "cow." This, she noted, was contrary to Education.

In the girl's first story the moral was expressed with a beautiful poem at the end, where death does not distinguish between poor and rich. The second "story" ended with a metaphorical sentence, in which she compared students with the foundation of society in general: if the foundations of a society are bad, then its buildings will not last long. Clearly, the girl compared the teacher to a mason not doing his job properly. By creating this story, the young story-teller was asking for help, trying to relieve herself and her classmates from an ongoing pressure and disappointment. I later found out that it was common practice for teachers in the region to mistreat their students and this young girl was only revealing the symptoms of a much larger problem, which was the lack of teacher training in the region.

In both instances, the need for a hero to save the students from this kind of treatment and the name-calling and abuse by teachers became the priority themes in our Dialogue with this community. It was apparent that teachers all over Jaghori, who for many reasons had themselves never been trained, needed intensive guidance. It was also evident that protecting and sustaining the tradition of storytelling will bolster the self-confidence of these young girls and will also help them heal.

As of today, the first part of the Dialogue project, the teacher-training component, is ongoing as I write and has already borne fruit. Having paid close attention to the storytelling skills of the girls—and to the content of their stories—we decided that a local institution was needed to carry out our mission and objectives, which were, essentially, to improve and serve the lives of our young teachers, as well as to provide confident teachers for the very young children. After a year of collecting data, asking for grants, and subsequent trips to the area, the Afghan Academy project was conceptualized and founded in November, 2005. The village of Chel Bughtu, district of Jaghori, is now the site for a brand new building with classrooms, a dormitory, and a kitchen. The Academy is training young female teachers and their male relatives in education, health skills, and vocational programs. The Academy will use non-traditional pedagogical methods such as storytelling, so that communities can educate their young. This project will establish the first of a projected twenty small, regional campuses, all over Afghanistan.

The Dialogue method—developing interactions that identify the strengths of the community, in this case, the strengths of the girls, and figuring out how their strengths could be used in service of the community—was a logical way to address community development challenges in war-ravaged Afghanistan. The fact is that storytelling is still alive and vital in this country, despite the fact that the venerated art of the *rawi* has been severely compromised everywhere, especially in places such as Kabul, where people suffered the most and where culture was most threatened.

Practitioners of community development know that the one of the best methods to learn what people are thinking about is to listen to their stories. Listening to and reading through stories while knowing where we are—being aware of our cultural, physical, and spiritual environment—is a formidable way to imagine new approaches to solving community problems. Here, in Jaghori, storytelling helped address problems related to the community's need for teachers and for justice.

As long as we have storytellers and stories, we have a powerful resource for developing projects and dialogues within communities. Fighting poverty, illiteracy, and injustice requires innovative and non-traditional approaches for development. Speaking with young girls in Jaghori, learning about their commitment to storytelling, and then reading their stories so profoundly inspired by the legacy of traditional storytellers, we were able to construct a solid basis—the Afghan Academy—for recognizing and employing the community's young women and for serving the district today.

Wahid Omar was born in the Afghan capital of Kabul. In 2005, under his leadership at the University of Kabul, forty-five projects were implemented in Afghanistan ranging from building schools and community centers, teacher training, water improvement projects, micro lending, to humanitarian aid and relief efforts. He has won many awards for his teaching and writing and collects Afghan folklore. His Ph.D. is in Oral Tradition and Community Development and will be completed in 2008.

References

Hosseini, K. (2003). *The Kite Runner*. New York: Riverhead Books.
Taylor-Ide, D. and Taylor, C. (2002). *Just and Lasting Change: When Communities Own Their Futures*. Baltimore, MD: Johns Hopkins University Press.

19
Sins Invalid
Disability, Dancing, and Claiming Beauty

PATTY BERNE

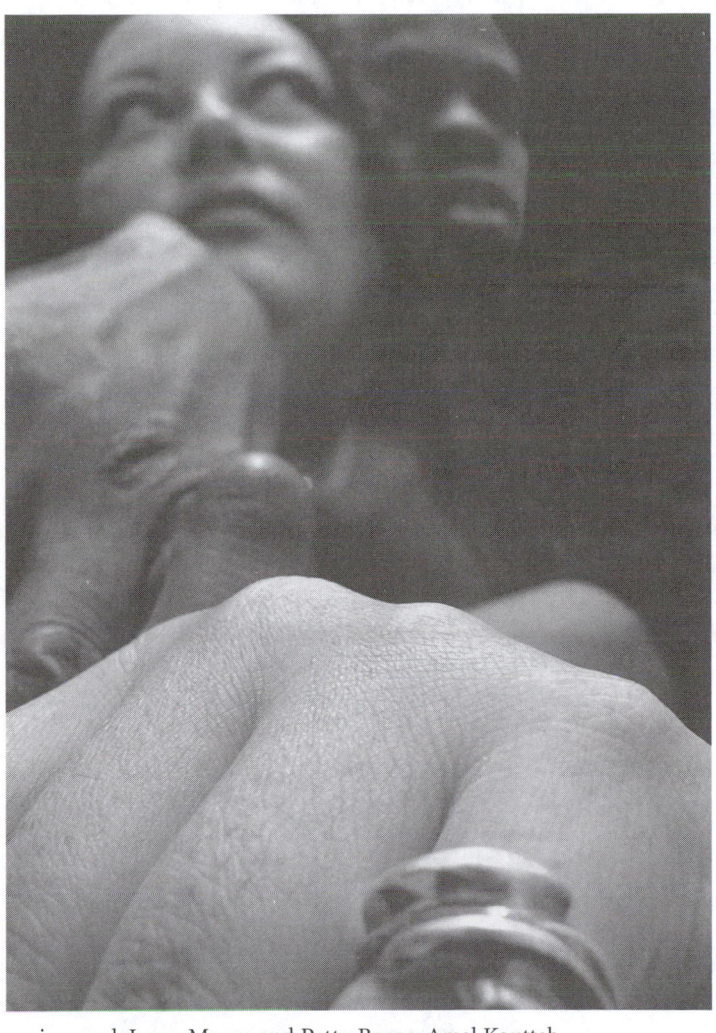

Two peas in a pod: Leroy Moore and Patty Berne; Amal Kouttab

Like many good stories, the early threads of this one were woven over dinner, a large bowl of saffron-laced *paella*, steaming on the table between two good friends. Leroy Moore and I were excited over his recent collaboration with Todd Herman—a film entitled *Forbidden Acts* that intertwines Leroy's randy poetry with tasteful yet explicit cock and body shots—*and* sharing dismay that most people can't seem to conceive that people with disabilities are sexual, let alone sexy.

> my forehead pressed hard against the cool wall
> sweat slips across the base of my neck
> leaving a salty trail for your tongue to track
> should you choose to follow.
>
> i inhale slowly in synch with your fingers' penetration.
>
> your wrist corkscrews circles getting smaller
> a zen garden in my flesh
> and i am pinned by your round shoulder to the wall and i open
> my mouth to taste plaster breathing
> you a wordless whimper of ecstasy.
>
> you hiss into my ear that i am a good puppy girl
> open all the way for you my cunt my heart my ass my mouth my mind
> everything
> open to your fucking vulnerable and so wanting.
>
> a knuckle presses the base of my hole and you uncurl a third finger up
> between my walls and you begin to thrust and i begin to chant your
> name daddy
> daddy please feed me daddy
> and you do filling me with a deep breathless undulating fuck
> each push taking more and your arm begins to pound.
>
> my mind spins a cacophony of screams to the meter of your voice
> because here is your sweet girl sweet girl sweet girl tighter
> good whore daddy's whore pretty whore tighter
> little toy fuck toy baby toy squeeze touch
> touch there daddy please scratch there there please and i am spread
> open pumping you stretched out needing you moan i push ignite ignite
> we ignite to
> catch pulses pulses it pulses and i catch
> fire branded and i

come to you
alive
with awe.

—patty berne
sins invalid 2006

We've both been disabled since birth, and bluntly, we're both pretty hot, and we both humbly know it. Still, every day throughout the day we each struggle with the disconnect between what we know to be true about our beauty and the passion of our lives, and what the world seems to believe, that we are less than, undesirable, pitiable . . . it's hard, to know that you have been blessed while others seem convinced you've been cursed.

Leroy F. Moore, Jr.
Excerpt from *Swimming against the Stream*
Sins Invalid 2006

Mmm, my sperm
here it comes
watch out!

My sperm has history swimming against the stream
My sperm has been rejected, feared, studied and labeled
dangerous by the mainstream
My sperm has caused scientists to write books
Politicians to write laws
Doctors to write prescriptions
My sperm put the fear in Charles Darwin, slave masters and Hitler
My sperm has women running to the doctors

My sperm has been swimming against the stream

My sperm gave birth to the eugenics movement
My sperm is in test tubes marked "DAMAGED!"
My sperm has been swimming in deep shark infested waters
My sperm, you think could cause one, two or worse a whole
generation like me . . .

So, being an activist and an organizer, we did what we know how to do—organize. And a performance event on sexuality and disability was in the process of being born—*Sins Invalid: An Unshamed Claim to Beauty In the Face of Invisibility.*

Well, truth be told, at first it was going to be a small video screening for a few friends in a local café . . . and our early working title still conjures up images of bloody puddles in my mind. But the universe often offers unexpected gifts, in this case manifesting as our friends and veteran artists Todd Herman and Amanda Coslor. We told them about our idea and they offered to collaborate, contributing massively toward the aesthetics, contacts, available resources, and experience. *Sins Invalid* then had a dedicated core group, moreover, a family. And to top it off, we then had a fiscal sponsor—The Dancing Tree.

But, let's backtrack for a second—what's so innovative about this show?

Well, besides the obvious "*have **you** ever been to an erotic event featuring people with disabilities?*", let's take a look at the context in which we live. We know that our culture maintains embodied and enforced "norms," norms that constrict all of us with unmet expectations and fears of the repercussion of not "measuring up." Regardless of where we identify on the spectrum of sexuality, gender, size, ability, age, class, etc., the boundaries of our normalcy get policed. And when we transgress boundaries by having different abilities, gender presentation, etc., we are at risk of social and economic alienation, hostility, threats to safety/violence, and the deepest acts of dehumanization—the implied and at times explicit message being that "***they***" (insert any oppressed group here—people with disabilities, African descended people, poor people, immigrants without state documentation, and so on . . .) are a different kind of human, "***they***" don't feel or think as we do, "***they***" don't deserve what we have, "***they***" are less than we are.

To bring the issue to the body, the definition of the "normal" body is becoming ever narrower, to the extent that even the natural process of growth and aging is seen as a problem to overcome. People with disabilities are often seen as "flawed" beings whose hope of normalcy rests in the "medical model."

Hold up—you gotta trust that this tangent into political framing is central to the telling of the story, OK? Cool.

The "medical model" is a way of looking at a person with a disability. The "problem" resides in that person's body, and the solution is to "fix," cure, or in some way modify that disabled person to fit into existing conditions and frameworks.

Hhhmmm . . . there's something missing in this medical model . . . can it be an analysis of power?

The disability rights movement articulated another lens of viewing disability—the social model. With this view, we understand that the "problem" resides in sociopolitical and economic structures which exclude an array of people and abilities, and the solution is social and institutional change.

This should resound familiar with folks from a social justice perspective. But still let's make sure we're clear. Let's say I go to a building which has stairs; my wheelchair does not climb stairs. Is the problem that I cannot walk up stairs? Or is the problem that the building owner and architect did not create a building which allows entrance to people with a variety of means of mobility? Is the problem my body? Or is the problem being excluded because my body is different from the building owner's?

As people with disabilities, we are not oppressed by what we can or cannot do with our bodies or minds. We are oppressed by the systemic prejudice, discrimination, segregation, and violence we face because we do not fall within a perceived "norm."

And the real irony is none of us does.

As social justice advocates, we know there must be avenues for resistance to oppression and celebration—and here is the power of Sins Invalid. We challenge dominant notions of the disabled body and sexuality because we understand it is key to challenging the oppression of people with disabilities; moreover, our performers offer stories and visions affirming our strength as people with disabilities, creating beauty in which we are centered.

So, meanwhile, back to our laptops and cell phones, we had a show to create—yowza!

Leroy, Amanda, Todd, and I began meeting in my tiny plant-filled living room to plan the show. A call to artists was placed and by the end of an arduous selection process we had a phenomenal group of artists defying norms, committed to speaking their truths about their bodies, their desires, their visions for the world, and—not surprisingly given who we are—folks were mostly brown and black, mostly queer and genderqueer, 100 percent compelling.

Powerful people with stories to teach—from hatakni 'ron daniella, Angolan in ancestry and living genderqueer with multiple disabilities, storytelling about his childhood masturbation before he slowly strips to the deep thud of a triphop track to reveal his sinewy body and a ten inch dildo—to mixed race crone-to-be solidad decosta delivering spoken word on living intersexed with eye contact so direct it burned the seat cushions; from dignified and flirtatious Lee Williams, an African American man perched in his wheelchair and in his 7th decade of life entering the stage and baring his

> *heart with the grace earned only through experience—to shy smiling Noemi Sohn describing the sexual and comic tensions of her first kiss in her home country of the Philippines while swaying to Marvin Gaye in the meter of cerebral palsy; from spirit infused Lisa Thomas-Adeyemo recanting poem, vignette and song in sensual mahogany tones—to Ron Jones, deeply thoughtful and artful moving in his meditative recreation of sunset skinny dipping; from fierce femme Leah Rae "spittin' poetry like fire, upliftin' . . ." to Lady Venus in full "fat 'n fabulous" burlesque glory as the MC.*
>
> *And that wasn't even the video artists—Todd Herman, Thanh Diep, Leroy Moore, Oriana Bolden, John Killacky and myself.*

Next, we had to develop the look of a show which was simultaneously erotic and communicating resistant politics. It turned out to be easier than one might think, because people claiming their bodies and desires for liberation are tender and powerful and fierce—and that's sexy.

A central part of our process was leadership development. As a whole, the progressive left in the U.S. has not addressed its ableism, making itself less than hospitable to people with disabilities (ableism is a set of practices and beliefs, embedded in institutions, which privileges people without disabilities and reinforces that non-disabled people maintain power). Regrettably, the radical left has not done much better. At the same time, to quote Ann Pointon and Chris Davies, in their preface to Millee Hill's essay "Black and Disabled in the Arts," "The disability world contains the same schisms, 'isms' and inequalities that exist in society generally, and the world of disability arts is no exception in reflecting institutional racism."[1] We saw and continue to see Sins Invalid as a place where people with disabilities can incubate a radical political analysis and their skills as artists, particularly those who don't see themselves represented in the ranks of disability rights/disability culture/disability studies due to race, class, gender presentation, etc.

Given this priority, our process looked like a hybrid between a community-based organization and a performance—facilitated meetings where we shared updates about the show as a whole, performed for each other to hone the on-stage work, and engaged in political discussions about our message; one on ones between performers and Leroy Moore or myself to support the process of disclosing both personally and politically on stage—after all, folks were exposing both their bodies and souls; and, for a performance event, a great deal of collective decision-making . . . that is until "tech."

Tech was, well, in my opinion . . . hell. The only thing that got us through it was the trust that had developed, the collective commitment of the group, and the intermittent splash of brilliance. But it was still wildly stressful. Things had to be done, and decisions made—quickly. It didn't help that many folks, including me, were learning what one does during tech as we went along (design the show in the theater space; coordinate lights, sound, and performer cues amongst all tech operators).

Note to reader: event organizing and running a performance are two very different beasts!

Nor did it help that, given cost, we had a tech **day**. Lots of people have a tech **week**. There were last minute coordination mishaps between the theater's technical director and the lighting interns from the local high school. We had equipment failures, including last minute projector freezing and mics not working. Leroy injured his back moving a table, a performer showed up ill, a minor conflict between personalities erupted . . . it was wild.

And, when the lights went down and a hush went through the audience, the magic unfolded. Three hundred people witnessed disabled artist after disabled artist, talking about desire, displaying our bodies and doing it in a way where **we** were setting the terms of engagement. We moved the audience through a new paradigm, with emotions in the theater shifting from voyeuristic eroticism to intimacy to loss to anger to risk to aroused by a new vision of embodiment.

It was beautiful. Sacred for some. A healing happened in that theater. Artists boldly claimed their bodies as whole and perfect, inviting others to join, and they did. The love in the room was palpable. The respect was visceral. In hindsight it's hard to explain—but I think most transformations are. At the show's close, we had a sustained standing ovation. For the night, we were done.

As I'm sure many organizers out there know, right after the magnetism of an event, there's an equal and opposite push away from the intensity, a required respite, which can feel like emptiness. There's a loss—there's so much syn/energy in the centrifuge of an event that after the motor stops . . . well, there's a deflation. Which is why, partly for political process and partly for emotional closure, we held debriefs . . . We debriefed and heard pluses and deltas from performers. We held a separate debrief for our logistics people, Ann Icardi and Maurice Campbell. And as a core group, Leroy, Amanda, Todd, and I debriefed, processed and processed some more, identifying what we were proud of, what frustrated us, and what we would do differently if there were ever a next time. And then, in the weeks following, we received feedback from friends who'd seen the show. People said they were surprised that a show on disability and sexuality could be so hot. On the web, we found people with disabilities who'd been in the audience blogging about us. Scholars in disability studies approached us. And it became clear, our impact wasn't just on that night—we had made a lasting impression on people. We had asked people to think and it seems that people did.

Solidad DeCosta
Excerpt from *intersexed is how it intersects*
Sins Invalid 2006

I don't think you can handle my body!
my curves swerve like a bat outta hell
and my lines define something mixed
you see, I am different—not just reddish
brown mixed-race different or pansexed dyke
different, for while all those things are a
part of me, they are not all of me/there's more/

When I was born, I was whole
My body reflected the realities of both Hermes
and Aphrodite . . .

No longer full of shame or dread, I am whole again,
and my scars just mark the path to my past
and the rest is just facts which is not the same as truth
because if the medical definition of your biology
is the only reality, where does that leave me?
For I do not consent to my invisibility, I shatter
the glass freak cage and tell it on the mountain
my fountain is receptive, my news is representative
and my life is anything but done . . .

So, after a month or two hiatus, we started the process again, but this time with a few changes, including a longer timeline.

One important piece of feedback we heard was the need for points of entry into the process. (Of course there were volunteer opportunities on the night of the show, but clearly that's rather limited.) So in Spring 2007 we facilitated a series of writing and performance workshops for people with disabilities, and we expect to facilitate two workshop series in 2008. The organizational process around the performance is another component with which we'd like to engage community members, so in 2008 we hope to seed an internship program.

A commitment made after last year's event was to pursue foundation funding. AEPOCH Foundation expressed a strong belief in our vision, and started us off on a solid footing. With those funds we hired development consultant extraordinaire Elaine Beale, who pitched hard and we've now received additional grants from the San Francisco Arts Commission, the Zellerbach Family Fund, Hewlett Packard Foundation, Potrero Nuevo Foundation, and the Rainbow Grocery Collective.

With the additional funding, we're running the show two nights this year, with a serious crew—a stage manager, assistant stage manager, and lighting designer.

And the show this year—it's another full on production, with ten live performers and three video artists. We have artists coming to perform from around the U.S. and one artist flying in from France. We are in the thick of it; in fact, this text is being written fifty-three days until the show. We can't describe the show quite yet as it has yet to happen, but we can predict that it will change people's perceptions on disability and sexuality, and hopefully lead into deeper political shifts.

We believe deeply in our work, our process, and our politic. We've gained strength from Audre Lorde, Paul Robeson, Eli Clare, Marlon Riggs, Otto Rene Castillo, Millee Hill, so many teachers. We want to magnify our message and engage a greater audience with a claim of beauty and justice for all people; we've decided to visually document the process and event. This is an incredible opportunity, of course a whole other layer of work, and at the end of the day we expect it to be more than worth the effort. Because we have stories to tell and a movement to build.

Lateef McLeod
Excerpts from *Living with Joey*
Sins Invalid 2007

"Just swallow" / You say to me / And I really do try / Cuz I be wearing tight fits / Like Rocawear jeans, big Ekco shirts, Gap hoodies / And when I am really GQ in a tailor made suit / And drool does not go with a tailor made suit / You know I try to look suave 24 7 / So there shouldn't be a problem with me swallowing, right? / Well I have to remember to swallow / Every minute / Every hour / Every day / That means when I roll down the street / Swallow / Whenever I talk to someone / Swallow / When I exercise / Swallow / When I go to school / Swallow / Cuz I don't want anyone to see me drool, especially you / You always say that it makes me look gross / And it is not my attention to gross you out / So I try to swallow like a mad man / I / (swallow) / Try and / (swallow) / Consciously do something / (swallow) / That everyone else / (swallow) / Does unconsciously / (swallow) / And you still / (swallow) /

Can't understand / (swallow) / Why / (swallow) / Can't I / (swallow) /
Learn to swallow / (swallow) / All the time / (swallow) / It is like /
(swallow) / To toss you a tennis ball / (swallow) / Telling you /
(swallow) / To throw it / (swallow) / In the air and catch it / (swallow) /
Every 15 seconds / (swallow) / And yell at you / (swallow) / When you
drop the ball

Swallow / Just swallow / Come on and swallow / You know you want to.

Maria R. Palacios
Excerpts from *My Sexy Disability*
Sins Invalid 2007

My disability is sexy.
Sexy like Incan sunsets
that paint oceans
and skies
and awaken the moon in your eyes
when you're with me.

My disability is sexy.
Sexy
like the uneven curves
of South American mountains;
sexy like rose petals
and red lips;
fields
of eucalyptus and pine,
dreams of a derailed spine
and the smell of sex
between my poems.

I am sexy.
Sexy like coffee and books;
cream and sugar to taste.
Go ahead and turn my page.
Read me.
My words
are dragonflies

and shooting stars,
the ridges of my scars
and the grand canyon
of my cleavage.

My disability is beautiful
and sweet.
I'm sweet
like arroz con leche,
and flan,
sweet
like ripe watermelons,
like the scent of mint.
I am cinnamon
and sin.
I am my own
Ave Maria;
Catholic girl gone bad,
21st century Frida Kahlo.
I paint my sexiness
with words.

Sins Invalid recognizes that we will be liberated as whole beings—as disabled/as queer/as brown/as black/as genderqueer/as female or male bodied—as we are far greater whole than partitioned. We recognize that our allies emerge from many communities and that demographic identity does not determine one's commitment to liberation.

Sins Invalid is social and economic justice for all people with disabilities—in lockdowns, in shelters, on the streets, visibly disabled, invisibly disabled, sensory minority, environmentally injured, psychiatric survivors—moving beyond individual legal rights to collective human rights.

Our stories, imbedded in analysis, offer paths from identity politics to unity amongst all oppressed people, laying a foundation for a collective claim of liberation and beauty.

Patricia Berne is a founder and managing director of Sins Invalid, which she supports through a vision of justice which includes the right to sexual expression. Her day commitments include acting as Project Director on Race, Disability and Eugenics for the Center for Genetics and Society participating on the Board of Directors at San Francisco Women Against Rape.

Note

1   Ann Pointon and Chris Davies, preface to Millee Hill, "Black and Disabled in the Arts," in *Framed: Interrogating Disability in the Media*. Eds. Pointon and Davies (London: British Film Institute, 1997), 184.

Further Reading

Sins Invalid: www.thedancingtree.org/sinsinvalid

IV
The Power and the Limits of Stories

Introduction

The authors in this part are looking at storytelling as catalyst, as personal property, as the dearest resource of the exile, as a vehicle for transmitting pluralities of truth and viewpoint. We are thinking of the four chapters at the end of the volume as speculative. They are not tied so much to specific projects as they are more general considerations of the power and the limits of storytelling-with-consequences in the public square. More than the project-based chapters, these chapters engage, to some extent, with questions of "storytelling" and "telling truth."

Cate Fosl writes about the ways that Fannie Lou Hamer, Rigoberta Menchu, and Anne Braden—all profoundly influential human rights activists and key movement actors—delivered autobiographical stories over and over in public to galvanize social activism. Hamer, Menchu, and Braden entered and shaped human rights movements when these events were at their ascendant, most optimistic, if dangerous, moments. They encountered attentive "masses," ready for recruitment, ready for voices that claimed that the world was mutable; that justice could occur because oppressive forces could be penetrated and laid low. Reimagining the world this way created the possibility of reimagining *the self* as a new, more politically potent entity.

Christopher Colvin also writes about the place of storytelling in the life of social justice movements, in this case post-apartheid South Africa. Colvin describes how journalists, documentarians, academics of various sorts, and others kept on showing up, after the Truth and Reconciliation Commission process was over, one after the other and endlessly asking the victims of the apartheid regime for their stories—their accounts of trauma. Those persons who "possessed" trauma stories complied as best they could, serving up their stories for global consumption, until this kind of servitude began to seem grotesque: for whose benefit was the teller telling?

Colvin asks about the price to the trauma-teller of "owning" what becomes a consumable story. He asks about the price to the ethical project when one is pressed to tell a story tailored "in bites" to the needs of the marketplace. Colvin concludes that, arguably, the potential for storytelling as compensatory, in the aftermath of great violence, is fatally compromised. If members of the traumatized group withhold their stories, the global eye is condemned to blind ignorance. If the storytellers decide to assert their ownership of what happened to them, as "intellectual property," as an attempt to control what is "theirs," the costs are fatally steep.

Together, the Fosl and Colvin chapters raise interesting issues about *when* storytelling occurs on the movement-making continuum, from the *unfolding* to the *unraveling* of mass activism—and also how the identity and interests of an audience are crucial to assessing the meanings of storytelling, including their potential as sources of generative energy.

Myra Mendible's "Imagining Cuba" explains how stories and storytelling are strategies for exile groups competing among themselves for The Past. The exile, she writes, uses stories for keeping the past—and personal dignity—alive. Also, the exile uses stories as construction sites for repairing the traumatic interruptions that are the exile's life. Perhaps most affectingly, Mendible explores story as the most valuable and trustworthy "container of assets" that the displaced person possesses. Reviewing her own life as exiled child, then as grown-up "in between," Mendible catalogues how the exiled person uses stories to construct bridges and boundaries between the old and the new and to accomplish tasks associated with transmitting various kinds of legitimacy to one's children in the new world. Mendible concludes that the exile's truth is necessarily ambiguous, a condition which makes stories a perfect engine for transmitting meaning, in this case, in South Florida.

Underscoring and extending the idea that stories are inevitably ambiguous, Martha Minow assesses the usefulness of storytelling to law, and by extension to analytical thinking generally. Moving across terrain from droll to quotidian to deadly, Minow extols the value of stories because of their power to "disrupt . . . rationalizing, generalizing modes of analysis with a reminder of human beings and their feelings, quirky developments, and textured vitality." Minow tellingly identifies narrative as a productive "antidote for social science rationality" at the same time that she recognizes the fundamental "incompleteness" of stories as a way of solving problems.

In the end, the quartet of speculative authors is only glancingly concerned with the question of whether to endorse a relationship between storytelling and a concept as singular and rigid as "truth." Ultimately these authors are, on the other hand, seriously concerned with the political valences of stories in the public square. One by one they consider the ways that storytelling facilitates "thinking freshly" in places where groups are locked (when we're lucky) in verbal wars over political truths, that is, struggling over whose vision of the past is believable and which vision of the future is best, and how the people gathered in the square can realize, as Minow puts it, their "capacity to act together" with coherent and effective civic intentions.

The speculative chapters, together with the chapters from the field, shed reflected light on the disastrous consequences that ensue when political story-telling becomes the sole prerogative of political operatives—a group that uses storytelling only to facilitate the consolidation of power. (Think "swiftboat-ing;" and "Harry and Louise" ads against national healthcare policy; and that untrue mantra, "weapons of mass destruction.") When this happens, as it does all the time in the United States, most typically and consequentially in shaping our national political campaigns, the operatives and the politicians they work for, with the help of media, shut out the people as sources of narratives that matter. Then we get war and no national health care, and other maleficent outcomes, such as illegitimate elections. Each of the chapters in this book makes a splendid case for the voice of the people, and for the ways that the power of the people inevitably resides in the collective stories they tell.

20

Anne Braden, Fannie Lou Hamer, and Rigoberta Menchu

Using Personal Narrative to Build Activist Movements

CATHERINE FOSL

I first encountered Rigoberta Menchu's storytelling in early 1985, when I hosted a small group of community women in my suburban Washington, D.C. home to meet her. I had never heard of Menchu at that time, and knew precious little about the plight of Guatemala's Mayan peasant poor. That changed as a result of the evening Menchu spent with us. She was a reserved young woman dressed in hand-woven, brilliantly colored fabrics, and she spoke softly, hesitantly, and with a translator in a tongue not her own (Spanish). The focus of the evening turned out to be her own life story, and her hesitation diminished as her tale unfolded. The contours of her past were riveting, adding detail and validation to beliefs I already held generally about brutality, injustice, and corruption in Central American dictatorships. What I took most from her account was an empathy that heightened my awareness of Guatemalan injustices and made action more compelling. That experience was widely replicated among young, left-leaning, mostly white urbanites like those gathered in my living room, many of whom went on to participate in the burgeoning movement against U.S. corporate and military intervention in Central America.

I did not know it then, but Menchu's narrative had recently been published as a book.[1] Thousands would soon read her testimonial—or hear it as I had—and her saga would help to spark an international solidarity movement of oppressed indigenous peoples, her role in which won Menchu a Nobel Peace Prize in 1992. The details of her account would also become highly contested, however, when a U.S. anthropologist challenged their factual accuracy, igniting a debate among social scientists, literary scholars, and intellectuals more broadly as to the role of "truth." More on that later. Still, one might argue that the net result was positive insofar as her widespread telling of her story in both oral and written form brought far greater public attention to the cause on which the story centered and raised the consciousness of thousands, at least, of non-Guatemalans regarding the social and economic conditions in that country.

Later in 1985, I attended an anti-racist workshop in North Carolina, during which I heard another gripping personal narrative told by an older white woman named Anne Braden. Braden gave an impassioned account of a conversion of almost religious intensity she had undergone as a young adult in the 1940s, from being a white southerner who accepted tacitly racial segregation and the privilege it conferred on her to becoming a lifelong crusader against segregation and white supremacy. She described the process as a painful one, "turning myself inside out and upside down," insofar as it had compelled her to reject the most basic of beliefs with which she had grown up, as well as to confront the complacency of her own family of origin. Braden spoke in tandem with an African American activist, Sadie Hughley, but most in the audience were young, white, progressive-minded, political women, like myself, who were deeply inspired by an elder of their own skin color who had so thoroughly broken with the lessons of her past. I found myself mesmerized by Anne Braden's story, and over the coming decade, it would become interwoven with my own as I entered a graduate program in U.S. history and chose her as the subject of my dissertation. Once I began spending sustained time with Anne as I interviewed her and occasionally accompanied her to public speaking engagements, I heard her recount that story of her political transformation many times.

My initial experiences with both Menchu's and Braden's personal narratives took place more than twenty years ago, but the power of those encounters and others like them figured significantly in my path into both social justice campaigns and the academy. Women like Menchu and Braden exposed me to what was, for me, a new brand of storytelling—one in which seasoned activists recounted personal experiences that created identification between narrator and listeners in ways that galvanized social action. Not only did narratives such as these propel my involvement in anti-racist and anti-imperialist social movements of the 1980s, but they triggered my thinking more generally about how narratives facilitate or inhibit social change. In 1985—the same year I met Menchu and Braden—I began to collect oral histories of women activists, an interest that would ultimately send me into doctoral study in modern U.S. history and a professional path that would set me to collecting and interpreting such narratives for probably the rest of my life.

Becoming a scholar of the southern freedom movement, I soon learned that although Anne Braden's "racial conversion narrative" (as literary scholar Fred Hobson has labeled it) was more unusual among white activists of her generation insofar as only a small number of southern whites committed their lives to that movement in the 1950s and sixties, many more women in the civil rights movement used their own "stories" as tools for mass mobilization.[2] The most famous of them, perhaps, is Fannie Lou Hamer, an African American sharecropper and Mississippi native who first heard the message of freedom at age 44 during a voter registration drive through the delta conducted by youthful workers of the Student Nonviolent Coordinating Committee (SNCC). Hamer's subsequent attempt to register earned her only threats and eviction from her home by the plantation owner. Although such defiance made her day-to-day life considerably harder in pre-voting rights Mississippi, Hamer remained resolutely committed to the promise of civil rights, and over the next months and years she withstood dramatic torrents of repression that included one beating in a Montgomery County jail so brutal that it did permanent damage to her health.

Hamer did, however, take away an important resource from those traumatic moments: her memories of them, which she frequently recounted in speeches and in interviews for the rest of her life. Those vivid retellings of her personal experiences, which she interwove with trenchant political and socioeconomic analyses, became widely known and revered among civil rights activists who saw how successfully she roused masses to action. Hamer's rhetorical talents culminated, perhaps, with her impassioned testimony to the Credentials Committee of the Democratic Party at its national convention in mid-1964. Those remarks were broadcast briefly on national television, detailing the brutality and degradation that dogged her life in Mississippi—and that of any African American seeking voting rights or other, more basic dignities. The inflammatory potential of Hamer's testimony being broadcast to millions so alarmed President Lyndon Johnson that he called an impromptu White House press conference and demanded the pre-emption of her comments. Hamer's voice became legendary in civil rights historiography because of the power of her personal narrative, made more powerful perhaps by her ability to punctuate her speeches with soulful, *a cappella* renderings of freedom songs that deepened the emotional impact for listeners. According to attorney Eleanor Holmes Norton, who met Hamer through SNCC, Hamer's civil rights oratory was rivaled only by that of the Rev. Martin Luther King Junior.[3]

Personal Narratives as Political Acts

This chapter reflects on Hamer, Braden, and Menchu's storytelling experiences in order to explore the personal narrative as a strategy employed by social justice activists seeking to prompt a collective consciousness that can propel sociopolitical action. While many of the projects described throughout this anthology have been collective in nature, no overview of stories told to change the world can be complete without an analysis of the role of the personal narrative in that project. The individual telling of one's own story has been central to movement-building in most if not all modern social justice crusades around the globe.

The personal narrative is, of course, but one of the varieties of stories that drive social movements, to which speech acts of many sorts are essential in the formation and enactment of a collective identity and mass demands for change. Scholars such as Francesca Polletta, for example, have offered compelling interpretations of the stories activists tell themselves within movements to "sustain and strengthen members' commitment," but the personal narrative is a particular variation of that larger set of movement stories.[4] While an analytical dividing line can be drawn between individual and collective narratives in movements, the personal narrative has a foot in both camps in some important ways. By nature an individual's story, and one that positions its teller as a mediator, the personal narrative recounted in service of social justice also has a dimension of "witnessing" or "author-izing" an experience previously marginalized (as, for example, in the case of "coming-out" stories). Telling one's own story thus has a collective purpose and can work as a consciousness-raising, even a community-organizing tactic.

As Kay Schaffer and Sidonie Smith have observed, the very framework of recent social movements such as civil, women's, workers', gay, and human "rights" are motivated by personal stories or cases that call injustices into focus.[5] In that sense, someone may "witness" or "testify" in service of social justice claims in a range of extra-legal settings. In the case of women's testimonies, one might argue (and Sidonie Smith has, in other writings) that a woman who tells her own story necessarily crafts a self differently and more disruptively, challenging prevailing ideologies of gender whether she intends to or not, because of the history of patriarchy that has muted or silenced women's voices.[6] Even though women activists may occupy a vast range of social conditions depending on their race, class, sexual identity, nationality, etc., it is clear from the most cursory glance at modern social movements that personal narratives made political have been of strategic importance for women activists fashioning collective identities, both in feminist crusades and in other kinds of reform campaigns.

In literature and in life, members of marginalized groups have historically looked often to their personal experiences as the basis for larger social claims. African American literature, for example, was born of slave narratives, which were in the nineteenth century one of the few avenues ex-slaves had for publicizing their critiques of slavery, which they developed by revealing the brutality of their own experiences enslaved. Women's autobiographies and autobiographical fiction then became the building blocks of feminist theory in the late 1960s because they were the most coherent body of literature that foregrounded gender critically in a canon that had all but locked women out. These examples pertain to personal narratives that were written and published, and that literature has indeed flowered in the modern world, especially in the years since World War II. Literary theorist Leigh Gilmore reports, for example, that the number of books published in English and labeled "autobiography" or "memoir" tripled between the 1940s and the 1990s, and similar booms in that genre have punctuated other cultures around the world.[7] In fact, this literary outpouring has been so vast and so diverse that calling it "autobiography" has given way in some circles to the more expansive category of "life writing" that recognizes variations such as letters, diaries, oral histories, and even autobiographical fiction.[8]

Although many of these published life writings are also consciousness-raising or movement-building projects, another medium of personal stories for social change lies in oral autobiographical narratives issued in the form of individual speeches or testimonials before groups of people who are changed or inspired in at least some small way as a result of the hearing. I prefer not to draw a sharp distinction between the oral and written forms, and in fact two of the three women discussed in these pages (Menchu and Braden) followed their spoken narratives up with published accounts that cover much of the same ground and share many common purposes.[9] Much of the exploration here is applicable to both oral and written narratives. Yet written texts sometimes raise different considerations having to do with marketing and commodification, as the controversies surrounding the "truth" of biographical details in Menchu's book so amply demonstrate. That particular dispute has played itself out in many venues, and I do not wish to rehash it here in discussing Menchu's story.[10] Because I am ultimately more concerned with historical, rhetorical, and feminist interpretations than with literary ones, my emphasis remains primarily on my subjects' spoken words and on the dialectic between narrator and listener, between individual and collective identity, between self and other.

Embodiment—among the most widely explored elements in feminist scholarship today—creates a different sort of intimacy between narrator and listener than that experienced by a reader. While the impact, the feeling of connection even, may be no more powerful for one who listens than one who reads, the bond created with a written text and its author is at least more solitary and self-contained. Physical presence produces a kind of immediacy and reciprocity that is dialogic or at least creates an opportunity for dialogue. The reciprocity available to a speaker from her audience is either absent or at least delayed in the case of a writer, who has no opportunity to experience her reader's response in the moment it occurs, only later (as in fan mail, for example). If in fact one accepts the most basic of postmodern precepts on the interactive nature of a text, the dialectic between teller and listener would almost necessarily alter at least a bit the story that results.

Most interpreters would concede that the immediacy of person-to-person contact is a part of what galvanizes social action. Although my first exposure to Rigoberta Menchu contained at the time no element of "research," I can still remember the vividness of seeing her and hearing her tell her story. In the case of Hamer, younger activists who recalled later her effect on their lives routinely commented on the power of her telling and particularly on her punctuating or interspersing speech with song—by its nature an oral dimension of her narrative presentation.[11] Over the years of researching my biography of Anne Braden, I had occasion to observe her deliver her personal narrative on dozens if not scores of occasions to diverse groups of listeners. Although I rarely (if ever) recorded her interactions with her audience in any manner even approaching methodical, I was struck by how routinely powerful were the responses to her telling of her own story and by the frequency of intense interpersonal encounters that followed in audience discussions or at the end of a program.

If nothing else, the spoken words of Menchu, Braden, and Hamer call into play the performative aspects of personal narratives employed for political ends. For Hamer, the addition of song has been crucial to how audiences received her speeches emotionally. For Menchu, traditional Quiche dress and use of a translator influenced my own and other North Americans' reactions to the story. In the case of Braden (who had excelled in the theater in college), the performative elements are perhaps less striking, but the contours of her narrative have a consistency over several decades' duration—without ever seeming "canned" or rehearsed—that is interesting. Her story is also different from the other two in its emphasis on her "conversion" from conventional southern white post-war society. Her oral delivery contained a tone of atonement—a quality not quite but almost ministerial—that seemed to enhance the story's power by relating it to southern religion, historically an influential force in southern culture.

Empowerment Narratives

Since Menchu, Braden, and Hamer deployed their stories mainly—or at least centrally—for the purpose of movement-building, their accounts are also what sociologist Robert Benford has called "participant narratives" because they are created and reproduced within the movement.[12] I would suggest that these three narratives and others like them might fruitfully be delineated further as "empowerment narratives" because the plot structure of each of the three stories moves from its author's disfranchisement, impoverishment, and stasis to strength, substance, and resistance.

Empowerment narratives such as these also connect to another body of work known as "trauma narratives" insofar as each woman's story situates her within a painful and problematic youth and turns on her emergence from its trauma.[13] In Menchu's case, her childhood was one of poverty, malnutrition, coffee-picking, exploitation, and loss resulting from the savagery of the Guatemalan army against her parents and brother. Similarly, Fannie Lou Hamer was one of twenty children born to a poor sharecropping family on a Mississippi plantation whose owner put her to work picking cotton when she was only six years old. Hamer's first four decades were spent largely resigned to an unyielding form of segregation and racial hierarchy reinforced with violence in order to deter challenges to the system. At age 42, having endured flagrant racism, back-breaking field work, and the concomitant loss of two pregnancies, Hamer was also involuntarily sterilized, one of thousands of women of color to be subjected to that procedure.

Braden's narrative presents a departure from the other two women's systematic deprivation insofar as she grew up in relative privilege even amid the Great Depression. Loved and supported by her middle-class southern family, Braden was a happy, deeply religious child with only glimpses of the moral dilemmas she would confront as a young adult. The beneficiary of an education at an elite Virginia women's college, she began, in 1945, a promising career in newspaper journalism back home in Alabama. Her suffering was not economic but psychological and moral as covering the Birmingham courthouse beat revealed to her the two separate and unequal forms of justice meted out to whites and blacks, for whom "ravishment" (incidents in which an African American man looked longingly at or refused to show deference to a white woman) was still a capital crime at that time in Alabama. As Braden began to notice the everyday degradations that southern white culture visited on blacks, she also observed the blatant perversions of Christian principles on which segregation depended and which her white friends and family tolerated with denial, dysfunction, or drink. The result was a kind of sickness she later characterized in her 1958 memoir as "of the spirit," writing that "finally I came to realize that no one can go untouched by segregation in the South . . . Either you find a way to oppose the evil, or the evil becomes a part of you and you are a part of it, and it winds itself about your soul like the arms of an octopus."[14] One might reasonably ask whether such trauma was less profound than the sorts that involve violence or wreak physical suffering, but in Braden's account, the experience clearly caused her considerable anguish and prompted a sharp turn in her life's direction.

The empowerment that follows the trauma in each of these three narratives works on several levels. The most salient is in the plot. All three narrators resolve the traumas of their early lives with resistance that originates from and brings them into a collective movement for change. Menchu became politicized gradually throughout her youth *vis-à-vis* the close community of Indian peasants among whom her father was a leader in organizing an agricultural workers' union. Braden's awareness of her complicity with southern racial hierarchy evolved slowly as she entered adulthood, but she renounced her earlier values and immersed herself in anti-racist and working-class activism soon after meeting for the first time others working collectively for racial and economic change. The galvanizing factor, perhaps, was her love for the man who became her husband, Carl Braden, a Marxist and labor journalist with whom she formed a lifelong partnership based not only on romance but on a shared commitment to social action.

Hamer's embrace of resistance was the most dramatic, and in some ways the most unexpected of the three. Forty-four years old, she threw off what appeared to be resignation to the oppressive conditions of her life in the Mississippi delta almost immediately after her first encounter with the young voter-registration activists of the Student Nonviolent Coordinating Committee, who arrived in her town in 1962. The day she first tried to register, Hamer failed the literacy test and was denied. The bus she and other would-be registrants rode on was stopped and ticketed. Then the day ended with threats from her employer-landlord of eighteen years so intimidating that she left home and went into hiding rather than back down. "If SNCC hadn't of come into Mississippi, there never would have been a Fannie Lou Hamer," she said in speeches and interviews later.[15] Within weeks she had been brought into SNCC's inner circles, and began traveling the South to organize. That story of her empowerment became one of the tools through which she recruited others.

While retracing their own processes of empowerment, Braden's, Hamer's, and Menchu's projects were at their vital center about empowering those who heard or read them toward greater understanding of and participation in organized forms of resistance. The issues and campaigns on which the three women sought to raise others' consciousness were different (though overlapping). Yet, these three empowerment narratives share a structural feature beyond that of plot development. In each case, the narrator weaves her own individual life plot—whose contours I have roughly tracked—with a more generalized political and economic critique of racism, of sexism, and ultimately of capitalism. That layering effect is what produces the whole story, a story that may be reproduced and used for movement-building.

By placing her individual life plot at the center of what is, for the most part, an essentially political action, each of the narrators considered here also asserts the implicit claim, "I matter," or "My story is worth hearing." Ironically, perhaps, considering the humility that has been widely commented upon in all three women, each becomes not just an individual, but a kind of exemplar. Such tales invite others to put themselves in the narrator's position, to enter an empathic understanding that calls on shared humanity. To the extent that such narratives inspire or empower, they do so in ways that point more toward a move beyond differences than to the sort of appreciation of differences—or organizing based on one form of difference—that has animated identity-based politics of the past four decades or so. To use Braden as an example, speeches in which she recounted her personal narrative may have appealed most poignantly to whites, southerners, and women—and perhaps most poignantly of all to white southern women. But I have also observed and heard expressed an equally powerful impact her words had on African Americans. For some, her testimony revealed that white people could indeed share a worldview; for others, her very conversion represented the possibility of success for the cause of racial justice.

The final dimension of empowerment in these narratives is that of the self. Hamer, Menchu, and Braden were political women who employed their own narratives to create solidarity with listeners, as tools for fashioning collective identities and collective movements. Much of the focus of this chapter has been on their audiences, but what about themselves? Can telling one's story ever ultimately fail to be about oneself? In the telling and re-telling of their empowerment journeys, each of the three was also defining, and redefining, herself.

That self no longer stood alone, however. Initially empowered by the first social movement organization she became a part of (for Menchu, the agricultural union; for Braden, the post-World War II southern Progressive Party; for Hamer, the SNCC), each experienced a sort of figurative death and rebirth within a more collective identity. Telling that story over and over became a source of renewed commitment, with the self reconstructed repeatedly in front of others who were or might become similarly committed and thus widening the collective. The story of each of the three soon became a familiar narrative to which others in the movement could refer or rely upon. Anne Braden used to love the phrase, "No turning back." For a white woman, even one like Braden—who was repeatedly excoriated as a Communist and a race-traitor—turning back was probably more of a possibility than it was for either Menchu or Hamer.

Yet telling one's story could become, for them all, a way of anchoring the self to the movement. The literary scholar and novelist Carolyn Heilbrun has argued that women write themselves into existence through autobiography.[16] For these women, and for others whose personal narratives have become forces for changing the world, the same may be true of storytelling.

Catherine Fosl is director of the recently established Anne Braden Institute for Social Justice Research at the University of Louisville, where she is also an associate professor of Women's and Gender Studies. Her biography of Braden, *Subversive Southerner: Anne Braden and the Struggle for Racial Justice in the Cold War South* (Palgrave Macmillan, 2002; University Press of KY, 2006), won the 2003 Oral History Association Book Award and was named an Outstanding Book of 2003 by the Gustavus Myers Center for Human Rights. In 2005, she was awarded the Catherine Prelinger Award of the Coordinating Council for Women in History for her achievements as a non-traditional scholar, and she was a Social Science Research Council sexuality fellow in 2005–06.

Notes

1 *I . . . Rigoberta Menchu: An Indian Woman in Guatemala,* edited and introduced by Elisabeth Burgos-Debray (New York: Verso, 1984) was the first English-language edition. The text was initially published in 1983 in Spanish.

2 Fred Hobson advances this terminology and analyzes such narratives by a variety of white southerners, Braden included, in his *But Now I See: The White Southern Racial Conversion Narrative* (Baton Rouge: LSU Press, 1999).

3 Kay Mills, *This Little Light of Mine: The Life of Fannie Lou Hamer* (New York: Dutton, 1993), 85. Mills's book gives a full account of the synopsis of Hamer's work offered here. Her speech to the Credentials Committee of the 1964 Democratic Party convention appears on pp. 119–20.

4 Francesca Polletta, "Plotting Protest: Mobilizing Stories in the 1960 Student Sit-Ins," in

Stories of Change: Narrative and Social Movements, ed. Joseph E. Davis (Albany: SUNY Press, 2002), 31–52 (quoted 48).

5   Kay Schaffer and Sidonie Smith, "Conjunctions: Life Narratives in the Field of Human Rights," *Biography* 27:1 (Winter 2004):3.

6   Sidonie Smith, *A Poetics of Women's Autobiography: Marginality and the Fictions of Self-Representation* (Bloomington: Indiana University Press, 1987), esp. 175.

7   Leigh Gilmore, *The Limits of Autobiography: Trauma and Testimony* (Ithaca: Cornell University Press, 2001), quoted in Schaffer and Smith, "Conjunctions," 21.

8   See, for example, Shari Benstock's essay, "Authorizing the Autobiographical," in her *The Private Self* (Chapel Hill: UNC Press, 1988), 10–33. The Personal Narratives Group uses a different term but takes a similar position in its collectively authored *Interpreting Women's Lives: Feminist Theory and Personal Narratives* (Bloomington: Indiana University Press, 1989).

9   Anne Braden, *The Wall Between* (New York: Monthly Review Press, 1958; reissued Knoxville: University of Tennessee Press, 1999); see n. 1 for the citation for Menchu's book.

10 The conflicts provoked around Menchu's book appeared in various periodicals both scholarly and popular soon after the publication of a 1998 volume by anthropologist David Stoll, repudiating the factual accuracy of portions of her story. The most complete accounting of the dispute and the commentaries it prompted (including Stoll's response to the compilation) appear in Arturo Arias's edited collection, *The Rigoberta Menchu Controversy* (Minneapolis: University of Minnesota Press, 2001). Most recently, Schaffer and Smith summarize the contestations surrounding the Menchu book on pp. 16–18 of "Conjunctions."

11 See, for example, the interviews used in Mills, *This Little Light,* and in many that refer to Hamer in Doug McAdam, *Freedom Summer* (New York: Oxford University Press, 1988).

12 Robert D. Benford, "Controlling Narratives and Narratives as Control within Social Movements," in Davis (ed.), *Stories of Change,* 54.

13 It is beyond the scope of this chapter to provide a deeper analysis of these works as trauma narratives, but it would be interesting to speculate on those connections. For more on women's trauma narratives, see, for example, Suzette Henke, *Shattered Subjects: Trauma and Testimony in Women's Life-Writing* (New York: St. Martin's Press, 2000).

14 Braden, *Wall Between* (1999 edition), 13 & 30.

15 Mills, *This Little Light,* 41. The biographical material earlier in this paragraph comes from Ch. 2.

16 Carolyn Heilbrun, *Writing a Woman's Life* (New York: W.W. Norton, 1988).

Further Reading

Anne Braden Institute: www.louisville.edu/annebradeninstitute

21

Trafficking Trauma

Intellectual Property Rights and the Political Economy of Traumatic Storytelling in South Africa

CHRISTOPHER J. COLVIN

"Signs of Injury" in Circulation

In the last two decades, the scope of intellectual property law has been greatly expanded to include a variety of objects, images, and ideas that might be called "cultural property."[1] Songs, artworks, stories, graphic designs, totems, and ritual artifacts have increasingly been brought under the umbrella of a variety of "rights regimes" that seek to protect the rights, especially of marginalized indigenous groups, to maintain control over and benefit materially from these "objects/products" of their culture.[2] This chapter considers a particular—and perhaps peculiar—cultural form that is only now beginning to emerge as a form of intellectual property in need of "protection."

Traumatic storytelling is an increasingly common activity in post-conflict, democratizing societies, an activity that produces an ever-expanding volume of narratives of traumatic suffering and recovery. These narratives, solicited by truth commissions, journalists, academics, and therapists, now circulate the world through particular relations of production, exchange, and consumption and structure—what I describe below as a "global political economy of traumatic storytelling." Some victim-storytellers in South Africa are pushing for the recognition of these stories as a form of intellectual property and are seeking a variety of protections against the manipulation and marketization of their stories of abuse. How this situation came about and what it might mean for the public sphere's engagement with images and narratives of abuse are the subjects of this chapter.

My first encounter with these disillusioned "victims of the TRC" (Truth and Reconciliation Commission), as they sometimes identified themselves, came through the monthly meetings of the Khulumani Support Group, a victim support and advocacy group in Cape Town. Khulumani is composed of victims of apartheid-era political violence and the Cape Town group was started in coordination with the Cape Town Trauma Centre, a non-governmental organization (NGO) offering trauma debriefing and counseling to victims of political and criminal violence. The group emerged out of monthly meetings that the Trauma Centre and Khulumani held jointly to provide advocacy services to victims and to gently introduce them to the principles and benefits of counseling.[3]

Part of every monthly meeting was devoted to "storytelling." At each meeting, there were typically between three and seven people who spoke. The stories were usually short, the speakers calm and measured in their narration. They began with a brief introduction, continued through a summary of key events and people and ended with a comment on how they were doing today. These stories were "tight," reduced to the essential elements needed to make the point. During the storytelling, there was little intervention from the facilitators. After the story, a facilitator would offer some very quick comments about the psychological experiences of the speaker and audience. After these brief comments, the floor was reopened and new speakers came forward until time was up.

The process of storytelling in these meetings reflects both the model of memory laid out by the Truth and Reconciliation Commission[4] as well as some of the features of what Levy and Sznaider have termed "cosmopolitan memory":[5] stories of traumatic suffering, reduced to the most important, shocking, and morally obvious details of harm, circulated less as specific histories in need of specific interventions or response but more as "signs of violence," symbols of the moral bankruptcy of apartheid and the means of group identity formation through a common rejection of apartheid morality.

Elsewhere, I describe the narrative work of victims as "traumatic storytelling."[6] I use this term to underscore three characteristic dimensions of the particular kind of storytelling in which I am interested. First, it is storytelling specifically about trauma, the traumas of apartheid in particular. It is a kind of storytelling that does not easily admit the ambiguous or the unspectacular. Second, it is storytelling framed through the psychotherapeutic language of trauma. In particular, it is storytelling that narrates via the conventional psychodynamic stages of trauma: traumatic event followed by, in various combinations, numbness, intrusion, denial, anxiety, a narrative "working through," and, finally, acceptance and integration through storytelling. Third, it is a kind of storytelling that can itself be traumatizing to the teller.

The TRC's investment in traumatic storytelling was in part a manifestation of the broader globalization of psychiatric knowledge about trauma.[7] Traumatic storytelling was not only something that was "of the moment" in global forms of public culture—on middle-class talk shows, magazines, and movies. It was (and remains) also a practice sustained by a range of political, institutional, and individual advocates. There is a large and growing network of "trauma centers" throughout the world.[8] Globalizing forms of trauma discourse and practice also run parallel with globalizing forms of political intervention. Peacekeeping troops, conflict resolution experts, diplomats, scholars of democratization—all can often be found in the same hot zones of post-conflict intervention as trauma counselors and debriefers. These experts at political and psychic reconstruction are inevitably accompanied by journalists and researchers who are eager to report on the latest forms of post-conflict healing and eager to circulate the latest stories of traumatic violence. They reproduce these traumatic stories and circulate them globally for the consumption of a diverse array of audiences.

Taken together, these diffuse actors, institutions, and interests—and the narratives of suffering that are produced, circulated, and consumed—form a global network for the circulation of traumatic storytelling. This wide circuit of narrative flow is sustained by a constant stream of journalists, researchers, politicians, priests, and psychologists who fly to the next hot spot—today South Africa, tomorrow Iraq—asking permission to record, interpret, and circulate "victims' stories." These stories circulated beyond the spaces of monthly meetings and interview rooms, into other countries, other cultures, and other histories that were largely unknown to group members.[9]

Khulumani members had a keen sense of this wide-ranging flow of their narratives. They often spoke to me—sometimes with pride and sometimes with frustration and suspicion—about the fact that people in America, Holland, England, Sweden, Denmark, and "even the Ivory Coast" knew their story. These lines of narrative circulation were often described in great detail. Two group members, Monwabisi and Thembile, both remembered clearly every interview and informal encounter they had had with foreign researchers. When I knew the researcher as well, Monwa and Thembile would frequently ask if I had heard from them, if they had produced something with their stories, and if other people were learning about Khulumani and the situation of victims in South Africa.

Anxieties of Alienation: Commodifying the Signs of Injury

As their stories are increasingly documented and circulated within these widening global circuits of media, academic, and activist knowledge production, group members are increasingly anxious and frustrated with the personal and political implications of storytelling. They say that they, the victims, should not have to do so much work for so little gain. Traumatic storytelling has not brought them reparations, it has not eased their poverty, it has not forced perpetrators to confess or beneficiaries to admit their own liability. Only on occasion has it seemed to ease the psychological effects of trauma. More often than not, after the brief "intervention"—at the TRC or monthly meeting—they are left to go home alone with little follow-up support.

These criticisms were not unique to Khulumani. Complaints about the TRC and its storytelling practice were well established long before this support group got started.[10] The idea that this kind of storytelling might be a culturally foreign and inflexible mode of individual healing or that storytelling might be a limited and insufficient response to wider social, political, and material needs were not particularly new either. During the first few months of my work with the Trauma Centre and the support group, I indeed encountered all of these criticisms. I quickly discovered, however, another, unexpected aspect of storytelling that introduced a new level of complexity.

This new dimension was highlighted for me during the first monthly meetings I attended. Trauma Centre staff involved with the group had warned me that Khulumani had recently been reviewing their standard practice of allowing researchers to sit in on monthly meetings and ask for interviews afterwards. I had long been aware of their ambivalence on this issue and was preparing myself to be asked to stop attending future meetings. Instead of discussing whether or not to allow researchers to attend, however, I soon discovered that the group had been discussing the going "market price" for their stories, comparing notes on compensation with members of other groups who had recently worked with researchers and journalists.

The discussion was apparently remarkably detailed, with estimates for a standard one-and-a-half to two-hour recitation ranging from 100 to 150 rand.[11] Some complained these figures were too low and recommended a minimum fee of R200. Maureen said that she would charge no less than R500 because she told a good story. Shirley said that most researchers were from rich countries and "R100 was not a lot of money . . . [we] should negotiate for the benefit of the group as a whole . . . [we] should not forget that we have bargaining power." Many people in the meeting had had contact with researchers, or even worked as "lay" researchers themselves. There were also debates around how to choose group members who would participate in research and how to divide the potential proceeds of these narrative exchanges.

In the end, a provisional decision was taken to try and share out research "opportunities" equally and to divide any proceeds evenly between the individual and the group at large. Despite all of this planning, however, very little money changed hands in such a systematic fashion. Most researchers and journalists got away with paying nothing and those who did pay often conducted these transactions privately, with the standard price of a story ranging between R80 and R100. More often than not, however, when money did change hands, it was framed not as "payment" for a story, but as reimbursement for "expenses" (transportation and food).

Despite the lack of systematic exchanges of money for stories, however, it soon became clear that each group member's "story" had not only been objectified—as a "thing" that a member "had"—but had come to function as a commodity as well. As I spent more time with the group, and I saw the many connections that these narrative transactions produced beyond the boundaries of the group, I began to imagine the work of storytelling as part of a larger network of relations of production and exchange. For Khulumani, the most visible participants in this system were the Trauma Centre, the TRC, local and foreign researchers, and journalists and documentary filmmakers. Less direct relations of exchange included the government agencies victims applied to for social services, other NGOs they came into contact with, international funding organizations, foreign governments, local beneficiaries, perpetrators, and other victims.

What I encountered, then, when I started working with Khulumani, was a heavily storied and documented kind of victim-subject engaged in a process of narrative production and exchange with a range of interlocutors, near and far. In order to describe this phenomenon, and to look more broadly at the full range of its memorial demands and transactions, I developed a metaphor of the "global political economy of traumatic storytelling." By tracing the circulation of narratives, the involvement of a multitude of actors, and the creation of a range of new subjects, objects, relationships, and meanings, it is also a way of opening a discussion about some of the broader effects of the global fascination with the traumatic memories of victims of human rights abuses. In this chapter, I am particularly concerned with the consequences of Khulumani's reluctant embrace of this political economy and its emerging sense that their stories of violation were not only a kind of reified "object" they possessed, but a form of "property" that they "owned" as well.

Wrestling for the Means of Production

One effect of this market for narratives of suffering is that traumatic storytelling has become *the* major way many victims negotiate relationships with others. Their position in a field of relations between the international community, their national government, civil society, the media, and the academy increasingly depends on their ability to produce and circulate engaging stories of suffering and recovery. In the process, victims' stories become commodified objects that move out into the wider world and structure an entire network of subjects, objects, meanings, and relationships.

Some other effects include:

- the regulation of the narrative content and structure of stories wherein what sells and what doesn't becomes a part of shaping the stories people tell;
- the shortening of stories into easily consumable pieces of information that fit within the lines of a membership form, pension application, TV interview, or case history;
- the evolution of the idea that victims have a single story, "my story," a unitary, bounded, and unchanging narrative that incorporates all that is essential in the "story of a victim;"
- and an anxiety over alienation from their story once commodified.

Khulumani has taken the lead in countering some of these effects. I will discuss in this section and the next two brief examples that point to their growing conception of their stories as a form of intellectual property over which they should have more control. The first involves their attempts to renegotiate their relationship to the press during a conference on reparations they held in 2001. The second involves a documentary that Khulumani produced about its own members and which has subsequently become the object of controversy about the control over ownership of this documentary.

A significant evolution in Khulumani's strategy towards the media and the production and dissemination of their stories occurred during the planning for what was called the "Reparations Indaba." Khulumani wanted to host a two-day conference as a way to pressure the government to discuss its policy on reparations. Government, civil society, church groups, academics, the press, and other victim organizations were invited to attend and add their "voices" to the call for progress in providing reparations. The Indaba (isiXhosa for "news") was a way for Khulumani to pressure the government to report on its progress in responding to the TRC's 1998 recommendations on reparations and shame them in front of the media if its report wasn't satisfactory. It was thus to be a public stage for the dramatic presentation and performance of Khulumani's case against government neglect.

In planning for the Indaba, Khulumani's media strategy was discussed at great length. Members of the executive committee repeatedly told tales of having been abused by the press, describing rushed requests for interviews at awkward moments, insensitive or persistent questioning, and the publication of misspelled and inaccurate personal information. Shirley Gunn, the Khulumani chairperson in the Western Cape, argued that the "media doesn't care about building victim profiles" of individual victims and Maureen, another executive committee member, added that "these people are vultures."

They decided to wrest more control over the representation of their stories by putting together a series of performances and displays at the Indaba for the edification of visiting journalists. They prepared, for example, a series of short biographical summaries to ensure the accuracy of details about individual victims. They organized a display of some of the pictures I had taken during previous political protests and pasted accompanying newspaper clippings that narrated these events. There were plans to perform a play that Khulumani members had previously put together about their experiences—Shirley argued that "it will be very moving and these people need a jolt." She also planned for a video composed of still images of the "poverty and suffering" that victims were still living under.

Though the play and the video didn't materialize in time for the meeting, the photos and various stories and newspaper clippings formed part of Khulumani's coordinated effort to mobilize their stories in a variety of new and self-directed forms. All of this was part of a project to "fill in the picture" of victims' experiences for those attending and reporting on the Indaba.

Part of taking back some control also meant undertaking to document the Indaba itself. Though Khulumani solicited my help and help from the Institute for Justice and Reconciliation, and the Community Video Trust to produce audio and visual documentation of the event, the executive committee made it clear that this was an exercise in "internal documentation" and that neither the press nor we had any assumed rights to any of the material we produced.

Khulumani's attempt to gain greater control over the production and circulation of these stories culminated with a press briefing held a week prior to the Indaba. The briefing was intended to explain the reasons for the Indaba to members of the press who would then, hopefully, provide some thoughtful, in-depth reporting on the event the following week. It was also a way to engage some of the journalists in a discussion around responsible journalism of human rights issues. The response from the journalists gathered, however, was lukewarm. Sensing that little substantive discussion of media ethics was going to take place, Shirley closed the meeting, saying that as part of this new relationship to the press, Khulumani expected copies of all of the past articles on victims to be sent to them as soon as possible. She also announced, to her audience's surprise, that the short summaries of victims' stories would be available at the Indaba, but only at the end of the meeting and only to those journalists who attended all or most of the two-day event. This attempt to renegotiate Khulumani's relationship to the press was the most direct effort they had made so far to regain some say in how and where the details of their traumatic storytelling circulated.

Rumors and Rewards: The Khulumani Documentary

During my two years of fieldwork with Khulumani, this sense that the stories victims were telling were both object and property continued to grow. It was not long after I finished my fieldwork, however, that the starkest example of the growing commodification of traumatic storytelling emerged. Shirley had, during my fieldwork, started an NGO called the Human Rights Media Centre (HRMC) and one of its first projects was to produce a documentary of the Western Cape Khulumani branch. Twelve of the group members were recruited for the film, ideas for the film were workshopped with these victims and others involved or interested in the project, and the footage of these victims' stories was shot. The raw material was sent to a professor of film in the U.K. who had agreed to do the editing for free.

For their participation, those appearing in the film were given a small token fee and all signed contracts agreeing to let the HRMC edit, produce, market, and distribute the film. During the editing process, further workshops were held and a premiere of the film was finally held at the Baxter Theatre in Cape Town. Several hundred Khulumani members were bussed in and the partici-pants in the film were recognized for their participation. Shirley and the

HRMC began planning to submit the documentary to various film festivals and television stations throughout the world.

Since my fieldwork had ended, I kept up with these developments, but only as an occasional observer on the sidelines. In many ways, the production of the film had followed all of the "best practices" for inclusive and participatory documentary production. Fully informed consent was obtained from participants, the scripting and editing processes involved all participants, and the HRMC was careful to ensure wide participation at the screening from the Khulumani group as a whole and from the film's subjects in particular.

It surprised me, then, to hear a few months later that Shirley had "stolen" the film and was taking it overseas and making "hundreds of thousands of dollars" for herself and the HRMC. I had already heard that Shirley had had the documentary accepted at a number of film festivals in Africa and Europe and anticipated that some audience members might have inquired about how they might help the group or the individuals in the film. I was a bit surprised though to hear from other members of the executive committee who had been in the film that Shirley was using the film to raise money for her NGO. Having worked with this group for two years, I was used to the development of these kinds of rumors and did not really believe that Shirley had snuck off to get rich from this documentary. What struck me, however, was the language of complaint used by the participants in the film. They said Shirley had "stolen" the film, that she was "profiting" from "their" stories. They asked me, rhetorically, "Who does the film belong to? We are the ones who made it. It is our stories. It is our film."

I responded that I didn't think Shirley would make any money from the film and if she did get any compensation or donations that were not specifically earmarked for the group or individuals in the film, it would probably have to go to cover the substantial costs of producing the film. I asked what the contracts they had signed said about this issue. Everyone could remember signing the contract, but no one I spoke to had a copy. And no one could tell me any of the substance of these agreements. They quickly dismissed my suggestion that Shirley was not making money with the film and said that they had heard that a person in Ireland had given her $150,000. They didn't believe me when I said that sounded very unlikely.

What I want to point out here does not have to do with the internal dynamics of the group I worked with or the ability for research processes, no matter how ethically and carefully carried out, to be misinterpreted. Instead, I want to highlight the way group members came to see their stories themselves—and the film that carried their stories—as a form of controllable intellectual capital, a kind of property that they owned in perpetuity, regardless of who funded the film or what the contracts they signed contained. As with their earlier discussions around the "market price" of stories, the participants in the film never really pursued this issue with Shirley and, in the end, everything was ironed out. What is important, however, is the fact that these group members, through their contacts with researchers, journalists, therapists, politicians, and others, were continuing to develop a commodified relationship with their stories of suffering during apartheid.

Subject into Object: Pain, Politics, and the Public Sphere

That images and narratives of suffering like this haven't really been discussed in the debates on cultural and intellectual property rights is a bit surprising since these images and narratives have been in wide circulation for long time.[12] Of course, the kind of content in these stories—murders, rapes, torture, beatings, disappearances—and the testimonial context of their production make it difficult to imagine these stories as a kind of cultural or creative "product" in need of intellectual property protections. But this is exactly how Khulumani members have increasingly come to see them. And their growing perception of their stories as valuable commodities that should be owned and controlled by the storytellers themselves is a result of their ongoing contact with those participants in the global political economy of traumatic storytelling that continue to solicit and distribute these stories around the world.

So what to make of this strange commodification of traumatic narratives? Whose interests are served in this political economy of storytelling and should we understand Khulumani's attempts to wrest more control over their stories and over the testimonial process through the language of rights and property as a positive development? As with any discussion of intellectual property rights, we soon run up against the tension between protecting the producers of these products (in terms of both future profits and exploitation during the research process) and protecting the contribution these products make to the "public sphere." A balance between the interest society has in maintaining open access to information and the interest private individuals have in protecting the products of their intellectual labors.[13]

To be sure, to argue that traumatic storytelling is a form of intellectual property and its "producers" should be granted a range of protections is probably an effective strategy for Khulumani members to pursue. The ethical issues involved in taking the day-to-day stories of a particular group are difficult enough—taking some of the most intimate stories of suffering and loss and circulating them without any thought for or compensation to individual storytellers is much more ethically fraught. Most people would probably be happy to grant that storytellers who offer these traumatic narratives for the consumption of others should be treated with the greatest respect and the process and products of storytelling subjected to a variety of measures that would ensure victims were not further abused in the process.

But the ethical issues here are not necessarily best served by the further commodification of traumatic storytelling. For there is something about the logic and process of commodification itself that has negative consequences for Khulumani members and for discussions of traumatic experiences in the public sphere more generally. Many of the recent debates about the ethics of circulating images of atrocity have centered on the ability—or rather, the increasing inability—of these images to produce an effective ethical or political response in their consumers.[14] Some fear that we are being desensitized to these images the more they are produced and circulated by the global media. They argue that this overload of images makes the reality they attempt to represent seem less and less real, and thus less and less in need of response from those over whom these images are flooding.

I would contend, however, that the problem is as much about the objectification and commodification of images and narratives of suffering as it is about their overproduction. I have shown elsewhere that even in the context of the Khulumani's monthly meetings with Trauma Centre therapists, where issues of information overload were not at issue, the tension between seeing traumatic narratives as alienable objects and seeing them as the beginning of a dialogue and a social relationship was strong.[15] Like others circulating and consuming traumatic narratives, many therapists took stories to be "signs" of something else, of psychological trauma and recovery, of the effects of torture, or of the resilience of the human spirit. Khulumani members, however, thought that through their traumatic storytelling they were entering into a social and moral relationship, one that demanded recognition and response from their witnesses. Stories of their pain and recovery were not signs of some broader process outside themselves but a direct communication, an ethical challenge to their listeners, one that they believed deserved a response.

The commodification of traumatic storytelling, however, makes it more and more difficult for members to secure such a response. For it takes stories of pain and privatizes them, removing them in effect from the public sphere and making them—for those listening—a question of consumption rather than ethical recognition and response. In this way, the scope for engaging with traumatic images and narratives in the public sphere in a way that does not objectify them is narrowed. This objectification of traumatic images and narratives is dangerous precisely because it obscures the social and political relations of production that made them possible in the first place—and here I mean both the relationships that facilitated the production and circulation of the stories themselves, as well as the relationships that enabled the violence in the first place. In the end, the use of intellectual property rights as a conceptual framework for protecting the rights of victim-storytellers, while perhaps well intentioned and/or strategic, runs the risk of compounding the negative effects of the global political economy of traumatic storytelling by further removing images and narratives of violence from the sphere of public debate and shared moral imagination.

Christopher Colvin, Ph.D., M.P.H., is a lecturer in social anthropology at Stellenbosch University. He is continuing his work with Khulumani but has also begun research with a men's HIV/AIDS support group in Cape Town. He also teaches in public health at the University of Cape Town and consults privately.

Notes

1 Richard Handler, "Cultural Property and Culture Theory," *Journal of Social Archaeology* 3:3 (2003): 353–65.

2 C. Berryman, "Toward More Universal Protection of Intangible Cultural Property," *Journal of Intellectual Property Law* 1 (2004): 293–333; J. Boyle, *Shamans, Software, and Spleens: Law and the Construction of the Information Society* (Cambridge, MA: Harvard University Press, 1996).

3 Eric Harper and Christopher J. Colvin, *The Torture Project at Cape Town's Trauma Centre for the Survivors of Violence and Torture* (Cape Town: Cape Town Trauma Centre for Survivors of Violence and Torture, 2000).

4 Richard Wilson, *The Politics of Truth and Reconciliation in South Africa: Legitimizing the Post-Apartheid State* (Cambridge: Cambridge University Press, 2001).

5 Daniel Levy and Natan Sznaider, "Memory Unbound: The Holocaust and the Formation of Cosmopolitan Memory," *European Journal of Social Theory* 5:1 (2002): 87–106.

6 Christopher J. Colvin, "Performing the Signs of Injury: Critical Perspectives on Traumatic Storytelling after Apartheid," Doctoral Dissertation (Department of Anthropology, University of Virginia, Charlottesville, VA, 2004).

7 Joshua Breslau, "Globalizing Disaster Trauma: Psychiatry, Science, and Culture after the Kobe Earthquake," *Ethos* 28: 2 (2000): 174–97.

8 Derek Summerfield, "A Critique of Seven Assumptions behind Psychological Trauma Programmes in War-Affected Areas," *Social Science and Medicine* 48:10 (1999): 1449–62.

9 See Levy and Sznaider, "Memory Unbound," for a discussion of "cosmopolitan memory," part of a theoretical model for what happens to these memories as they circulate and cross-fertilize with other places and other memories.

10 Fiona Ross, "On Having Voice and Being Heard: Some After-Effects of Testifying before the South African Truth and Reconciliation Commission," *Anthropological Theory* 3:3 (2003): 325–42.

11 Roughly 15–20 US dollars at the time.

12 One notable exception has been the debates around war photography. Much of this debate, however, is less about ownership of these images and more about the ethics of producing, circulating, and consuming these images.

13 D. Lange, "Copyright and the Constitution in the Age of Intellectual Property," *Journal of Intellectual Property Law* 1 (1993): 119–34.

14 Jean Baudrillard, *The Gulf War Did Not Take Place* (Bloomington: Indiana University Press, 1995); Luc Boltanski, *Distant Suffering: Morality, Media and Politics* (Cambridge: Cambridge University Press, 1999); Susan Sontag, *Regarding the Pain of Others* (New York: Farrar, Straus and Giroux, 2003).

15 Colvin, "Performing the Signs of Injury."

Further Reading

Khulumani Support Group: www.khulumani.net

22

Imagining Cuba: Storytelling and the Politics of Exile

MYRA MENDIBLE

> Borderlands are physically present wherever two or more cultures edge each other . . . Living on borders and in margins, keeping intact one's shifting multiple identity and integrity, is like trying to swim in a new element, an "alien" element . . . not comfortable but home.
>
> —Gloria Anzaldua

For those of us accustomed to navigating the fluid borders dividing our "Cuban" and "American" cultural identities, the condition of being both and neither at the same time is indeed not comfortable but home. We are, in Gustavo Perez Firmat's catchy phrase, "born in Cuba, made in the U.S.A." We are members of that group referred to as the "one-and-a-half" generation, a designation that attempts to capture the "in-between" status of *cubanos/as* who emigrated to the States as children or adolescents and have lived, as Firmat calls it, "on the hyphen." I am Cuban-American, exile, refugee, naturalized citizen, ethnic, immigrant, *gusana*.[1] To native-born Americans, I am simply Cuban; to Cubans on the island, I am too *Americanized* to be genuinely Cuban. The "in-betweens" cohabit two or more identities at once; we are insiders/outsiders, both Cuban and American and yet neither simultaneously. Our stories resonate with different languages, cultures, and subjectivities, producing oblique glimpses of a world where personal and collective memories collide and co-exist. We navigate waters as turbulent and treacherous as the Caribbean Sea itself, but they are our waters and our familiar shores bordering the distance.

This chapter registers my attempts to chart a course through these treacherous waters, to make sense of the passionate polarities that have divided Cubans on the island from Cubans in Miami for decades. In many ways, it is about the difficulty of establishing a grounded identity in a public space that reverberates with the high-pitched ideological conflict between Havana's and Miami's vociferous elites. But just as importantly, it is about the power of storytelling to reshape images of self and community in ways that can

239

transcend factionalism or discord. Storytelling is here imagined as a creative and constructive force for change—as a political act. Given the intensity of debates dividing U.S. Cubans from Cubans on the island on such issues as the U.S. embargo, the challenge to locate and pursue an elusive thread of connection between us is no less urgent today than it was in 1959, when Castro's revolution triggered the Cuban diaspora. Many of the "in-between" generation remain separated from Cubans on the island by a sea of silence, and from each other by misunderstanding, frustration, hostility, or indifference. I have heard fellow Cubans in the U.S. dissociate themselves from "Miami Cubans" and Cubans in Miami denigrate *marielitos*.[2] I have seen the images through which Cubans in the U.S. are gazed and judged, and have encountered the distortions and prejudices these images support. In this chapter I attest to the formative role that storytelling plays, hoping to reclaim at least one voice in a chorus of voices silenced by the very people who presume to speak for me and for all Cuban exiles.

Growing up in Miami, the Mecca of most Cuban exiles, I learned to understand the nuances of exile politics and thus to negotiate a place for myself. For much of my early life, I was oblivious to the petty divisions and antagonisms that could turn "insiders" into outcasts. As one of over two million Cuban immigrants who settled in the South Florida area following the Revolution, I was raised a mere ninety miles away yet a world apart from my homeland. Growing up Cuban in a U.S. city where Cubans are in the majority meant that I could be an insider, could feel at home anywhere in Miami where my food was served and my language spoken. It meant that while I was part of a minority by national standards, I grew up as just one of the family in Cuban Miami, spared many petty prejudices that minorities often face. As a teen, I was adept at crossing borders, at being both the *cubanita* next door and an Americanized young woman who loved rock music, went braless, and straightened her hair. My friends and I spoke our own hybrid tongue, the *Spanglish* that even American girls in Miami learned to use in intimate chatter. Only later, in my adult travels beyond the city's borders, would I recognize the mutability and relativity of that "insider" status: I did not have to go far to become the outsider, an object of suspicion or curiosity. I could travel a mere hundred miles south or north or west of Miami and encounter looks that said "go back where you came from." Yet these markers were more fluid still: during a return visit to Cuba, I was shocked to discover that I was an outsider in the land of my birth as well.

As a carryover of my Cuban heritage, family stories were fundamental to the formation of my identity. Kept alive in exile, they shaped and sustained certain values, forged a communal and individual sense of self, and transmitted a vision of the past that helped guide me towards the future. Growing up Cuban in Miami meant that my birthplace remained a living memory. It was alive on the streets of *calle ocho* in Little Havana, in the language we spoke at home, and in the stories that nurtured my childhood. We had fled Cuba just two months after Fidel Castro and his Revolutionary Army occupied Havana, settling in Miami for what my parents regarded as a brief sojourn. Year after year, my mother safeguarded our property titles in a small metal box, convinced that someday we would reclaim the life left behind. My father's loss was less tangible; his memory served as his metal box, and it stored a wealth of stories rich in detail and drama. Years of exile never faded my father's memories of home. Although his gratitude to our adopted land was unquestionable, my father never forgot his first love. He yearned for her, idealized and idolized her, held her in his memories. She was *his* Havana. Eyes full of emotion, he called her "the Paris of the Caribbean," his graceful, exuberant city that never slept. He knew every nook and cranny of her, and she clung to his senses—her vibrant rhythms, pleasant and familiar smells, sultry breezes, and gentle sun.

It is therefore not surprising that my father loved recounting incidents from his life in Havana. Recalled in exile, these tales assumed for me the status of myth: they were about a place I did not remember, about a birthplace I had left as a child and could only envision as a set of characters and settings described in my father's stories. Later I would realize that as entertaining as his tales were for their drama and colorful detail, they were also instructive, helping to instill a sense of pride in me for who I am and where I come from. They also provided glimpses of a man I did not know—for my father the construction worker in Miami was not the picaresque protagonist of his tales. Like many children of his generation, my father grew up poor and without much formal schooling. As one of thirteen children, he was literally dancing for his food by the age of twelve, spinning a mean Charleston for the rich American tourists who frequented the local racetrack. My father loved retelling the story about the American major league team owner who had insulted him by disdainfully tossing a penny into his tip box. The wiry boy had looked defiantly at the man in the white suit, taken the coin out from among the pile of bills and tossed it back with equal disdain. On a personal level, this story was to teach me about dignity in the face of prejudice, humiliation, or insult. But exile would infuse even this most personal event with cultural significance: my father would come to represent Cuba itself—defiant, proud, and staunchly independent in the face of its rich and powerful neighbor to the north. Thus would the personal blend into the political, and thus did his stories bestow a vision of both the man and the country I would not otherwise know.

Other stories described his life as a child of the city, a boy nourished as much by the sights and sounds of Havana's nightlife as by the local *fondas* (eateries) that often provided free meals. Havana fed his love of music and dance, as there were always impromptu gatherings where tabletops became conga drums and work-weary men and women came alive to the rhythms of rumba or *guaguanco*. During these street gatherings, social and racial distinctions dissolved in communal celebration: hard-edged factory workers might recite poetry to the strains of a Spanish guitar while teary-eyed old women puffed contentedly on their husbands' cigars; the young could be initiated into a Cuban ritual through the "Guantanamera," a ballad-style melody comprised of a traditional refrain interspersed with improvised verses. My father told how by joining the circle of adults, he learned to compose his own lyrics on cue and thus participate in a communal song that had endured for generations. To me, these tales of home provided a personalized history that countered the less forgiving, sometimes hostile images later reflected by my public world. To my father, storytelling was the only way he knew to cross the boundaries of time and place, to unite me—his Americanized *cubanita*—with her heritage and her birthplace.

My parents would never set eyes on their homeland again, but both kept their respective metal boxes intact: *mami* sifting through her faded titles as a way to retain her dignity during years as a hotel maid on Miami Beach, *papi* sorting out tales to impress and instruct his increasingly alien offspring. Growing up elsewhere—away from the "home" I knew only through pictures, legal documents, and stories—I came to understand that my mother's obsession with property titles and my father's preoccupation with storytelling shared a purpose. My parents' "metal boxes" were meant to safeguard my inheritance, the legacy they hoped I would claim. Each contained the only assets my parents believed they could offer: *mami's* promised the financial security that eluded them as immigrants; *papi's* offered a history I would not otherwise learn. In the end, my mother's tangible assets would prove the more illusory and immaterial, while my father's stories served as a lifeline to the Cuban half of my identity. These shared memories fostered in me the sense that I belonged to a colorful, sometimes dysfunctional, sometimes extraordinary extended family. That storytelling was more than an entertaining pastime—that it served to unite generations of displaced and fractured communities across time—was a history lesson that I would learn later. I would realize that my father's stories were meant to safeguard not only our family's but an entire culture's history in exile.

History and memory share much the same function in shaping community: both employ imagination and experience to look into the past; both are subject to revision; and both are indispensable in forging and maintaining connections to the past and to each other. My concept of history does not here refer to those authorized and fact-based reconstructions of the past that I studied in school, but to the body of communal and personal memories transmitted through time and subject to reinterpretation and reinvention. This conception of history is certainly more fluid and tricky, more tangential, anarchic, and subjective. Yet it is no less powerful in its didactic significance or formative function. Recounted and remembered, events are "kept alive" and granted authenticity (if not accuracy); the past is given shape, accorded value, and preserved. Through this sharing of memories and telling of stories, we redefine our sense of community and foster our connection through blood and history. Given the primacy of storytelling in the formation of national identity, it is not surprising that competing groups tinker with the past to fashion more positive, self-serving stories based on history but creatively embellished by memory. As historian Charles Maier points out, memory "mingles private and public spheres . . . [and] conflates vast historical occurrences with the most interior consciousness."[3] This fusion of public and private history articulates aspects of Cuban exile group identity and contains the seeds for both discord and solidarity. It is a richly textured and polyvalent voice indeed that speaks to us through these collective memories, a chorus of conflicting stories that deny us the comfort of tidy, official History.

So it was that as a teen growing up in Miami, I identified with the Cuban exile community. I shared the memories of loss that haunted my parents and other Cuban-born adults. I understood the rage, the mourning, the painful longing that fueled public protests and other expressions of Cuban exile identity. I moved between this familial world defined by exile and the world I shared with my American friends, who regarded my family's preoccupation with politics with curious bewilderment. They could not understand why so many Cubans in Miami did not simply *move on*, live in the present as Americans, and shed their obsession with Cuba's past and with Fidel Castro. How could they know that lives had been forever changed and a people radically divided by events in 1959? How could they relate to the passionate displays of patriotism and fiery rhetoric that shaped Cuban exile politics in Miami? To the inhabitants of the world outside this exile enclave, politics had very little to do with daily life, while to me, it was intimately personal. In my familial world, Castro's latest words or deeds informed dinner conversations and news flashes about Cuba sparked impromptu street demonstrations or heated arguments among friends and family. In my home away from home, Cuba was always an absent presence, the subject of gossip exchanged over *café cubano* at the ubiquitous coffee stands and the object of passionate emotions vented on local radio talk shows and news editorials. It was a world where the butcher bore the scars of torture endured during twenty years as a political prisoner and my neighbor's brother had been executed by a pro-Castro firing squad. This was not a world where politics was just about an occasional election.

An exile community's historical consciousness is deepened by two kinds of experience: direct participation in the events or emotional engagement through oral testimonies, memoirs, autobiographies, familial lore, and imagination. Since I left Cuba at the age of five, I possessed few memories born of my own reality. Instead, I relied on the many stories I remembered, the diverse people I met who shared their private memories of Cuba's past. At home and on the street, I heard stories fueled by rage and disappointment. In those stories, Cuba was a nation violated—her people scattered, oppressed, imprisoned, executed, or lost at sea. She was the Republic whose possibilities had been cut short by *comunistas*, by traitors and despots. Later, my university studies offered other versions as well. If conditions in Cuba were so ripe with potential; if the island had sustained a healthy, vibrant economy; if there was little evidence of discontent—then why did the Revolution happen? To my adult mind, my father's stories seemed unreliable, like memories filtered through the eyes of a lover. I began to question contradictions, inconsistencies, partial truths. I longed to know "the real story."

For my vision of Cuba was always filtered through multiple lenses, each casting doubt on the other and evoking conflicting emotions and conclusions: shifting my perspective from Cuban to American or vice versa could destabilize any conviction or cast doubt on any opinion. Personal histories avowed in private circles crumbled under public scrutiny, as newspaper and television accounts often contrasted with local images of self and community. Like others of the "in-between" generation, my knowledge of Cuban history stemmed from secondary, often contradictory sources. It was mediated by my parents and later filtered through an educational system that measured Cuban history only in relation to its own cultural myths and perspectives. On those rare occasions when Cuba was mentioned during my formal schooling, it was as a representative Communist Other to Democratic America—as an island nation defined by loss and lack. Cuba's complex history, filtered through this narrow lens, served to affirm the virtues of capitalism or to admonish young Americans who may be lured by pop culture images of el Che or Fidel. The U.S. stood as an example of democracy and justice defined against its Other: Latin America. Understandably, my view of Cuba from that perspective was that it had always been a "banana republic," its history simply a string of strongmen dictators, racists, and regressive initiatives. In this version, Cuba's long war for independence from Spain is named the "Spanish-American War," obscuring the fact that a generation of Cubans, led by a military *leadership* comprised of 40 percent Afro-Cubans, paid for that victory with their own blood. This script calls for the U.S. to play enlightened democracy to Cuba's "Third World" role. It ignores the U.S. government's role in imposing their own segregationist policies on Cuba's military during its occupation, and neglects to mention the fact that unlike the U.S.'s War of Independence, Cuba's articulated a vision of racial equality and harmony.

Yet for years I felt destined to carry these remnants of a tattered and dishonored heritage like an albatross around my neck.[4] Stuart Hall's remark that identity is never stable but is "subject to the play of history and the play of difference" suggests that identity is an ongoing process of identification and association. In this sense, my *cubanidad* became as much a political choice as a question of birthplace or native language. But it was a choice implicated by the stories and memories I internalized as my own—personal and cultural narratives born of family lore, historical events, hearsay, and personal experiences. Historical memory nurtures our sense of belonging: it fosters connection and kinship, a shared vision of an imagined home place that is indispensable in shaping personal and national identity. But Cuban exiles and their bicultural sons and daughters carry the fragments of a shattered history like baggage. Forty-six years of migration and separation have eroded and confused our memories, leaving gaps, absences, and conflicting images, each account filtered through personal experience or perspective. At the same time, we hear voices proclaiming their authority to dictate our memories, to view the entirety of a collective past through narrow and myopic lenses focused on the speaker's own interests. Often, these interests conflict with our own experiences or distort images of self and community. We cling to a thread of connection even as we feel our grasp slipping with each negative depiction of Cubans or each public incident of intolerance among our own people. Like many of my generation of Cubans raised in the U.S., I have regarded my ancestry with mixed feelings, torn between a need to reject the identity conjured by these dominant perspectives and a desire to connect to my heritage without shame. Indeed, as Margaret Ferguson has remarked, exile is "the metaphorical name for the experience of ambivalence."[5]

Exile defines the present only in relation to the past; it perceives "the world always in terms of relations: nostalgia, the fictional recreation of better times in relation to a negative reading of the present."[6] This predicament sheds some light on an older generation of Cuban exiles who confound the "in-between" generation with their inability to act upon the present. Many are caught in this labyrinth of history where all paths lead to the past and there is no exit to the present. Any vote cast, and position taken, any alliance formed in the United States seems bound to this obsession with the past. Such a preoccupation with the past makes exiled and displaced peoples particularly keen on storytelling. They seem to sense its profound influence, its formative and instructive role in shaping identity and recording cultural memory. Perhaps, as Michael Ugarte remarks, "to be displaced is to be obsessed with memory."[7] The story of exile expresses its own poetic, "its own language, conceits, and motivations." Ugarte's analysis suggests that regardless of specific context, exile's voice records the experiences of loss, absence, separation, and fragmentation that seem to characterize the migratory experience. Most significantly, exile gives rise to a polemic that "brings into play a series of ideological and historical disputes whose battle ground includes the new home as well as the old."[8]

In the context of Cuban politics and discourse, Cuba's complex history is reduced to a polemic between pro-Castro/anti-Castro scenarios. This dichotomy, which Francisco Valdes aptly locates in elitist Miami and Cuba factions, is founded on contrasting versions of the past.[9] It rejects complexity in favor of a singular and myopic vision. Each side constructs a notion of *cubanidad* founded on imagined communities past and present. The dueling factions in Miami and Havana have instigated and fueled hostility among Cubans since the ascension of "Fidelismo" in 1959 and the subsequent influx of Cuban refugees to the U.S. Both sets of elites have constructed unilateral and ossified versions of Cuban history that support their respective agendas. On the island, the circles of power that regulate all aspects of life, the government and the party, have dictated and disseminated Cuba's official story. These elites cultivate a romantic image of themselves as heroic Davids slaying—or at least defying—the menacing Goliath of the North. From this perspective, Cubans who emigrated after Fidel's 1959 triumph are labeled *gusanos*, worms who greedily abandoned the homeland in favor of U.S. capitalism. Miami's elites, on the other hand, encompass a loose assemblage of business leaders and politicos who have amassed wealth or position in the U.S. and wield it to promote their own agendas. They are in direct opposition to Havana's elites, and as a group, express an interest in "freedom" and "democracy" only to the extent that these remain abstracted enough to serve their own aims. Both factions have cloaked themselves in nationalistic fervor to invoke their cause and monopol-

This effigy of Fidel Castro, photographed by the author on a recent visit to Miami, serves as visual testament to the endurance of stories shaping politics and culture in Cuban Miami

ize political power, and both have resorted to disinformation, suppression, intimidation, and even violence to control their constituencies.

Of course, both sides disseminate and validate their version of Cuban history. On this side of the Cuban divide, Cuba's history reads like an echo of Milton's "Paradise Lost," while on the other, present-day Cuba emerges as "Paradise Found" when compared to selective memories of Batista and *yanqui* imperialism. Both sides have continued to insist on the authenticity of "their" story, rejecting any reconfiguration of Cuban identity that might destabilize or challenge their authority. While these polarized and stalemated speakers have set the tone of Cuban political and social discourses in Miami and Havana, neither represents the actual and complexly diverse communities they profess to care so much about. Instead, each side has constructed self-serving notions of *cubanidad* founded on imagined communities past and present. Cuban exiles that cling to this singular vision memorialize the pre-1959 past as the moment of solidarity and communality, and only insiders to this vision may share its glory. Miami's elites have been granted access to the U.S.'s political machinery, and they have wielded their influence by financing pro-embargo campaigns and "representing" the Cuban exile community on the national stage. *Their* opinions on everything from the embargo against Cuba to whether six-year-old Elian should stay in the U.S. are the ones televised on national news programs, *their* views are held up by the media as representing "the Cuban exile community" or "Miami's Cuban community." It is no wonder that many Cubans of my generation have moved away from Miami and dissociated themselves entirely from the identity essentialized as "Miami Cuban." The easy identification I felt growing up among fellow Cubans could have dissolved in the face of these camps.

But many of the "in-between" generation occupy the interstices between these elites' conflicting narratives. We have rejected the inflammatory rhetoric on both sides of the Cuban border and sought to reconcile the opposing historical perspectives these represent. For me, the many stories I remember and the memories I keep in my own "metal box" have helped to humanize the most easily demonized. They have helped to soften even the most embarrassing public displays of *cubanida*. The stories I long to hear do not aim to produce a coherent narrative of Cuban identity; nor do they gloss over the ugly aspects of our collective history or supplant them with idealized patriotic musings. Thus I keep listening, knowing that for every story of vengeance there is another of reconciliation. As Cubans struggling to come to terms with our differences and yet longing for connection, we can live with this ambiguity. In fact, we can make it home.

Myra Mendible is Professor of Literature, Cultural Theory, and Ethnic/Gender Studies at Florida Gulf Coast University. She has published widely in peer-reviewed journals and is the editor of an anthology ironically titled, *From*

Bananas to Buttocks: The Latina Body in Popular Film and Culture, published by University of Texas Press in 2007.

Notes

1 A derogatory term for those who emigrated from Cuba after Fidel's 1959 takeover. Literally translates as "worms."
2 Another derogatory reference, in this case against those who migrated to the U.S. as part of the 1981 Mariel boatlift. Castro forced boat captains to include some criminals and mentally disabled people onboard the vessels carrying family members out of Cuba.
3 C. S. Maier, *The Unmasterable Past: History, Holocaust, and German National Identity* (Cambridge, MA: Harvard University Press, 1988), 149.
4 The protagonist in Samuel Coleridge's poem, "The Rime of the Ancient Mariner" is compelled to tell everyone he meets the story of his crime against nature, for which he is forced to wear a dead albatross around his neck.
5 Margaret Ferguson, "The Exile's Defense: Dubellay's La Deffence et Illustration de la Langue Francoyse," *PMLA* 93:2 (March 1977): 277.
6 Michael Ugarte, "Luis Cernuda and the Politics of Exile," *MLN* 101:2 (March 1986): 327.
7 Ibid.
8 Ibid., 326.
9 FranciscoValdes, "Diaspora and Deadlock, Miami and Havana: Coming to Terms with Dreams and Dogmas," *Florida Law Review* 55 (January 2003).

References and Further Reading

Brock, L. and Castañeda Fuertes, D. (eds.) (1998). *Between Race and Empire: African-Americans and Cubans before the Cuban Revolution.* Philadelphia: Temple University Press.
Dehay, T. (1994). "Narrating Memory," in *Memory, Narrative, and Identity.* Eds. Amriitjit Singh, Joseph T. Skerrett, Jr., and Robert E. Hogan. Boston: Northeastern University Press.
Duke, C. (1983). "The Idea of Race: The Cultural Impact of American Intervention in Cuba, 1898–1912," in *Politics, Society and Culture in the Caribbean.* Ed. Blanca G. Silvestrini. San Juan: University of Puerto Rico Press.
Ferguson, M. (1977). "The Exile's Defense: Dubellay's La Deffence et Illustration de la Langue Francoyse," *PMLA* 93:2 (March): 275–89.
Halbwachs, M. (1992). *On Collective Memory.* Trans. Lewis A. Coser. Chicago: University of Chicago Press.
Hall, S. (1996). "Cultural Identity and Diaspora," in *Contemporary Postcolonial Theory: A Reader.* Ed. Padmini Mongia. London: Arnold, 110–21.
Llorens, V. (1967). *Literatura, historia, politica.* Madrid: Revista de Occidente.
Maier, C.S. (1988). *The Unmasterable Past: History, Holocaust, and German National Identity.* Cambridge, MA: Harvard University Press.
Perez Firmat, G. (1996). *Next Year in Cuba: A Cubano's Coming-of-Age in America.* New York: Doubleday.
Portes, A. (1998). "Morning in Miami: A New Era for Cuban-American Politics," *The American Prospect* (May–June): 28–32.
Ugarte, M. (1986). "Luis Cernuda and the Politics of Exile," *MLN* 101:2 (March 1986): 325–41.
Valdes, F. (2003). "Diaspora and Deadlock, Miami and Havana: Coming to Terms with Dreams and Dogmas," *Florida Law Review* 55 (January 2003): 283–317.

23
Stories in Law

MARTHA MINOW

One of my favorite stories is an old one about the walled city of Verona. Over time, the population inside the wall grew and the city became overcrowded. The problems from this circumstance mounted, until one day the Bishop decided something had to be done, and called a meeting with the Chief Rabbi.

The Bishop said, "The overcrowding in Verona has become unbearable. The Jews must leave."

The Chief Rabbi said, "Leave? But we have lived here for generations! Surely we should talk about so drastic a measure."

The Bishop replied, "But who should talk? We could have a debate. But everyone in town cares about the subject."

The Rabbi proposed, "We could hold it in the amphitheater; there is room for everyone."

But the Bishop said, "No one could hear us there. It will have to be a silent debate."

They agreed, and the big day arrived. Everyone turned out and watched expectantly as the Bishop began.

He raised his right hand up to the sky.

The Rabbi brought his right hand down and pointed to his left palm. The Bishop held up three fingers.

The Rabbi held up one.

The Bishop reached under his chair and brought out a wafer and ate it, and a glass of wine and sipped it.

The Rabbi pulled out an apple and took a bite.

At that moment, the Bishop leapt up and said, "You are right, the Jews can stay. We in Verona will have to find another way to solve our problem."

A crowd gathered around the Bishop, excited and perplexed. "We followed the debate very closely," one person said, "but what exactly was said?"

"Ah, the man was brilliant," said the Bishop. "I said, 'The Lord of All commands that the Jews leave Verona today.' He replied, 'But the Lord is here in Verona with the Jews, too.' I answered, 'The three aspects of the Trinity—the

Father, Son, and Holy Ghost—guide us on this matter.' And he answered, 'But there is just one Almighty, one King of the Universe.' I responded with the wafer and the wine to say, 'Jesus died for our sins so the Christians could be saved.' But he responded with the apple, noting 'We are all children of Adam and Eve.' And indeed we are; we are in this together; we will work it out together."

Meanwhile, another crowd surrounded the Rabbi. "Rabbi, Rabbi, Rabbi, what happened?" they cried. "I have no idea," said the Rabbi. "The Bishop said, 'The Jews of Verona must leave here today.' I answered, 'We are staying right here.' He returned, 'I will give you three days to pack.' I offered, 'We'll take a week,' and then he ate his lunch and I ate mine."

This story has endured for some time; and I confess, I never tire of it. I have used it in talking about problems in the adversary system, the difficulties of bilingual education, and the elements of luck in persuasion. Like a rich common-law decision, the story has multiple features that can be highlighted, depending on the context in which it is invoked.

At the most basic level, then, I suggest that storytelling offers real continuities with common-law reasoning; it dwells on particulars while eliciting a point that itself may be molded or recast in light of the story's particulars reviewed in a different time.

The story of Verona has something particular to say in this moment, in this discussion of narrative and law. It is a story about reaching agreement without full understanding; it is a story about the importance of perspective to human capacities to understand and to communicate; it is a story about the influence of experience and situation on perception, and the making of meaning out of human actions.

Each of these themes appears in contemporary debates about the place of stories in legal scholarship.[1] Some writers advocate the use of stories to promote practical problem-solving; some admire and some criticize the power of stories in conveying particular points of view or perspectives; some celebrate and others worry about the disproportionate use of storytelling genres by women of various races and men of color in legal writing. Rather than review those debates, I mean here to comment on them in three ways. First, I will review a recent effort of my own to approach a legal controversy by telling some stories about it; I will ask what works and what does not work in this effort. Second, I will consider how Hannah Arendt's defense of the political theorist as storyteller illuminates the motives and methods of storytelling in and around law. Finally, I will consider the promise and limits of storytelling as an approach to a legal problem in light of Hannah Arendt's conception of political theory as storytelling.

But before I do this, let me offer some opening observations. Stories seem to work, when they do, on many levels; they can produce an experience, an insight, and one or more emotional responses. With any given story, some people get it and some people do not. Some of those who get it do not like the experience and are troubled by it. Perhaps the story prompts a response that feels inconsistent with other strongly held views or intuitions. Perhaps the experience of a response to the story is itself troubling because it occurs on levels not easily summarized by principles, logical analysis, or other specific modes of reasoning that seem more generally accessible or rationally defensible. But the walled-city-of-Verona story raises questions about the accessibility of a given form of rational argument in a world of human and group differences. I will return to these observations when I conclude.

The Story of Kiryas Joel

Three Stories

I recently wrote a paper telling three stories about the Supreme Court's 1994 decision in the case of *Board of Education of Kiryas Joel Village School District v. Louis Grumet*.[2] You may know it as the Hasidic school case. The Supreme Court struck down a state statute creating a special school district for the disabled children of an ultraorthodox Jewish community in upstate New York. Construed as a violation of the establishment clause, the statute triggered five opinions in the Court and revealed the recurring disagreements about how to formulate legal doctrine in this area.

In conversations about the case, I was most struck by how many people thought the case was an easy one—and nearly all agreed with the Supreme Court's conclusion. Although unsure of my conclusion, I felt that the case was a hard one. I set out in my essay to communicate why and found myself telling stories. The first story is a short version of the history of the Jewish Diaspora— the dispersion of Jews from Palestine after the destruction of the Second Temple in A.D. 70. As a people without a nation, the Jews—and the governing authorities—devised ways to live apart that sometimes led to a certain amount of autonomy and self-governance and sometimes led to distrust, regulation, violence, and expulsion. Thus, the Jewish communities of Babylonia and medieval Europe retained control over domestic legal affairs, such as religion, education, family law, and civil litigation.[3] The tradition-bound, segregated Jewish communities provided some psychological sustenance and preserved collective Jewish identity in societies that largely despised Jews, excluded them from the economic and social worlds opened to others, and threatened them with physical violence.

The story I then told focused on the perhaps ironic turn of events presented by the Enlightenment and the ultimate emergence of constitutional democracies in Europe: in several countries Jews encountered opportunities to join the larger societies, but only if they surrendered their religious traditions. As a story within a story, I told of Moses Mendelssohn, who argued that Jews could "adopt the mores and constitutions of the country in which you find yourself, but be steadfast in upholding the religion of your fathers, too." And it was the conventionally Jewish-looking Moses Mendelssohn who was walking down a busy street in Berlin in the 1790s when he accidentally bumped into a large Prussian officer. The officer yelled, "Swine!" Mendelssohn returned with a courtly bow, replying, "Mendelssohn." It is a bittersweet commentary, perhaps, on what happens when members of a despised group claim equality while retaining their group membership. I explored similar tensions posed for Jews by the French Revolution and Napoleon's code; Jews repeatedly faced the invitation to citizenship if they would reconcile their religious beliefs and practices with the duties and conduct of the French people.[4] The destruction of the Jews during World War II, for many Jews, demonstrated the impossibility of this invitation.

I told this first story to frame the second story—the story of the village of Kiryas Joel in New York that led to the Supreme Court controversy. The first story gives a context to the effort by a group of Hasidic Jews to live in an enclave by themselves, to speak Yiddish, to dress in clothes more typical of medieval communities than late twentieth-century America, and to educate their children in private, single-sex religious schools. Called the Satmar, these people obtained incorporation of their residential area near the Catskill Mountains as a separate local government under New York law. Named for their founder, the village of Kiryas Joel, like similar communities of Satmar Hasidim, is viewed by its inhabitants as a form of homage to those who died in the Holocaust and as a living testament to the vitality of the way of life the Nazis tried to eradicate.[5] They also sought publicly funded educational and related services for their children with disabilities, as authorized by federal and state law. During the mid-1980s the state provided such services in the religious schools run by the Satmar, but Supreme Court decisions then forbade the provision of such public services in religious schools on the grounds that this could advance sectarian ends or entangle the government in religious activities.[6]

Some of the parents of disabled Hasidic children sent their children to the public school in the next town but found this an unacceptable option because of the "panic, fear, and trauma" experienced by children sent away to school with people who viewed them as very different from themselves.[7] So, at the request of residents of Kiryas Joel, the New York legislature authorized the village to set up its own public schools. The village exercised this authority to set up a school solely for students with disabilities, because the residents had no interest in having any other public schools. Citizen taxpayers and the New York School Board Association challenged the statute in court and claimed that this special school district violated the requirement to separate church and state.

The school itself is administered by people from outside the community, with entirely secular instruction under the direction of a non-Hasidic superintendent with twenty years' experience in bilingual and bicultural education in the New York City public schools.[8] Nonetheless, the entire student enrollment in the school comprises Hasidic Jews, some from within Kiryas Joel and some from neighboring communities. There is some evidence, though not in the record of the case, that whatever franchise is enjoyed by the villagers is effect-ively controlled by the rebbe through the auspices of his son, the rov.[9] The son announced his slate of candidates for school board and instructed all eligible voters to vote for them.[10] Dissent within the community exists, but it also tends to be followed by expulsion from the communal institutions.[11] Such facts were not in the record, because the challengers objected to the sheer creation of the special school district as an impermissible union of church and state.

The New York trial court, appellate court, and Court of Appeals all found the statute a violation of the establishment clause by using various versions of the Supreme Court's precedents in the area. Four members of the Supreme Court treated the statute as an impermissible "fusion" of governmental and religious functions;[12] the legislature, in this view, improperly delegated civic authority on the basis of religious group membership rather than general and neutral principles. One member sought to re-establish the precedent of *Lemon v. Kurtzman*,[13] which once guided establishment clause decisions, but received no attention by a majority of the Court across the several opinions. Justice Stevens found several specific factual points justified finding this an instance of establishment rather than accommodation of religion; Justice O'Connor agreed, but in her own opinion recommended revisiting the decisions made in the 1980s that prevented the provision of public services on the site of paro-chial schools. Justice Kennedy wrote separately, with the view that accom-modation of the Satmar is a permissible goal, but the legislature impermissibly configured a school district along religious lines.

The dissenting Justices Scalia, Rehnquist, and Thomas reasoned that the school itself posed no problems for the establishment clause, that the civil authority over the schools was explicitly distinct from religious authority, and that the motivation for the legislation was either secular or else a permissible accommodation of religion. Rather than pursue these or other doctrinal lines of argument, my story proceeded to consider why all organized Jewish groups, except the Orthodox, joined in opposing the school district in Kiryas Joel. I speculated that this line-up echoed the dilemma of assimilation created by the Enlightenment for Jews and other subcommunities.

Finally, my third story told the contrasting tale of the struggle for desegre-gation of schooling and other institutions in this country. Social movements, using lawyers, have struggled for both racial equality and inclusion of people with disabilities during the twentieth century. With this story as a larger con-text, the village of Kiryas Joel could be faulted both for secluding all of its students from integration with other kinds of children and for isolating its children with disabilities from education with its non-disabled children in the religious schools.

I myself struggle for a conclusion in the paper. I argue, perhaps weakly, that however much we may criticize the Satmar for failing to shoulder the financial costs of fully educating their children with disabilities in the religious schools (with no public aid), this is surely a decision the Constitution entitles them to make. Just as parents may choose private religious schools for some of their children, they may choose public schools for others. I also suggest that as desirable as desegregation may be as a public policy, the courts have curbed it at the limits of city boundaries, and it would be both curious and unfair to make an exception to this rule where disabled Hasidic children are involved. It is their education and their interests that must be considered. Thus, if the Satmar parents are viewed as making a good-faith request for secular public education within a secular town recognized by the state, their children are entitled to it. I tweak the Satmar by suggesting that their bilingual programs for Yiddish-speaking disabled children should be opened to their archenemies, the Lubavitch Hasids, but mainly I ask questions about how subgroups can both respect and resist the state in a liberal society committed to both inclusion and religious liberty. More generally, I propose evaluating similar proposals for special public schools for African American males only, for military academies for boys only, and for math classes for girls only at least in part by reference to competing narratives of particularity and narratives of inclusion.

What Works and What Does Not Work

What works about the stories I tell about Kiryas Joel? I think that they can shake up some assumptions. The case looks harder *with* than *without* the narrative of the Diaspora. Indeed, the case looks harder because of the emphasis on the details of the school for disabled Hasidic children: many people who read about the case did not realize that the school was for children with disabilities; others did not realize that the entire instruction in the school is secular and under the control of secular authorities. Some people tell me I have convinced them that the Court's decision was wrong.

Such comments make me nervous, because I am not sure I have convinced myself. Not that it matters much in terms of Kiryas Joel itself: within a month of the Supreme Court's decision, the New York legislature adopted a new law, written to permit any municipality to apply for a special school district, and granted approval under this statute to Kiryas Joel. The new statute is under challenge and will raise questions of motive and effect, but it is a new framework for the debate. But when we turn to other claims by groups to have accommodations in public schools that produce segregation, what terms of evaluation should prevail? I imply in my chapter that the juxtaposition of the story of the particular group with the story of social movements for inclusion can *prompt wise judgments*. Can good judgments indeed emerge simply with the collision of stories and narratives of the societal struggles for desegregation and integration? Must good judgments follow from such collisions, or might poor conclusions also be reached? How is this process of decision through contrasting stories better and worse than application of one set of norms, and how are stories better and worse in gathering together potentially conflicting norms?

On reflection, I think that good judgments *could* emerge when people turn over in their minds competing narratives about both a particular claimant and a larger social struggle, but there is no guarantee. Being able to appeal to some overarching principles and even some mid-level concepts lends at least the sense of some consistency in judgments across contexts and over time, which matters to the rule of law.[14] These kinds of consistency seem especially important where relations between the state and subgroups are involved; otherwise favoritism, unfair discrimination, and unreasoned whimsy seem only too likely. Yet stories implicitly identify some principles that can be universalized in the sense that any group meeting the terms of those principles should be treated the same way. Two such principles direct observers of the case of the school district of Kiryas Joel to consider and to treat as weighty: (1) the needs and interests of children, especially those with disabilities, and (2) the meaning of the proposed action in the lives of the subgroup and in the lives of others in the society. Whose meanings should receive state endorsement or state rejection?[15]

Perhaps my turn to storytelling stems from my own understanding that neither of these principles currently receives acknowledgment, much less a place of priority in prevailing legal analysis. I and others could and in fact do work directly on the project of advocating these principles,[16] but in that long period called the meantime, shifting from the fight over principles to the insights of stories offers another technique for persuasion. So the incompleteness of storytelling as a mode for decision-making may be both a defect and a virtue, a defect if one seeks articulated norms to guide future decision-makers, but a virtue if one knows that prevailing articulated norms are not the right ones.

There is for me a more troubling *shortcoming of the storytelling mode. By itself, it gives no guidance or suggestion about which stories to tell.* Here are small examples. In my published account of the Satmar Hasidim, I detailed divisions within the community and negative views held by others about it.[17] I also reported on earlier litigation by the Satmar objecting that the neighboring public school system failed to fully accommodate local Yiddish-speaking disabled children. I did not, however, report on an earlier suit brought by the Satmar in Kiryas Joel challenging the use of female bus drivers when male students were transported to the neighboring public school,[18] nor of their failed effort to assure that Satmar girls would be taught in the public school only by female public school teachers who spoke Yiddish.[19] Why not? I viewed them as irrelevant given that the public school set up in Kiryas Joel is itself coed with both male and female teachers, in sharp contrast to the sex segregation usually demanded by the Satmar.[20] But there is also no question but that these additional stories convey unattractive features of the community that I was trying to paint in a sympathetic light. Storytellers (and advocates) may do this, and there is no rule or guiding principle of selection for storytelling. To be sure, there are problems of selectivity in any human endeavor, including efforts at systemic theory building, because the limits of time, space, and attention invariably force authors to select which features, objectives, examples, and objections to discuss explicitly and which ones not to. In the very moment of treating one or another starting point as plausible, an author has selected, knowingly or unknowingly, from a range of possibilities.

The biggest check on selectivity problems in storytelling lies in the availability of another story, perhaps told by someone else. Indeed, as anyone who has told a story to a child—or been a child—may recall, the likely response to one story is the call to tell another. I tried to check the partiality of the stories of the Diaspora and Kiryas Joel with a counterstory about the social movements for school desegregation and integration in the United States. But the availability of counterstories does not indicate which counterstories should be elicited, obtained, or heeded.[21] If the counter or alternative stories are simply those told in response to an initial story, we face the specter of warring stories with no methods for testing them or for resolving disputes that they reflect. In another context, I have worried about this problem, given the contemporary prevalence in legal and political arenas of victim stories.[22] One who claims to be a victim invites, besides sympathy, two other responses: "I didn't do it," and "I am a victim, too." No wonder some describe contemporary political debates as exhibitions of "one-downmanship" or as the "oppression Olympics." Victim stories risk trivializing pain and obscuring the metric or vantage point for evaluating competing stories of pain. Victim stories also often adhere to an unspoken norm that prefers narratives of helplessness to stories of responsibility, and tales of victimization to narratives of human agency and capacity.

Intriguingly, Seyla Benhabib argues that Hannah Arendt's commitment to an existential sense of human choice helps to explain her own defense of storytelling,[23] and it is to Hannah Arendt's views that I now turn.

Hannah Arendt on the Storyteller as Political Theorist

A quirky, original thinker, Hannah Arendt is perhaps best known for her studies of totalitarianism in general and of Nazism in particular.[24] Recently, several scholars have explored how what may seem quirky or undisciplined in her work actually manifests a methodological commitment that Arendt made to narrative, in contrast to the prevailing methods of social science.[25] Thus, for example, she interwove narratives about individuals and discussions of works of literature in *The Origins of Totalitarianism* not as faulty pursuits of the empirical method but instead as commitments to narrative as the mode for lending meaning and understanding to human action.[26] Arendt distinguished action, which is creative and free of causal necessity, from behavior, through which individuals become predictable creatures of the mass;[27] she further identified social science as well suited to describing behavior, but narrative as crucial to capturing the meaning of human actions and conveying the availability of choices to each individual.[28]

Seyla Benhabib traces Arendt's commitment to narrative to her effort to connect her commitments as an existentialist with her identification as a German-Jewish intellectual living through the twentieth century.[29] From these vantage points, Arendt struggled specifically with the very problem I recounted in the story of the Diaspora. States so often accord rights to members of their own nation but not to members of other nations, like Jews, who reside within their boundaries. Drawing on the legacies of modernism and antimodernism, and the traditions both German and Jewish, Arendt experienced a great tension between universalism and particularism.[30] This tension is manifest in the contrast between Arendt as the modernist and Arendt as the storyteller of revolutions and witness to totalitarianism.[31]

More basically, Benhabib and others suggest that Arendt defended storytelling as the proper mode for political theory after totalitarianism, compared with rationalist social science techniques that look for laws of human behavior. Those techniques risk dulling the mind of observers against what is new and unprecedented. Social science rationality could treat horrors such as the concentration camps as capable of being explained and accepted by reference to prior events, rather than as radical departures that require a sense of rupture.[32]

Not only would such an explanation be wrong in Arendt's view, but it would also yield the worst moral response—passivity and acceptance rather than resistance and outrage.[33] Hence, in her explorations of the "banality of evil," the ordinariness of life within bureaucratic regimes, she adopted, perhaps paradoxically, the surprising view that horror can take the form of bureaucratic rule, with no one feeling accountable, as a way to shake up listeners so they would be on guard against future horrors. She struggled for modes of explanation that would demonstrate how every person can and must participate in the task of politics against the backdrop of totalitarian and mass societies that impair the capacity of people to act together as citizens.[34]

The task of the political theorist, as pursued by Arendt, is to confront the community with the challenge to think freshly in the face of the unprecedented and to reorient people to permit them to build a new future.[35] The method to be used must resist the tendency to present history as inevitable and analogous to the past or as the unfolding of historical necessity. Human beings are too unpredictable for these images to be correct, and, in any case, such images have poor moral implications, yielding compliance and predictable behavior rather than unpredictable and courageous human actions.

Storytelling can disrupt the illusion that social sciences create in the service of rational administration, the illusion that the world is a smoothly managed household.[36] Storytelling invites both teller and listener to confront messy and complex realities—and to do so in a way that promotes communication and thinking about how to connect the past and the future by thinking about what to do.[37] Rather than taking the view that only experts understand and act in the political world the political theorist who tells stories thinks about politics in a way that remains faithful to the capacity of citizens to act together.[38]

Arendt further suggested the moral resonance of the narrative form itself. This view seems to be echoed in works by James Boyd White and Martha Nussbaum, who emphasize the ethical relationship between author and reader, which is modeled especially in fictive narratives.[39] For Arendt, narratives are crucial in constructing a sense of the self in the face of traditions that have crumbled and human hopes that risk being forgotten.[40] The problem of selection does not trouble Arendt; she acknowledges that the storyteller selects and necessarily judges while excavating the past, just as a deep-sea diver finds pearls.[41] The storyteller uses bits of the past to unsettle the present and deprive it of peace of mind.[42] The story form is itself well suited to portraying the plurality of human viewpoints on any given event. Arendt argued that the narrator should never pretend to reproduce the standpoint of past actors, because that would disguise the standpoint of the author.[43] She also maintained that only through the variety of relationships constructed by many people seeing from different perspectives can truth be known and community be created.[44] Attentiveness to the partiality of any story, then, as well as to the perspectival nature of a shared social world, follows from the commitment to narrative.

As may be obvious, these interpretations of Hannah Arendt's work bolster my own struggles with the case of *Board of Education of Kiryas Joel* (not to mention the walled city of Verona). Like Arendt, I notice and value the capacities of storytelling to draw attention and disrupt the tendency to assimilate a new problem to the past and submerge it under general schemes.[45] Like Arendt, I see in the mode of storytelling the possibility of enacting and expressing insights about the partiality of any individual's viewpoint, as well as the hope that we can come to imagine the viewpoint and experiences of others. Like Arendt, I look to storytelling to arrest the ready reaction, to reorient people's minds to confront the future, rather than to accept the past. Like Arendt, I look to stories, which I acknowledge that I select, as a way to create a heuristic for making meaning of the past and pointing toward ways to act in the future.

Like Arendt, I find myself struggling with the limits of Enlightenment universalism, or what some call political liberalism, given the historical events of the twentieth century. In the name of universalism, particular groups have been oppressed; in the name of Enlightenment rationality, particular groups have been exterminated. At the same time, as more recent history suggests, the war of all against all is a likely result of a revival of particularisms.

Indeed, there seem to be a series of nested dilemmas or multiple versions of the same dilemma. There is the "Jewish question:" How much of their own identity must Jews (or any other subgroup) give up in order to enjoy the benefits of citizenship in a liberal state? The promise of inclusion in the world of rights-bearing individuals offers freedom from group-based oppression, but if the price is assimilation, it is too high. That price also gives a dark hint that inclusion, equality, and dignity are not truly in the offing.[46]

Similarly, there is the issue of modernity, which seems to invite the fluid movement of persons, capital, and ideas under the rubrics of political, economic, and intellectual freedom. Yet this same modernity seldom discloses the corrosive effects of mobility of people, investments, and ideas.[47] The mobilities that seem rational and compelling—and seem to fulfill contemporary political and economic theories—may neglect the places of meaning, coherence, stability, and commitment in people's lives.

There is, in addition, a parallel contest between intellectual methods, such as those of social science and some forms of philosophy, that seek the general and the universal but risk suppressing differences and disagreements. In contrast, commitments to narrative revel in particularity, difference, and resistance to generalization.

Finally, there is the tension between the general and the particular as goals for both intellectual focus and legal regulation. Should we desire explanations that are bigger than each particular, and laws that run across a vast range of particulars in search of predictability, power, coherence, and control, or do any general forms simply install one particular over others, suppressing by subsuming, neglecting by abstracting?

Hannah Arendt's work suggests that at stake in these dilemmas are both the meaning we choose to make of the twentieth century and the actions we hope to enable in the future. I do not want to sound grandiose but I do think that something like this is at stake in the contemporary debates over storytelling in legal scholarship. Storytelling similarly has resurged in other fields, such as medicine, history, religion, and political theory, biography and autobiography, fiction, and entertainment. If Arendt is right, these are causes for celebration.

Still, let me repeat the concerns already raised: Stories alone do not articulate principles likely to provide consistency in generalizations to guide future action; stories do not generate guides for what to heed or what additional stories to elicit. Stories on their own offer little guidance for evaluating competing stories. I might as well state explicitly another favorite story, and an old one.

The Rabbi hears in his study a dispute between two congregants. He listens to the first person carefully and comments, "You're right." Then he listens to the second person and concludes, "You're right." The Rabbi's wife, overhearing it all from the kitchen, calls out, "They can't both be right." "You're right also," says the Rabbi.

Offered as an illustration of the limitation of stories themselves to guide the evaluation of stories, this story also suggests a guide to the entire set of dilemmas that I have described. The guide is a posture of humility and acknowledgment of the partiality of truths. To generalize far beyond the context of that story, let me suggest the following: Modes of analysis and argument that maintain their exclusive hold on the truth are suspect. By casting doubt on alternative modes, they shield themselves from challenge and suppress alternative ways of understanding. They also render ordinary and explicable all they encounter: "To a hammer, everything looks like a nail." But some things are extraordinary and call for extraordinary responses. Methods of analysis that smooth out the bumps and subsume all under generalizations risk not only making this mistake but hiding it from view.

Some forms of social science reasoning—for example, the form of microeconomics recast as law and economics—run this danger. So do some forms of philosophic argument that convert all problems into terms amenable to a pre-existing framework, whether it be one inspired by John Rawls or one developed by Jeremy Bentham. So do some forms of legal doctrinal analysis that crank a fact pattern through the judicially crafted test.

Storytelling offers a worthy challenge to these modes. Stories disrupt these rationalizing, generalizing modes of analysis with a reminder of human beings and their feelings, quirky developments, and textured vitality. Stories are weak against the imperializing modes of analysis that seek general and universal applications, but their very weakness is a virtue to be emulated.[48] A story also invites more stories, stories that challenge the first one, or embellish it, or recast it. This, too, is a virtue to be copied. And stories at the moment seem better able to evoke realms of meaning, remembrance, commitment, and human agency than some other methods of human explanation. All this might change if theorizing picks up some of the themes of stories, but, then again, it might not.[49]

I suggest, in conclusion, that the revival of stories in law is welcome, not as a replacement of legal doctrine, economic analysis, or philosophic theory but as a healthy disruption and challenge to them. This is not about which must leave, stories or law, stories or social science, stories or philosophy, but about how they can live together, in and outside the walled city of Verona.

Martha Minow, the Jeremiah Smith, Jr. Professor, has taught at Harvard Law School since 1981. An expert in human rights and advocacy for members of racial and religious minorities and for women, children, and persons with disabilities, she also writes and teaches about law, culture, and narrative.

Acknowledgments

I thank my parents and siblings, who have always taught me that stories are the best way to make a point; Vicky Spelman, Avi Soifer, Cass Sunstein, Charles Fried, and Lucie White for helpful conversations; and Joe Singer and Mira Singer, who love stories.

Notes

1   See Kathryn Abrams, "Hearing the Call of Stories," *California Law Review* 79 (1991), 971; Randall Kennedy, "Racial Critiques of Legal Academia," *Harvard Law Review* 102 (1989), 1745; Daniel A. Farber and Suzanna Sherry, "Telling Stories Out of School: An Essay on Legal Narratives," *Stanford Law Review* 45 (1993), 807; Jane Baron, "Resistance to Stories," *Southern California Law Review* 67 (1994), 255; Angela P. Harris, "Foreword: The Jurisprudence of Reconstruction," *California Law Review* 82 (1994), 741.

2   *Board of Education of Kiryas Joel Village School District v. Louis Grumet*, 114 S.Ct. 2481 (1994). My paper, presented as the Harris Lecture at Indiana University and forthcoming in the *Indiana Law Review*, is "The Constitution and the Subgroup Question;" an earlier version was presented as the Beatrice K. Schneiderman Social Action Series lecture at Kehilath Anshe Maarav-Isaiah Israel, Chicago.

3   Naomi W. Cohen, *Jews in Christian America: The Pursuit of Religious Equality* (New York: Oxford University Press, 1992), 11.

4   Morton Borden, *Jews, Turks, and Infidels* (Chapel Hill: University of North Carolina Press, 1984), 110.

5   Jerome R. Mintz, *Hasidic People: A Place in the New World* (Cambridge, MA: Harvard University Press, 1992), 29.

6   *Aguilar v. Felton*, 473 U.S. 402 (1985); *Wolman v. Walter*, 433 U.S. 229 (1977).

7   Brief for Petitioner, *Board of Educ. of Kiryas Joel Village School Dist. v. Louis Grumet and Albert W. Hawk*, on writ of certiorari to the New York Court of Appeals, No. 93–517, at 6 (quoting Affidavit of Hannah Flegenheimer).

8   Ibid., at 11, Petitioner Appendix 115a–1171.

9   Exhibit 6 to Brief of Amicus, Committee for the Well-Being of Kiryas Joel, *Board of Educ. of the Kiryas Joel Village School Dist. v. Louis Grumet and Albert W. Hawk*, on writ of certiorari to the New York Court of Appeals, No. 95–517.

10 Ibid.

11 Mintz, 313–348.

12 114 S.Ct. 2481, 2487–2490 (Opinion of Souter, part II-A) (relying on *Larkin v. Grendel's Den, Inc.*, 459 U.S. 116).

13 *Lemon v. Kurtzman*, 403 U.S. 602 (1971).

14 Cass Sunstein's comments were especially helpful to me as I formulated these thoughts.

15 This question reflects my assumption that state neutrality is impossible in at least some cases pitting subgroups in the society against one another. I defend this assumption elsewhere. See Minow, "Constitution and the Subgroup Question;" Martha Minow, *Making All the Difference* (Ithaca, NY: Cornell University Press, 1990).

16 Martha Minow, "Rights for the Next Generation," *Harvard Women's Law Journal* 9 (1986), 1 (arguing for conceptions of children's interests); Martha Minow and Richard Weissbourd, "Social Movements for Children," *Daedalus* 122 (Winter 1993): 1 (same); Robert Cover, "The Supreme Court, 1982 Term-Foreword: *Nomos* and Narrative," *Harvard Law Review* 97 (1983), 4 (emphasizing the significance of local origins of meaning neglected by contemporary constitutional adjudication).

17 Minow, "Constitution and the Subgroup Question."

18 *Bollenbach v. Board of Education of Monroe-Woodbury Central School District*, 659 F. Supp. 1450 (SDNY 1987).

19 Mintz, 310.

20 Indeed, I suggest that this willingness to forgo sex segregation is a sign of the Satmar's good-faith deference to public norms in the public school system, justified internally in the community, however, by reference to an interpretation of Talmudic law. Minow, "Constitution and the Subgroup Question."

21 I mean to suggest here that a storyteller should seek out contrasting stories, rather than wait for them to present themselves. Too often the stories that go unheard are those of people with minimal access to power or resources to make themselves heard.

22 Martha Minow, "Surviving Victim Talk," *UCLA Law Review* 40 (1993), 1411.

23 Seyla Benhabib, "Hannah Arendt and the Redemptive Power of Narrative," in Lewis P. Hinchman and Sandra K. Hinchman, *Hannah Arendt: Critical Essays* (Albany: State University of New York, 1994), 111.

24 Hannah Arendt, *The Origins of Totalitarianism* (3rd enlarged ed. New York: Harcourt Brace, 1973); Arendt, *Eichmann in Jerusalem: A Report on the Banality of Evil* (rev. ed. New York: Viking Press, 1965); Arendt, *Men in Dark Times* (New York: Harcourt Brace & World, 1968).

25 David Luban, "Explaining Dark Times: Hannah Arendt's Theory of Theory," in Hinchman and Hinchman, at 79; Melvyn A. Hill, "The Fictions of Mankind and the Stories of Men," in *Hannah Arendt: The Recovery of the Public World*. Ed. Melvyn A. Hill (New York: St. Martin's Press, 1979), 275.

26 Luban, 101. See also Hanna Pitkin, *Wittgenstein and Justice* (Berkeley: University of California Press, 1993), 242.

27 Arendt, *Human Condition* (Chicago: University of Chicago Press, 1998), 38–9.

28 Hill, 283.

29 Benhabib.

30 See ibid., 114.

31 Ibid., 131.

32 Ibid., 122–3.

33 See ibid., 123.

34 See Hill, 284.

35 See Benhabib, 119, 121.

36 Hill, 284.

37 See ibid., 291.

38 Ibid., 275–6.

39 See James Boyd White, *Heracles' Bow: Essays on the Rhetoric and Poetics of Law* (Madison: University of Wisconsin Press, 1985) (stories construct worlds of meaning). See also Alasdair MacIntrye's *After Virtue* (London: Duckworth Press, 1981) (a similar theme but is more explicitly nostalgic for a past world of coherence); Martha Nussbaum, *Love's Knowledge* (New York and Oxford: Oxford University Press, 1990) (style itself makes a statement, and the style of literature expresses more fully how to live than linear philosophic argument can; conceptions of the good life are embedded in the very structure of imaginative works of literature, including the tensions and contrasting levels of attention).

40 Benhabib, 124, 130.

41 Benhabib, 122, 126. Perhaps the process of telling stories conveyed for Arendt even more basically the adoption of the role of judge for the storyteller: "Story telling reveals meaning without committing the error of defining it . . . it brings about consent and reconciliation with things as they really are, and . . . we may even trust it to contain eventually by implication that last word which we expect from the 'day of judgment' " (Arendt, *Men in Dark Times*, 108). The point is not that each story is true but that it is faithful to the reality of what happened and thereby lends meaning to it; imagining other people's perspectives would be crucial to storytelling in Arendt's sense—see Hill, 292, 297.

42 Benhabib, 126.

43 Ibid., 121.

44 See Nancy Hartsock, *Money, Sex, and Power: Toward a Feminist Historical Materialism* (New York: Longman, 1983), 254 (discussing Hannah Arendt).

45 It would be interesting to explore whether stories are more arresting when other modes of speech and analysis are dominant, but the long-standing place of stories in, for example, rabbinic tradition, suggests that stories can compel even against the backdrop of other analyses.

46 Arendt specifically argued that modern anti-Semitism is more pernicious than the traditional Christian doctrine that blamed Jews for crimes committed against Jesus, because in Christianity one can atone for one's crime by conversion, penance, or denunciation of one's associates. Modern anti-Semitism, "which erupts when Jews en masse begin to enter 'society,' without fully becoming its members," treats Jewishness as an undefinable essence that cannot change. The individual Jew loses an accountable self and instead becomes a specimen of the species Jew. Benhabib, 117.

47   See Michael Walzer, "The Communitarian Critique of Liberalism," *Political Theory* 18 (1990), 6 (arguing that the United States is in no danger of becoming a community, given people's geographic mobility, divorce rates, class membership mobility, and political party shifts).

48   Compare Elizabeth Janeway, *Powers of the Weak* (New York: Alfred A. Knopf, 1980).

49   Would these values be more dominant if storytelling itself became the dominant mode of academic discourse?